Against the State

AGAINST THE STATE

Politics and Social Protest in Japan

David E. Apter and Nagayo Sawa

Harvard University Press
Cambridge, Massachusetts, and London, England

This book is printed on acid-free paper, and its binding materials have been chosen for strength and durability.

Library of Congress Cataloging in Publication Data

Apter, David Ernest, 1924–
    Against the state.

    Includes index.
        1. Eminent domain—environmental aspects—Japan—
Narita-shi.   2.   Environmental protection—Japan—Narita-shi—
Citizen participation.   3.   Shin Tōkyō Kokusai Kūkō.
4.   Farmers—Japan—Narita-shi—Political activity.
I.   Sawa, Nagayo.   II.   Title.
HD1265.J32N3713   1984   387.7′36′095123   83-15338
ISBN 0-674-00920-7 (cloth)
ISBN 0-674-00921-5 (paper)

But their resistance does more than just reveal the truth about the other side; it has also developed into a sharp attack and a serious challenge against the state ...

While the idea of the farmers at the beginning was only to keep their land, this has changed in the process of the struggle. They came face to face with state power and grasped its substance—a state which would not allow them the minimum condition for their lives as farmers, to live and die with the soil.

Yuko Matsumoto, *A Report from the Front*

Acknowledgments

A BOOK OF THIS KIND, which is dependent on access to forbidden terrain and privy to intimate political concerns, rapidly accumulates debts and obligations. When Secretary General Kitahara of the Hantai Dōmei said to us, "Treat Sanrizuka as your second home," he not only offered hospitality but ushered us into a wider circle of confidence. We hope that he and other participants in the movement opposing the construction of the New Tokyo International Airport at Sanrizuka will feel that we have not abused that confidence. We have tried to provide a record which, if it does not reflect the point of view each participant prefers, is nevertheless faithful to the diversity of issues and principles involved and does justice to the wider significance of the struggle.

Three people who above all deserve our gratitude do not, unlike most of the others mentioned, appear in the text itself. They are Jared Lubarsky, Tatsuru Akimoto and Takako Hirose. All were present at the Kyoto-American Studies Seminar in the summer of 1979 when the idea for this book took shape. It was Jared who first suggested it. Takako's participation was crucial in the first summer's field research. Tatsuru worked with us from the beginning to the end of the field work, and many of his ideas found their way into this book.

Preliminary research was funded by the Fulbright Commission in

Acknowledgments

1979 and the Concilium on International and Area Studies, Yale University, in 1980. The main research support was generously provided by the Japan Foundation. To all these organizations we acknowledge our gratitude.

Some of the ideas applied in the analysis came from that lively company of scholars at Yale interested in problems of interpretation and critical analysis, the Whitney Humanities Center, where the senior author has been privileged to be a Fellow. The writing of the book was greatly facilitated by the latter's affiliation with the Fondation Nationale des Sciences Politiques and the Maison des Science de L'Homme in Paris, 1981–82. Thanks are due to Serge Hurtig, Guy Hermet, and Clement Heller for their helpful assistance.

As for those more directly involved, some of the most important acknowledgments we cannot make, out of deference to their wishes. It is in the nature of a movement like this one that certain key people must remain unidentified. They know who they are, however, and it is our hope that this indirect recognition of our gratitude will reach them. Most of those who should be acknowledged the reader will become well acquainted with in the text.

Crucial to us both in gaining access to the site and helping us to understand what our interviews meant, as well as placing this movement in broader context, were Kazuko Tsurumi, Professor at Sophia University, Kōzō Higuchi and Shizuo Ōta of *Rōdō Jōhō,* Satoshi Kamata, Yūichi Kōri, and Masayuki Takagi.* The last two, journalists with *Asahi Shimbun,* shared with us materials, manuscripts, and information. Much of the material in Chapter 7 is drawn from Kōri-san's book *The Story of Tomura Issaku* [*Monogatari Tomura Issaku*] (Tokyo: Asahi Shimbun-sha, 1982).

Other key figures included Tsutomu Kasé, farmer, poet, and former president of the Youth Department of the All-Japan Farmers' Union, who was deeply involved in the Sanrizuka struggle from its beginnings; Ichiyō Mutō, editor of *From the World* and an associate of the Pacific-Asia Resources Center, which publishes the magazine *AMPO;* Michio Matsui, former secretary to the late President Issaku Tomura of the Hantai Dōmei; and Isao Yokota,

* Japanese names here follow the English form: given name first and family name last. In the text, however, the Japanese name order is used (family name first). Authors of books are cited in the notes according to the usage that is appropriate in each case. For example, Japanese authors of books published in English will find their names listed in the English manner.

Acknowledgments

minister of the Ōizumi Church, who with the Tomura family made it possible for us to use the Sanrizuka Church as our research base and living quarters in 1981.

There are of course many others who deserve our thanks: officers and key officials of the Hantai Dōmei, such as Kitahara-san, Ishibashi-san, and Shima-san, all of whom will be more properly introduced in due course. Others on the opposite side—Yoshifumi Imai, former president of the Airport Authority; Tsuneji Hattori, former director general of the Ministry of Transportation; Yoshinari Tezuka, now chairman of the Japan National Tourist Organization; and Dietmen Katō, Utsunomiya, and Den—helped provide both a governmental and a political perspective.

Kazuaki Marumo and Teiichi Aoyama, both Senior Researchers of the Japan Techno-Economics Society, painstakingly analyzed the complex process of Japanese decision-making for us. Others who were extremely helpful were Yasuyo Kawata, one of the founding members of Amnesty International in Japan; Motomu Konno, now President of Tsuge Shobō publishing house; Mitsuru Ōami, reporter for the Japan Broadcasting Corporation, Chiba Bureau; Kaoru Wada, section chief of the Chiba Prefectural Government Airport Policy Section; Yoshinori Ide and Yasuhiro Okudaira, professors at the Institute of Social Science, University of Tokyo; Kenkichi Gomi, professor at the Department of Economics, Hōsei University; and Shōji Hayashi, chief architect of the Narita Airport.

We owe special thanks to five people for their many kindnesses: Takeo-san, Kishi-san, Takahashi-san, Daté-san, and, above all, Sumie Tomura, widow of President Tomura. She embodies in her quiet way the strength of the women of the Hantai Dōmei, who played such a crucial part in the struggle from the very beginning.

Finally, our thanks are due to Katarina Rice and Aida Donald of Harvard University Press for their wise counsel and editorial help, and to Mrs. Sheila Klein, who typed innumerable drafts of this manuscript with patience and good cheer.

D.E.A.
N.S.

Contents

Photographs

Introduction

ON MARCH 28, 1982, a mass rally was held in Sanrizuka Park
by farmers of the Sanrizuka-Shibayama Rengo Kūkō Hantai Dōmei
(the Sanrizuka-Shibayama Farmers' League Against the New Tokyo
International Airport), their militant allies, and supporting groups.
With anti-riot police in full regalia surrounding the park and helicopters circling above it, the following statement was read to the crowd:

> The whole world faces now a grave crisis of imminent
> war—nuclear war; the human being is thus threatened with
> holocaust and total annihilation. An urgent demand for
> peace expressed in anti-war, anti-nuclear protest is becom-
> ing more and more common not only among the Japanese
> people but also among people all over the world.
>
> We, members of the Opposition League and those who
> are rallying around it, have been fighting for 17 years
> against the construction of Sanrizuka military airport
> under the banner of "Stop war! Fight for peace!" in
> diametrical, violent confrontation with the state power.
>
> Now that anti-war, anti-nuclear struggle is gaining mo-
> mentum anew, we feel it our duty, as ones fighting in
> Sanrizuka—a fortress of people's struggle of the whole of
> Japan, to fill responsible positions in this struggle.[1]

Introduction

The audience included citizen groups, students, trade unionists, members of the Chiba branch of the locomotive union, and followers of sects manning fortresses in the area. Clad in combat costume and helmets, waving huge banners and flags imprinted with slogans attacking the airport, imperialism, and militarism, they proclaimed the most peaceful of intents. The staging area was significant in itself: Sanrizuka Park is the last remnant of the old imperial estate whose lands once made up most of the terrain on which the airport is being constructed. While the rally went on, planes took off and landed every few minutes from the one runway the government has been able to build, although passengers remained oblivious to what was happening just a few thousand yards away.

The statement read at the rally is not really so surprising. Many movements, after all, come to see themselves in heroic, moral terms as pieces of contemporary history. More interesting is how and why this movement was able to establish a common front with such a variety of people around so many issues of public protest. What makes this movement particularly special is not the magnitude of its claims, but the place and role it has come to occupy in the protest politics of Japan. This small place with few inhabitants came to be a symbol of the most abstract and pressing moral concerns. Sanrizuka, a rural pocket of Chiba Prefecture, became a "fortress of people's struggle" whose leaders claimed "responsible positions in this struggle."

There are, of course, many factors that must be weighed in the balance. Even frequent travelers to and from Narita International Airport would be surprised to hear it referred to as a military airport. Its chief commerce is the civilian and business traffic that is characteristic of a thriving industrial society. For the officials and political leaders who worked long and hard to make the airport a reality, all the claims of the farmers and militants except the farmers' self-interest can be put down to bombast, rhetoric, or irresponsibility. For some of them the confrontational events constituted rebellion. They took the rhetoric seriously enough to see in the conflict a challenge to the legitimacy of the government, indeed of the state itself. All sides—but for different reasons, perhaps—saw the airport struggle as a focal point.

In fact, the movement accumulated such a variety of principles that it appeared to be a fault line for all forms of citizen protest, indeed something volcanic; it was a place where all other cleavages joined to form a concrete disjunctive force in the community. As it gained momentum, the movement converted considerable numbers of citizens into partisans on one side or the other, with a wider and wider circle willing to suspend judgment rather than automatically supporting the government's position.[2] Public opinion became less passive, more interested and alert. On the fringes it was even passionate.

As the movement came to stand for struggle itself and the airport for the state, the state in turn became the symbol of imperialism, militarism, and nuclear holocaust, so particularly at issue in Japan. Skirmishes in the struggle over the airport took on wider significance. Old people invading the main hall of an imperial lodge during ceremonies celebrating the handing over of the imperial estates at Sanrizuka to the Airport Authority represented the end of the higher authority that preceded parliamentary government; it was a severing of a loyalty no longer required. The violent fight against surveyors invested the terrain itself with a kind of independence. Sanrizuka became a world partly outside the jurisdiction of the state. The fighting to preserve the towers and fortresses built by the farmers and militants came to represent the defense of the revolution. Taking over the airport control tower showed that the defenders could take over the commanding heights of power. Each of these events came to be seen as a logic of history in common with the logic of revolutionary movements elsewhere.

Accounting for this mixture of myth and logic, narrative and text, action and story, brings us to broader questions about the negative aspects of modern industrial life. For even in this most successful society, progress has its victims, its marginals. Our explanation must try to show, then, some of the costs of economic transformation, for these constitute the other side of corporate Japan, the other side of "Japan as number one." For if Japan today is a monument to discipline, intelligence, and hard work and Japan's political leaders shrewd guides to effective policy, there is, as always, another side to the story.

The airport, not yet complete but functioning, stands adjacent to Sanrizuka. Some of it is on land the emperor once owned, land that included large estates, experimental farms, and a horse ranch dating from before Tokugawa times. The landscape was sufficiently beautiful to have earned a reputation as the Barbizon of Japan. It was a place of much local pride and affectionate nurture over many generations. The transformation of the emperor's land, and of the farms and villages adjacent to it, into runways and terminals endowed the entire area with metaphorical significance. The government decision to put an airport there has been seen as rape, a violation of fertility, nature itself. But underneath all this charm there is another history to this land; the bitter struggles between peasant and lord, tenant and landlord. Both the charm and the bitterness have their place in this movement.

Whatever the traditions invoked, there was wide agreement within the movement that the airport would irrevocably destroy values essential to life itself. Hence the question of self-interest became the most trivial part of an organization that saw itself as defending an alternative politics and set itself against the general drift of society. It always represented a minority view, of course—all the more reason that as a protest army it marched up the hill of principle so quickly. Once confrontations and violence occurred, it became virtually impossible for the government to convince people to pack those principles up and march right down again to the practical world of bargaining and negotiation. The impossibility of bargaining did not come only from the confrontational atmosphere and from the different views of life. Rather, there were specific and significant political issues involved. The lack of effective due process in Japan is one of the important ones; other political issues that we will consider are the inadequacy of consultative mechanisms outside elite circles and the failure of local government to represent local interests. They cannot be separated from the visible effects of economic growth, which in the name of progress resulted in pollution, environmental disaster, and the desecration of Chiba Prefecture. While some of the worst effects of pollution are being mitigated, it took movements of this kind to force the government to act.[3]

If there was no modesty of principle involved in this conflict, then, it was for good and understandable reasons. The movement endured over a generation, not least perhaps because these and other claims put forward remained so adamantly nonnegotiable. The government had no proper way to deal with the representatives of the Hantai Dōmei, and in fact this was not an accidental deficiency but rather a strategy. It is what extra-institutional protest is about. The government's chief weapons were secret negotiations and private manipulation, against both of which the movement took every possible precaution, from mutual surveillance to self-criticism. It treated as traitors those who would favor negotiation or compromise. It reacted immediately against those who suggested temperate solutions. It was reluctant to back away from the largest principles to accommodate the most practical needs of the farmers themselves, a practice that in the end helped divide it. Some farmers will eventually be forced to give up the land needed to finish the airport. They cannot ignore either financial compensation from the government or the alternative land that the government promises to provide. Because the farmers have other commitments than those of the movement, the Hantai Dōmei tried to minimize the conflicts of interest by involving whole families, including wives and children. But the farmers are left with a complicated problem, nevertheless. Inside the airport area the issue is land. Just outside the airport area, irrigation will be the crucial issue, and noise pollution, and government funding. In either case if farmers want to preserve their way of life, they will in the end need government help in order to do it.

For almost an entire generation, this movement has remained much more than a farmers' movement, although farmers were and must be at the core of it. If it has involved whole families in the community, it has also served as a lightning rod for protest movements all over Japan: anti-nuclear, environmental, and peace groups, groups protesting discrimination against Koreans in Japan and those protesting discrimination against a pariah caste like the *burakumin*. It had direct links through its militant allies—the seventeen supporting sects, who maintained some thirty-three fortresses and solidarity huts scattered about the airport—with those fighting against the presence of American forces and nuclear ships.

There is no one starting point. Perhaps the best place to begin is with the "political economy" decision reached by the Japanese Cabinet in 1960 to emphasize industrial over rural development in a program popularly dubbed "income doubling." The principal objectives were to reduce the size of those sectors of the economy that were relatively inefficient and to divert the labor force into needed and better paying occupations. Regarded by the government as a forward-looking program of general economic and social improvement, it also marked Japan's coming of age as an industrial power and was seen as a way of putting firmly behind her the legacy of defeat in the war and the long years of poverty and reconstruction in the aftermath. The new airport was planned in part to handle the increased commerce projected under the new policy. The airport was also to be a symbol of the new role Japan would play in the world.

Violence itself began in 1965 when the Cabinet decided to construct an airport at Tomisato, near Narita City in Chiba Prefecture, to serve the rapidly growing needs of metropolitan Tokyo. It was to be a spectacular inland airport, efficient and beautiful, a showcase for people entering Japan. It represented the largest single project ever undertaken by the government. It was bound to be controversial. With only 15 percent of Japan's land area arable, virtually every proposed site for so large an undertaking simply had to be the subject of dispute. Assessments of relative costs and benefits and preoccupation with the technical problem of constructing such a complex facility disguised the political consequences. The airport decision could not help but stimulate hard bargaining and dirty politicking within the governing Liberal Democratic Party, so much so that those in charge forgot those not directly involved in making the decisions. They ignored the local people themselves.

At Tomisato farmers protested so violently that the government gave up its plan to build the airport there. Indeed, the campaign waged by the Tomisato farmers was so effective that their Hantai Dōmei became the model for the farmers of Sanrizuka, the new airport site, not far from Tomisato and adjacent to Narita City. Sanrizuka was more thinly populated than Tomisato, and much of the land already belonged to the imperial household. This time the opposition would be, the government assumed, less strong and less effective.

The government's decision to transfer the site had been made in secret. Yet the government considered the decision a testimonial to its own flexibility—that is, as a response to public outcries at Tomisato. There was something to this view, although the farmers of Sanrizuka and adjacent Shibayama did not see it that way. For them it was an outrageously arbitrary act. Feeling betrayed by the government they had believed in, they looked on Liberal Democratic politicians as duplicitous enemies interested in self-enrichment and aggrandizement—a view not far off the mark, as the Lockheed scandals would later suggest. Asking themselves how Haneda, the main airport already serving Tokyo, could suddenly have become obsolete, they found a ready answer in the demands imposed by the escalating Vietnam war. The proposed Narita airport became a "military" airport, a symbol of U.S. imperialism and Japanese subservience to American military needs. In turn the farmers saw their own resistance as part of a common "front" with "progressive forces" in Vietnam and elsewhere, and as part of a peasant struggle of classic proportions, especially after some of them had visited China during the Cultural Revolution.

When the defending farmers were joined by representatives of New Left sects, some of whom had elaborate supporting networks reaching out to various trade unions and citizen protest groups, Sanrizuka became a "mobilization space." The movement remained hospitable to all opposition forces that supported its cause as long as they did not try to dominate the Hantai Dōmei. The main supporting group that did try to interfere, the Japan Communist Party, was expelled from the site. The movement also eschewed terrorism: it refused to allow members of the Japanese Red Army or other violent terrorist factions to participate in the struggle. Within these limits, all opposition groups were welcome.

The original concern of the farmers was that they were being forced to give up their livelihood as farmers. Indeed, one object of the Cabinet's decision to shift to industrial priorities was to drive small farmers off the land. It was the airport itself, however, that was of immediate concern, as in Tomisato. Farmers began their activities peacefully enough. They petitioned local prefectural and national authorities, enlisted the support of Dietmen, particularly from the Japan Socialist Party, and got help from members of the Japan Communist Party. But despite such efforts they found that normal channels were blocked; they could not make their views count. It was from this rather specific perspective, farmers protecting their way of life, that the movement began. Then, as peaceful methods gave way to violent ones and as confrontations resulted in mounting casualties, people came to think of the affair in other terms and to question why in a parliamentary and democratic state it was so hard for small groups to obtain an adequate hearing, and why succeeding Liberal Democratic Party governments remained so insensitive to those unable to manipulate the dominant political factions, no matter how legitimate the claims involved. Indeed, violence seemed to be virtually the only recourse except surrender for people who felt passionately about the rightness of their cause.

Once it became clear to the farmers that the government would hold firm and that officials would remain unmoved by farmers' pleas that their way of life was being taken away, most farmers quickly sold out, taking advantage of what seemed at the time generous compensation terms. Within a year after the first ten farmers sold out, all those in the first-stage construction area had followed suit except one old woman, Ōki Yone, who steadfastly refused to give up her house. Poor, without family, but of great presence, her opposition became an inspiration for farmers and the militants who came to help them. Opposition stiffened not only among farmers still left in the area designated for the second stage of construction but in the nearby Shibayama area as well. Farmers there were affected less by land acquisition than by noise pollution, changes in ground water levels, and irrigation changes, all injurious to a predominantly rice-growing area. Shibayama has primarily wet farming (rice); in Sanrizuka, on the other hand, there is primarily dry farming (vegetables). Both kinds of farming were affected by the airport construction itself and by the roads, rails, and other facilities cut into the landscape.

Relations between the Hantai Dōmei and the authorities deteriorated rapidly. Confrontations occurred more frequently and with greater ferocity, especially after 1967, when New Left sects and representatives of the Zengakuren, the All-Japan Student League, first came to the site. Militants built solidarity huts and fortresses at various sites around the airport, stationed more or less permanent cadres in them, and then began working for the farmers, providing them with free labor, publicizing the struggle, and politicizing and radicalizing them. The farmers had not lacked political experience, of course, but theirs was mainly of a different kind, with party bosses and behind-the-scenes negotiation. Students used tactics developed in the student movement. As violence escalated, farmers employed techniques they had learned in World War II. Supporters mobilized from universities, trade unions, and the peace movement built and maintained defenses and held rallies and meetings designed to attract public support and raise money.

Some of the farmers had been members of the Japan Socialist Party and a smaller number had been members of the Japan Communist Party, but most were firm supporters of the Liberal Democratic Party. Until 1960 the LDP had been relatively responsive to their needs. Now they saw this party as the instrument of their betrayal, and, indeed, as testimony of the failure of parliamentary democracy itself. The more hostile farmers became toward the state, the easier it was for them to accept militants who previously had seemed foreign to them.

The militants had behind them a history of successful organizing and confrontation, beginning when a coalition of various student and citizen protest groups opposed the revision of the U.S.-Japan Security Treaty—the AMPO riots of 1960. This movement, the first mass action organized by New Left students, became the "model" in the Sanrizuka struggle. A variety of sects and organizations—student organizations like Chūkaku-ha, Liberation, Fourth Internationalists, and Zenkyōtō, and broader citizen protest groups like Beheiren—came to live with the farmers on the site. Many of them remained in Sanrizuka, having dropped out of schools and universities; some indeed became internal exiles, cut off from their roots in society. But among these "militants," only a small proportion, mostly leaders, considered themselves professional revolutionaries. Mainly the stream of recruits came from high schools, colleges, and universities. Junior civil servants, clerks, and individual members of trade unions also came in considerable numbers to protest and fight.

There was also a larger support group of intellectuals, among them journalists, writers, professors, and filmmakers, attracted to the movement both because of its specific aims and as a symbol of all the things they considered to be wrong with Japan. For them Sanrizuka was another example of the Liberal Democratic Party's corrupt and manipulative politics and of its attentiveness to big business and to the United States. Senior government officials were, they thought, working hand in glove with those who would profit most from the airport. As the Lockheed scandal and other revelations of corruption became public knowledge, none of this seemed implausible. What was written in the journals, books, and pamphlets about the affair made the airport into a symbol of all the evils of corrupt party politics. Virtually the entire catalog of Japanese political sins were laid at the airport's door—so much so that the Sanrizuka struggle overshadowed the Minamata movement, a dramatic struggle of fishermen and their families poisoned by mercury. In the Minamata case the issues were for the most part more focused; even the broader issues at Minamata had less to do with the state itself than with its carelessness and its failure to consider the human problems of pollution and environmental disaster. Both Sanrizuka and Minamata were vivid examples of government indifference to the social tragedy of public and private development projects.

MANY PEOPLE both inside and outside Japan are surprised to find that the Sanrizuka movement is still going on; if nothing else, the magnitude of Japan's accomplishments has made many of the concerns of the sixties and seventies seem academic. On the other hand, many activists would argue that their original concerns—such as constitutional revision, remilitarization, and the problem of growing Japanese imperialism—are only now becoming visible as public issues of major concern. No doubt the big debates on these issues will intensify. But they have become increasingly separated from the Sanrizuka movement itself. In any case, the public mood is more conservative than a few years ago. It may be that as these matters are debated the New Right will be of more concern than the New Left.

Moreover, Japan's economic position has changed. Twenty years after the program of income doubling was announced and a high proportion of small farmers joined the industrial labor force, Japan displaced the United States as the premier producer of automobiles. Today Japan plans a second-stage revolution using computer and robot technology far beyond the capabilities of virtually all Western competitors. Moreover, Japan's accomplishments have not been accompanied by the usual social pathologies—high crime, violence, and increasing divorce rates. Families remain intact, and there is little generational conflict.[4] A highly selective and competitive educational system ensures a stream of extremely well instructed and capable "recruits" to the various roles and networks of organization that make up modern Japan. Social stability is well preserved. Security of tenure is a social obligation. Relations between employer and employee remain remarkably close. To an outsider, Japan seems to be passing from a scientifically derivative society to an innovative and creative one without visible or apparent major social crises.[5]

In fact, this is by no means the case. It is true that compared to other democratic societies Japan has managed with extraordinary ability. The qualities of its population, the sense of duty, skill, hard work, are well known. But precisely because of Japan's successes, the size and intensity of opposition in Japan, the duration of the struggle, and, indeed, the role of the left as an oppositional force, all of which have been a part of Japanese life since the Meiji restoration, tend not to be taken into account. The Sanrizuka struggle is a reminder that farmers, with their history of conflict, and the Left, with its history of violence, have indeed intertwined many times in the past, both in the immediate vicinity of the airport and in similar situations over many years. Opposition in Japan is old and has been unable to make its views prevail, either in the days of imperial power or today under the continuous rule of the LDP. Violence, then, is endemic to protest.

What happened at Sanrizuka? This small area became the symbol of extra-institutional protest in Japan, a metaphor of government oppression, and a sign of the state itself. As the struggle evolved, the movement became heroic, epic, and remarkable both in its own eyes and within a wider circle of supporters. It had its heroes and villains, its failures and triumphs. Its protagonists believed that it would gather strength and momentum, leading to a great disjunctive and "overdetermined" moment. Then not only would the cause triumph but revolutionary change would occur. The narration of episodes served as both litany and logic for a movement creating a *mythologique* embraced by both the old farmers, grandfathers all, and those young militants who left home to come and work for them, sometimes marrying their sons or daughters, and in general defending them within an increasingly radical alliance. So the broadest principles were married to the most immediate concerns, in a rhetoric reflecting and appropriate to the escalating violence of the confrontation with the government.

A key factor is indeed violence. The combined opposition sought to isolate the airport physically by constructing fortresses around it at key points. Mobilizations not only served to focus attention on specific issues but were occasions in which surveyors, architects, builders, engineers, and indeed the airport workers themselves were transformed from instruments of construction to destruction; their activities despoiled the land, the patrimony, the sacred soil itself. Displaced grave sites became violations of ancestral propriety. Wounds and deaths were the final expressions of desecration. The Airport Authority, which had the central responsibility for building and running the airport, became not only an instrument of an insensitive bureaucracy of which one might approve or disapprove, but an agency of government serving as a partner of the United States in a capitalist, imperialist alliance for remilitarization. Thus a moral architecture was created within the Sanrizuka crossroads, a mobilization space that intensified as the bulldozers cleared the land of trees, houses, farms, and people. The movement fought back with Molotov cocktails, with sticks, with farm implements. But no matter how many pitched battles they won, they could not prevent the building of the first phase of the airport.

On both sides violence was endowed with legitimacy and legitimacy with violence. The incidents were not isolated from other protests in Japan and must be seen in the context of a legacy that goes back a long way. Prototypes can be found in the turn-of-the-century conflicts brought about when Meiji governments sought rapid industrialization and simultaneously fostered militarism. Not all those who fought back were on the left; indeed, some were on the right, or what might in retrospect be considered the right. What both right and left shared then were anti-imperial and anti-bourgeois attitudes. But the left was by far the more significant participant, and from such struggles it has a long list of heroes and martyrs, not a few of them rural in origin. There is an indigenous radical inheritance that resides in peasant as well as in worker movements.

The radical tradition also includes various strands of Protestant Christianity, pietism, and Tolstoyan influences. Students who became socialists often did so after an involvement with Christian precept. Another strand is Marxism, particularly the Marxist discussion groups that preceded the Communist Party itself. The leader of the Hantai Dōmei, Tomura Issaku, was himself not a Marxist but a devout Christian who saw the struggle in terms of Christ and the disciples. It was he who connected radical Christianity to radical sects, and both of them to the farmers' movement, deliberately converting the implements and events of rural work and life into a semiotics of violence.

The movement was arrayed, however, against a national state that had good reasons for self-congratulation. Its policies had facilitated the reconstruction of Japan. Government officials were sure of themselves and the correctness of their decisions. They had sympathy for the farmers' plight, but they could not, after all, be expected to have infinite patience when what was at stake was a self-evident public good. Farmers had a genuine grievance because they had not been treated with the respect they deserved. But amends could be made, and the government was willing to do that if the movement would allow them to get on with the construction. As this did not happen, the government blamed the militants who appeared to be the main obstacle. The militants were after all subversive in their self-proclaimed objectives and irresponsible in their actions throughout Japan. They had no right to be involved, the government thought; they were outsiders in Sanrizuka. By inciting farmers to violence the militants stiffened the government's views. One can see why by recalling a mass rally of the left, with speeches delivered as if words were bullets. On the platform, delivery is more important than meaning, and signaling more important than thought. No matter how diverse the rally's makeup—farmers, trade unionists, students, old people, young mothers with babies strapped on their backs—the government could easily convince itself that a radical anti-logic was at work, an anti-logic aimed at exorcising all the mediating and bargaining methods on which the government depended.

THREE MAIN THEMES underlie this book; the first two are given special prominence while the third is embedded in the text so as not to intrude into the events themselves. The first theme is the Sanrizuka struggle, which, as we have said, deals with the other side of Japan's success story. The conflict in no way diminishes the magnitude of Japan's accomplishments but rather suggests the country's social overhead costs. The Narita Airport is of course functioning, albeit in somewhat truncated form; to that extent the government has won. But the airport has also been a government failure in terms of the time it has taken to build and the disruptions it has produced in so many people's lives.

The second theme, deriving from the first, is a more general one: it is the problem of violent protest in democratic societies. We do not consider violence a necessary reflex to oppression. Rather, we want to examine, in many-sided terms, how violence evolves. As well, we want to show how the most marginal people in a society bring up the most central issues—a circumstance that makes a democratic government less, rather than more, responsive, because it cannot allow its policy to be determined by minorities utterly lacking in political power or economic significance. Not even a socialist government can become hostage to its poor or deprived; it must cater to the needs of a larger spectrum of citizens or risk alienating their support. But the way a government limits its political obligations lies in how it defines its responsiveness, and to what clienteles. There is always a danger of violence where obligation leaves off, especially when there are large supporting clienteles for the protesting groups and a wider circle of public sympathy.

The third theme, a very different one, is the problem of modern social science theories. In the recent past we have witnessed the decline of functional theory, the ebb and flow of structuralism, and the emergence and domination of political economy, of both the pluralist-liberal and the neo-Marxist or dependency persuasions. Simultaneously there have been remarkable advances in operationalism, descriptive empiricism, and quantitative analysis, both statistical and formal, applied by means of survey and other methods to the vectors, forces, interests, and classes of which society is composed. The common defect of all these, from the present point of view—that is, from the perspective of a case study—is that they omit what might be called the cognitive dimension of daily life and action in favor of overkill theories in which case materials become merely illustrative. Despite lip service to the principles of induction, what emerges are results too generalized or too superficial to add much to understanding. Our emphasis here is on the people who do things in a context which is in part of their own making. They are not mere surrogates for larger forces. Nor do they consider what they do to be separate from what goes on in the rest of society or the world. They understand very well how specific events take on broader meaning in both Japanese and comparative contexts. But it remains a complex business, as we hope to be able to show by using several interpretive schemes—functional, structural, and phenomenological.

One advantage of so small a case is that we can combine several approaches in an overall intellectual strategy that allows us to distance ourselves from any one point of view while entering into the lives of those involved. Early chapters suggest something of the social structure of the communities, introducing the main individuals and their families. The reader will get to know them, get a sense of how involved their lives are, and will learn their names, the places they inhabit, where they came from, the rules and obligations they live by, and what the movement has meant to them.

The three main groups of participants are farmers, government officials and politicians, and militants (defined as members of New Left sects that have built and manned fortresses and solidarity huts in the area). For each group we will provide the background necessary for understanding the context of the events themselves. The perspectives of each group will be treated in turn, with sympathy. As will be clear, there is no final right or wrong on such issues, nor any monopoly of truth or point of view.

The Japanese government still thinks that it has been motivated primarily by consideration of the general welfare, although its protagonists will admit to a perhaps too limited perspective. Some agree that the official position has been too arbitrary, narrow, and quick to assume that unbridled growth brings self-evident benefits. As for the more sinister charges of corruption and remilitarization, there is little evidence for these in any narrow or legal sense. But if one moves to a different plane, to that of the farmers or the militants, one sees that a different kind of "evidence" is involved. There is a drift in Japan to the right, both within and outside the government, and the public mood is daily becoming more conservative. With the coincident prosperity and growth have come renewed pressure for remilitarization, not least from the United States. Some people see in Japan's successful penetration of East Asia a new expression of the old "Japanese co-prosperity sphere." For them a new corporatism rides roughshod over the older sensibilities, obscuring social problems by the dynamics of its power.

As for the militants, when the government "denies their authenticity" they claim even more insistently that they are fighting against all the inequities and wrongs of Japanese life. Their role is to struggle against capitalism, imperialism, government arbitrariness, and those organized forms of the left associated with the Japan Communist Party (and, to a lesser degree the Socialist Party). And there is no doubt that for a time their activities struck a responsive, if limited, chord in the broader spectrum of Japanese society.

There is a great diversity of views in this movement, sometimes hidden or expressed in a secret or guilty manner. Many people told us that we would not be able to understand the movement. We have taken this to mean that there are many meanings. All need somehow to be sifted and examined. For no matter how unique each meaning is, each is essential to the others, to the totality of meanings without which no one of them can be understood.

This brings us directly to the problem of methods. We use three, and they are ordinarily hostile to one another. The first, or functionalist, is concerned mainly with broad characteristics of social structure and politics. It derives generally from anthropological and sociological principles associated with British and American field methods and with comparative analysis. The second, or structuralist, deals with what might be called the structure of cognition in action; it derives from a French and European tradition emphasizing representations, symbols and signs, rhetoric and actions. Treating events like a text, it decodes them according to their metonymic and metaphoric status in a dialectically organized framework of binary expressions.

Each of these two approaches fills in gaps left by the other. The functionalist approach, more empirical and descriptive, enables us to incorporate certain assumptions about marginality, functionality, and development.[6] But alone it does not penetrate much below the surface of events, except in very schematic terms. The second enables us to probe more deeply into the way people think and act. The danger in the structuralist approach, increasingly recognized, is that the observer will impose his own views on the subject; art will take away from science in the very act of transcending it. The way out of the methodological predicament is our third emphasis, the phenomenological approach. Special effort has been made to reconstruct the everyday lives of those who live and work in the area or who are otherwise involved in the Sanrizuka conflict. Only a very small case study will allow such an approach. Because of the size we can show the small worlds in the large and the large in the small.

Our analytical framework will not be made more explicit in the text for several reasons. First, we hope that we have been able to integrate the three approaches successfully, despite their somewhat contradictory emphases, and embed them within the context of a story that reveals the richness and variety of the movement. We do not want to talk about metaphors or show how symbols are structurally derived, but rather to provide their substance as descriptive ingredients. Second, we do not want to dilute the main arguments with methodological controversies that can be of only parochial interest. The focus is on politics and the political. Within that frame our obligation to the participants is to bring out the diversity of their views and circumstances. All are survivors. They have the touchiness and rights of those who have gone through a great deal and have seen virtually everything in the course of the struggle. They deserve respect on all sides. Finally, most difficult of all, these approaches are not much good for what might be called "dealing with silences." For if the participants are good at defining by their words and actions what they do want to say, often with great delicacy, they leave it to the observer to interpret by means of interminable discussions and reflection what is left out. One pokes at the interstices of their words and deeds by means falling somewhere between detective work and literary explication, neither of which would merit the grand methodological titles described above.

In writing this book we have deliberately allowed a literary aspect to take precedence over the social science aspect of our story (with apologies to our fellow political scientists). It must be made clear that we do not profess an Olympian outlook. We want to read this struggle like a text, the text like a narrative, and the narrative as a moral logic of politics.[7] We believe that a good deal of politics is motivated by movements of just this kind, movements acting out extra-institutional modes of protest, initiated by marginals of one kind or another who almost never succeed on their own terms. These are the occasions when the ordinary business of making policy, even good policy, is simply not enough; we are obliged to pause and ponder what such events imply for the future of democracy.

These, then, are a few of the concerns that we bring to the crossroads at Sanrizuka where the trouble begins. It is a very ordinary crossroads, reaching out to what is still a predominantly rural land-scape. There are certain things about it that are unfamiliar to many of us, but by and large most of what happens there also happens everywhere else as well. Its uniqueness can easily be overstated. It remains a place where, as Lafcadio Hearn wrote in 1904, "no ordinary person shuts his door to lock out the rest of the world. Everybody's house must be open to visitors: to close its gates by day would be regarded as an insult to the community ... Only persons with very great authority have the right of making themselves inaccessible. And to displease the community in which one lives ... is a serious matter. When a community is displeased, it acts as an individual. It may consist of five hundred, a thousand or several thousand persons; but the thinking of all is the thinking of one."[8] Even for his day, Hearn exaggerated. There was, and is, plenty of disagreement. But around Sanrizuka even now the farmers' houses are still remarkably open to visitors. It is the airport that has its doors locked and its gates closed to all except the authorized. Authority has become too inaccessible. And although each of the communities we will examine has not always acted as an individual, they are all very displeased.

I

Two
Crossroads

Among men, the Japanese are probably the fore-
most makers of patterns. They are a patterned
people who live in a patterned country, a land
where habit is exalted to rite, where the exem-
plar still exists, where there is a model for everything, and the ideal is actively sought, where the
shape of an idea or an action may be as important as its content, where the configuration of
parts depends upon recognized form, and the
profile of the country depends upon the shape
of living.

Donald Richie, *Katachi*

1
Sanrizuka and Shibayama

THE BEST WAY to go to Sanrizuka is by bus, for then you enter almost immediately into the life of this small crossroads backed against the New Tokyo International Airport, some seventy kilometers from Tokyo itself. From a plane, the way most people come to the area, you would never know that the crossroads exists—the landscape, factories, farms, roads, and houses all dwindle into insignificance. There is a fast train that stops nearby. But the train is not a good way to travel. It sticks to its own route and minds its own business. The bus, especially the one that starts some kilometers away at Narita City, is much better: it meanders and stops and starts for passengers. In this rural setting the bus's schedule leaves time for greetings to be exchanged, and there is a relationship between the driver and the travelers, whose composition varies according to the rhythm of the day.[1]

If you go to Sanrizuka, perhaps the first thing you will become aware of—indeed cannot ignore—is the sound of jets and the noise of trucks en route to the warehouses and terminals of the airport. Twenty years ago there was nothing much here except quiet villages and farms and a crossroads at the edge of the imperial meadow and horse ranch. In Tokugawa times (1600–1868), the estates provided horses to the Tokugawa shogunate and other powerful feudal lords. Today they are gone; only a few reminders are left.

Two Crossroads

In the old days people used to come visit the estate and the friends and relatives living in the surrounding hamlets and villages. Even then the hamlets were small, from twenty to twenty-five households. Today many are even smaller, reduced by the airport and the events attending its construction. Weddings, funerals, firefighting, celebrating—these activities still go on in the hamlets and villages of the area. It would be a mistake, though, to consider the people who live there as rustic or traditional. Even in the old days when the crossroads consisted of not much more than a small hotel, a fish shop, a post office, and some commercial buildings and storehouses, it was a post stop for the Tokyo stage and the people of the area were shrewd and successful farmers. Since Meiji times (1868–1912), experimental agriculture had been done at the imperial estate. Local farmers built up poor-quality soil until it became some of the best farmland in Chiba Prefecture. Visitors to Sanrizuka used to come to observe and learn about these innovations. Some came to wander in the imperial meadow, especially in spring when thousands of cherry trees were in bloom. Others simply passed through to one of the hamlets dotting the area—hamlets like Heta, an old village with many large thatched-roof houses and thick-walled storehouses, and bonsai and gardens cultivated over many generations, or Tōhō, where settlers came, many after World War II. In this area there were originally lords and peasants, then landlords and tenants; there are mainly farmers today.

Even now, despite the airport and the commerce that passes through Sanrizuka en route to it, the bus from Narita City still drops you off into a world of rural exchange. On three sides the roads still lead to hamlets, villages, fields, and farms. Sanrizuka itself has grown to about four hundred households, but the surrounding countryside still has the look of things in their proper places, the head of the household on his farm, the household in the hamlet. If nothing is really old or traditional, nothing is wholly new. There has been no rupture with the past.

It is important to have this overview in mind before boarding the bus at Narita City to go to Sanrizuka, although a great deal can be observed through the bus's windows. Small factories and housing estates are displacing the farms. In this area farming is difficult—which is one reason why so many farmers have given up. They remember that until very recently it was a dull way of life, often brutish, and sometimes regrettably short. It is not surprising, then, that many farmers, mainly poorer ones, accepted the government's offer and left for other pursuits as soon as the opportunity presented it-self. Those that are left are real farmers, devoted, dedicated, extraor-dinarily hard working. Their farms show their dedication.

You see them in the field, men and women, husbands and wives. The women wear trousers and conical hats and do more of the heavy weeding and back-breaking labor. Their husbands have benefited more from the technological revolution. Chemical fertilizers and two-wheeled tractors with attached carts and other pieces of me-chanical equipment have made men's life easier; and in the home new appliances have made life a bit more attractive for wives. Men and women keep to their traditional division of labor. Despite im-provements, however, the work is still demanding. Few children suc-ceed their parents in full-time farming even when they inherit the land. Farming is more attractive to the old than to the young. This is a particular concern of the Youth Corps of the Hantai Dōmei. Some of its members have explored ways to farm collectively, which is more attractive to educated young people, and to use organic farm-ing methods.

Because of the imperial estate and its experimental agriculture, Sanrizuka was never a quiet place. Even before the airport there was plenty of commerce and exchange, both of products and ideas. It is an area where both left and right ideologies had made their appear-ance before the war and where intellectuals had come, some to teach in the local high school. Occasionally poets and philosophers came to stay at the imperial estate. National politics were important in the area, too. After the war, LDP factions had local bosses in Sanrizuka. Many of the farmers in the Hantai Dōmei had once been tenants, of course, but that ended in 1946 and 1947. Only radical nostalgia would confuse these farmers with "peasants." Although some visitors note a certain picturesqueness of visage and costume and think of peas-ants in Vietnam or of the Chinese who made up the Eighth Route Army, the farmers of Sanrizuka and of neighboring Shibayama do not fit that pattern.

Nevertheless, they are fighters. On some of their fields the forts and solidarity huts of the militants have been constructed. The more radical and militant the sect, the more bristling the fort's appear-ance. On desolate patches of land one sees billboards in huge, angry Chinese characters that proclaim the people's struggle against the airport. In the middle of a field adjacent to the airport where three farmers still live, there is a huge windmill built by militants as the symbol of the Hantai Dōmei. The road around the area is heavily guarded, giving the airport a besieged look. There is a feeling of tension at every turning of the road, every path, every gate. If as a solitary walker you were to explore the road, you would be followed by two sets of binoculars, those of the militants from their fortresses and those of the police from their steel watchtowers. You would probably be followed by a police jeep or offered rides by detectives in civilian dress. If you drove in a car driven by a militant from one of the sects, you would probably be followed or stopped and questioned by the police.

But the solitary walker is not what matters. What concerns the police are the hundreds or thousands who pour into Sanrizuka by bus, train, taxi, and car when the Hantai Dōmei calls for a mass mobilization. Then the fortresses fill up with defenders; the solidarity huts become staging areas; the houses of militants in Sanrizuka and the farmers' compounds in the hamlets and villages become places of meeting, discussion, organization, decision. Rallies are held at the center of the old imperial estate, now a park, or at Yokobori cemetery, not far away.

In Sanrizuka, a few surviving buildings and lodges of the imperial estate slowly decay, their thatched roofs caving in. There, too, where the local residents have their tennis courts and families walk in the woods that are left, one finds the main mobilization space of the Hantai Dōmei. Around this spot the ordinary life and commerce of Sanrizuka go on.

Those who use the airport are quite oblivious to this space, for neither the airport bus nor the train goes through Sanrizuka. The freeways to Tokyo, entered just beyond the main gates of the airport, innocuously pass by buildings and farms, some of which are backed up against the airport fence itself. From above, looking down, all one sees is small houses and barns, ribbon-like roads, rice paddies and fields, all looking so miniaturized, neat, and carefully tended that the overwhelming impression is one of nurture and peacefulness. The traveler cannot see the fortresses and solidarity huts strategically located around and adjacent to the airport. Watched and guarded both from inside and out, threatened at regular intervals by police in full regalia who pound on the gates and shout, are the cadres who live more or less permanently behind high walls and fortifications.

NEITHER the visual images of peace and neatness, nor the violence which has accompanied the construction of the airport, provides a true picture of daily life in the area. Explosive confrontations aside, Sanrizuka maintains its equilibrium very well. It has gradually become a commercial and shopping center for the small-scale activities appropriate to the surrounding hamlets and villages. Among its four hundred households are ex-farmers who sold their land to the Airport Authority and bought new houses in Sanrizuka with the compensation money. A few inhabitants are militants who came to the fortresses or participated in the movement and then married and settled down in the area. More and more of those who live there work at the airport as clerks, attendants, engineers, technicians, and bus and taxi drivers. They live in Sanrizuka because it is a nice place to bring up children, convenient to where they work, and not far from Tokyo.

Several sites within Sanrizuka are of particular interest. Of great symbolic importance to the movement are the home, compound, and church of the still revered former Hantai Dōmei president, Tomura Issaku, who died of cancer in 1979. Tomura was a Christian, an artist of no mean merit who produced remarkable modern sculptures, and as well a businessman who had inherited a farm machinery and implements shop in Sanrizuka. Across the street is a second important site: the kimono shop and home of Kitahara Kōji, secretary general of the Hantai Dōmei before the movement separated into two factions. An ex-navy noncommissioned officer, the headman of the Sanrizuka crossroads, and a city assemblyman at Narita City, Kitahara is a key figure in the Hantai Dōmei's relations with outside supporters. Just beyond Sanrizuka in one direction is a third important site, the headquarters of Chūkaku-ha, the most powerful sect in the area and one of the most militant in Japan. Its headquarters is a combined fortress and solidarity hut with high walls and a lookout day and night. Chūkaku-ha also maintains a watchtower and hut on the land of Ishibashi Masaji, who became the acting president of the Hantai Dōmei after Tomura's death. His small farm lies a few miles beyond Sanrizuka in the opposite direction from the Chūkaku-ha headquarters, near several of the farmers still resisting land acquisition for the second stage of the airport construction.

These four locations define Sanrizuka for the members of the movement. Their focus of attention is on the road that skirts the airport and the partial no-man's-land where the second stage is being planned. There, opposite neat farms, are desolate patches where the government has constructed watchtowers, fences, moats, gates, barbed wire. It is the object of the militants and the Hantai

Dōmei to keep pressure on the government so that it will give up the construction project. They want to make the airport into a facility so ugly and alien that the government will become a "prisoner" inside, beleaguered within a fortress of its own making. At a minimum the farmers want to "teach the state a lesson"; on that they all agree. After that their views differ. A few hope for revolution. Some want the airport torn down, its runways plowed up, and its farms returned to their original and pristine state. Others want to prevent the second stage from being built. Still others want to force the government to "apologize," to admit its error, or to establish better principles and practice of due process and consultation. Some farmers are out to get the best possible compensation from the government and are involved in private negotiations. Whatever their views of the matter, one thing is clear: All the farmers are old. Time is not on their side.

The area to the east, north, and south of Sanrizuka itself is increasingly built up with shops, houses, motor parks, filling stations, restaurants. Farther out the landscape remains predominantly rural, although there is a patchwork quality to the distribution of land for farming. Some farms are in Sanrizuka itself. Some factories rise up out of undulating fields. West, at the fourth quartering of the crossroad at the center of Sanrizuka, the road is blocked by a chain-link electrified gate topped with barbed wire. Surrounding the gate are spotlights and high watchtowers. The police stationed here wear—in both winter and summer, no matter how intense the heat or humidity—heavy blue uniforms with long padded tunics, helmets with transparent visors that come down over their faces, thick padded neckguards, high gauntlets, and thick gloves, and they are armed with long curved metal shields and long staves. The traveler cannot go through but rather must turn to the right past the fence. Just inside the fence the main 4,000-meter runway and airport buildings are in full view. The second and third runways have not yet been built nor the land for them fully acquired—hence the need for the second stage of the construction project. Necessary backup facilities are also planned, and a pipeline for fuel is presently under construction. Plans for a Shinkansen, a bullet train, to and from Tokyo have been suspended.

A hotel complex has been built outside the airport. Of nondescript design, it is for the most part indifferently maintained. There has been little money for proper maintenance, and use has been far less than anticipated, in part because the airport opening was delayed for so many years by the Hantai Dōmei. The hotel complex continues to lose money. Slowly the space between Narita City and Sanrizuka is beginning to fill up with facilities of this kind. It does not take much imagination to anticipate how all will blend imperceptibly into the large, increasingly industrialized suburban sprawl that has engulfed the rest of Chiba, so much so that Sakura and Chiba City, once rural towns, are now part of greater Tokyo.

If one were to stand at the center of the crossroads and ask where the roads go and who lives there, the answer would be different for each quadrant. The north and south quadrants immediately adjacent to the airport represent areas chosen for the projected second stage. There the farms, hamlets, and villages are predominantly pro–Hantai Dōmei, and there one finds the solidarity huts and fortresses of the political sects. To the east and west, looking beyond the immediate range of the airport, are houses and farms, nurseries and gardens, and small factories. The landscape shades off into the last pocket of rural life in the prefecture.

Indeed, it is this larger rural area where concern is greatest over the impact of the airport. For along with the construction aboveground there is an underground jungle of drainage ditches, sewers, pipelines, cables, conduits, and so on. These have altered the ecology of the area. Water levels have dropped; wells have gone brackish and have dried up. The age-old irrigation system that is crucial to wet farming and rice production has largely been destroyed. As an advance outpost for an encroaching industrialization, the airport is a sorry advertisement.

But many people in Sanrizuka feel that despite its drawbacks the airport is there to stay, the price of progress. No longer is it much of a topic of conversation among the farmers and construction workers who eat at one of the three Chinese restaurants along the road near the fence, their shoes lined up neatly as they sit in the booths on raised platforms. Pictures of airplanes are on the restaurant walls. One restaurant is said to be favorable to the militants, the other two indifferent or pro-airport. Closer to the crossroads, adjacent to a Shell filling station and some new construction, are the bus park, supermarket, post office, police station, and hotel that make up the crossroads itself. Behind their modern façades most of the buildings are old. In the old days, as we have said, those who had business with the imperial ranch would stay and observe agricultural experiments, new equipment, and new livestock breeding techniques imported from the west by the Meiji government. Travelers en route to the many hamlets and villages scattered about would stop in Sanrizuka for the night. The old hotel is still there, hidden behind a modern sliding-glass door front. Its clientele is of course quite different today. Through the entrance one can see that some of the shoes deposited by the guests and lined up neatly along the inside steps are very expensive.

Close by are two supermarkets, some small shops, and a fish store now expanded into a sushi shop run by the younger generation of the proprietors of the fish store. Next door to the sushi shop are the post office and the police station. The police, neatly uniformed and relatively popular, are not at all like the riot police. During a festival they drink beer or whiskey with the town elders and keep a relaxed eye on the younger generation to see that things don't get out of hand. They direct traffic, chat with the inhabitants, and act as neighborhood wardens.

The traffic is always heavy. On weekdays there is a great deal of truck traffic, not only to the airport but also to bring farm equipment and make general deliveries to Sanrizuka. In the late afternoon on Sundays, especially in the summer, traffic tends to back up for a long way. The cars are filled with children and grandmothers who have spent the day visiting relatives, or at the beach some twenty-five minutes away, or on a tour of the temple complex at Narita. People from villages that have long since disappeared under the bulldozer may come back to visit still surviving hamlets or to go to a funeral, wedding, or other solemn occasion. Family members meet in Sanrizuka to dine in one of the many small restaurants. The food is good and eating out is not much more expensive than eating at home.

The general atmosphere of conviviality extends to those ex-farmers or part-time farmers, about sixty of them, who accepted the government's offer of compensation at three times the market price and sold their land. One might think that the members of the Hantai Dōmei would give them a cold shoulder, but this is not the case. Except for a few who clearly betrayed the movement, there is considerable understanding and sympathy between those who left and those who stayed and a recognition that each household must make its own decisions in its own way. In any case, many of those who did sell, and then built or bought new houses in Sanrizuka, voice regret at having sold when they did. Delays in opening the airport prevented the concessions that many had obtained from being profitable. Inflation rapidly ate into the benefits they originally received. Some built rather big houses that have proved to be too expensive to maintain and today are getting tacky. For many, finding alternative occupations to farming has not been easy.

But not everyone lost money on the airport. Some houses in Sanrizuka are splendidly opulent. Built in a modified Chinese style, with blue ceramic tile roofs that curl upward at the ends, they are imposing structures. Some have large gardens with carefully tended bonsai. Many have a large upstairs, generous windows, and out-buildings. In a country where the size of rooms is measured by the number of tatami mats covering the floor, these houses are large indeed. Some of them belong to contractors and subcontractors working at the airport or adjacent sites. A few, it is said, belong to speculators who received inside information from politicians and made a killing selling land, negotiating concessions, and acting as go-betweens. Some are owners of larger shops within the terminal building or neighboring hotels. Some are proprietors of automobile repair and sales establishments, restaurants, and other local businesses. Sanrizuka is not poor. The streets are deliberately narrow, with a nice mix of houses, small shops, and eating places along them. Farther out are groves of trees and bamboo, and beyond them the older and more established farms.

There are two twenty-four-hour taxi services and a bus service to the airport. Mostly they cater to passengers traveling between Tokyo and the airport, but there is also a great deal of local movement by taxi. Engineers, merchants, and others are buying houses in Sanrizuka or in hamlets nearby, preferring to live in old houses than in large, new complexes. Often they send visitors home by taxi; pre-payment is part of the pattern of hospitality. Near the bus stop are billboards advertising the Kabuki Theater in Tokyo, the stylized face and hair of the actors standing out arrestingly. Below the adver-tisement, perhaps pasted over the lower portion, are many copies of a small announcement or two—maybe a notice that Chūkaku-ha will hold a mass rally in Tokyo at which members newly released from jail will speak, sharing the platform with representatives of the Hantai Dōmei.

The bus stop is conveniently located across the street from the sushi shop, in a diagonal space adjacent to some shade trees and shrines. A few of the stone monuments, stelae, and carved deity fig-ures are quite old. The latter usually wear an apron, a cap, or some other article of clothing. Food offerings are placed in front in small, cheap cups. Occasionally someone will leave a sprig of flowers. In the area under the trees, dark and untended, old newspapers and paper cups blow about and catch in the grass and weeds. Some of the ref-use blows over from the supermarket across the street, the one that is opposite the hotel and diagonally across from the sushi shop. The supermarket sells California almonds, raisins, rice, and tuna fish and looks much like a supermarket anywhere, with standard brands of packaged food, canned goods, and produce. Farmers' wives shop here. There are a few more exotic products—octopus and squid, seaweed, many kinds of noodles, both Chinese and Japanese. They are shelved near the Coca Cola. The aisles are narrow, and the shelves are tightly packed. There is a profusion of sweets—cookies, cakes, candies. The supermarket also sells batteries, pharmaceuticals, and clothing, despite specialty shops for all these things nearby. The clothing for sale includes the baggy blue pantaloons worn by farm women for work in the fields, a symbol of the Women's Corps of the Hantai Dōmei. There are, in addition to farm clothes, dress socks with monogrammed brand insignia; round white children's hats that are almost a uniform in the summertime; men's underwear, including jockey shorts and T-shirts; a rather good assortment of men's work, dress, and sport shirts; and ties, belts, gloves, and caps. The supermarket also sells three sizes of pillows, tatami mats, and T-shirts printed with peculiar slogans in English.

Most people go to the supermarket on foot, but those that drive can park on a kind of cement apron in front, or across the street next to the bus stop and the shrines, where there is a cleared but dusty field. The supermarket is open quite late and on Sunday, as are most of the shops at the crossroads. Crossing the street at the crossroads requires caution. There is a great deal of traffic, not only cars, trucks, and buses but also motor scooters, motorcycles, and bicycles pedaled by the very young and the very old. Congestion is made worse by cars parked on the sidewalks or partly in the roadway, obstructing the flow of heavy trucks through the narrow intersection. The congestion is particularly bad at the supermarket, which is always crowded with housewives. Another supermarket, not far away, on the other side of the intersection, is owned by an American chain. More brightly lit and modern than the first, it sells mainly packaged goods, ice cream, soft drinks, bread, cakes, crackers, sandwiches, frozen foods, and heat-and-serve T.V. dinners. It has no fresh produce. Peaches, watermelon, eggplant, and other local vegetables and fruits can be bought in season only in the first supermarket, the more crowded and scruffier one, or in the family grocery stores that also sell beer, tea, sake, and soft drinks. Within easy reach of the bus stop there are also a tailor's shop, a tatami mat repair place, a general store, a radio and electronics equipment place, an appliance shop, and a bicycle, motorcycle, and motor scooter sales and repair center.

Most of the buildings are old ones with converted fronts. Similar shops a little further out of town are new.

It is only a few steps from the crossroads to the farm machinery and repair shop of the Tomura family, which occupies a long, narrow compound running between two streets. It was established by Tomura Issaku's grandfather, who came to Sanrizuka to make tools, copying the designs of tools being imported for use on the imperial estate. The shop is still being run by the Tomura family, and Mrs. Tomura, a lady of great dignity and simplicity, inhabits the family house. Scattered about are a number of outbuildings, including the Sanrizuka church. Adjacent to it, until recently, there was a long, yellow building that was originally a church, then a kindergarten, and finally a dormitory for militants; it was torn down in 1982. At the entrance to the compound and at various places inside it, somewhat casually distributed, are Tomura's large, rusted iron sculptures. They are powerful and dynamic, like the man and the movement he came to exemplify. The house opens inward to the compound. In one window is a faded decal urging support of the Popular Front for the Liberation of Palestine. Children's toys and bicycles add to the clutter of scrap metal, old tractor engines, and the spillover from a workshop in the back.

At the opposite end of the long compound stands the Tomuras' small but elegant church with its small shaded yard and gate. There is little life left in it. Across a narrow lane, in the kimono shop of Kitahara Kōji, the telephone rings every few minutes and there is constant activity. When Tomura was alive there was no question of who had the moral authority of leadership. After his death the location of power became more ambiguous. In any case, Kitahara was different from Tomura in every way. Where Tomura was austere and a bit Olympian, conscious of thought and action both in art and in the movement, Kitahara was a more directly political person. He became an important link between the Hantai Dōmei and supporting groups—Hiroshima peace organizations, Okinawan rights groups, and various sects, most particularly Chūkaku-ha. Kitahara has been arrested and beaten a number of times. He depends heavily, as Tomura did, on the active support of his wife. Although in principle both men saw the Sanrizuka movement as a way of liberating women, their practice in the home fell short.

Also near the crossroads are a nursery school, a community center for older people, and a Shinto shrine, all sharing the same trees and sandy yard. It is here that on festive occasions lanterns are strung out and concessions set up, their stands festooned with colored lights and gaily painted flags, fishes, and other items of cloth or paper that flap and wave. The concessionaires sell all manner of small insects, foods, beer, and ice cream. There are shooting galleries, barkers, and a calligrapher to mark one's ancestral remembrance on a piece of white paper to be placed on a board or a shrine.

Perhaps the ugliest building in Sanrizuka is a large cement block of flats for airport workers and others, with its garbage bins prominently displayed in front. Still much the most impressive building is what remains of the emperor's detached villa, a large, sprawling structure with an elaborately thatched roof, wings, and quarters for women and servants. Weeds have grown up around it and the gates to the green chain-link fence around it are locked. (The two main government symbols in Sanrizuka, one the airport and the other the emperor's lodge, are both surrounded by locked fences.) In the garden, now overgrown, are large stone monoliths with poems etched into them in Chinese characters. Despite neglect the building has lovely lines and a gracefulness, not to say a modesty, that gives it its uniqueness. Now, in somewhat forlorn isolation, it is ignored by the local inhabitants. Part of one wing has fallen in completely and weeds have grown up inside.

If one follows the road from the crossroads south toward the airport entrance itself, one can see, just at the end of the main runway, the remains of a large steel tower. Built by the militants, it stands on top of a three-tiered cement building containing rooms manned by representatives of sects. From the top of the building it is possible to peer directly into the runway and watch the planes taking off and landing. Stacked inside are helmets, staves, electronic and camping equipment, futons, pots and pans, and first-aid equipment. A farmer lives at the base; his land is farmed by militants. Across the road at a police barracks, parked buses containing airport police in full regalia wait for any contingency. One can see why they wait if one climbs to the top of the cement and steel tower. At its base are the remnants of hundreds of automobile tires that were doused with gasoline and ignited, sending up flames that lit up the sky for miles around. The tower, then the scene of many dramatic events, was much bigger than it is now. It has been torn down repeatedly by government cranes and bulldozers, only to be rebuilt by the militants. A little further down the road, the windmill, brightly colored, shifts with the wind. The windmill is within sight of three embattled farmers who live nearby and three adjacent fortresses bristling with barbed wire and high stockades. The police in their watchtowers on the other side of the fence keep their telescopes trained on the farmers, the forts, the windmill, and anyone who passes along the road.

As you travel away from the Sanrizuka crossroads and from the airport itself, the landscape changes radically. The land becomes more sloping and manicured, almost like the English countryside in Cambridgeshire, with narrow winding lanes and well demarcated and tended fields. The glass and plastic greenhouses that dot the landscape enable the farmer to continue his growing season throughout the year. There are many pastures; horsebreeding is still done in the area. Some of the thatched farmhouses date from Tokugawa times. Tucked behind trees and gardens is an occasional thick-walled storehouse or treasure house, its windows constructed like the doors of a safe. There are large nurseries growing evergreens in twisted and shaped forms under the supervision of masters of gardening, while adjacent to them modern factories stand out sharply in the predominantly rural setting, constructed of brightly colored plastic and light steel.

Toward Shibayama and the sea the landscape changes again. In Sanrizuka the main crop is vegetables, mostly peanuts, potatoes, watermelons, eggplant, tomatoes, pickles, and corn. In Shibayama, especially in the lower regions near the sea, rice farming predominates. There the intense green of the fields is punctuated by the bent figures of men and women. The women, in their conical straw hats and baggy trousers, do most of the hand labor, and at certain times of the year work in the paddies waist deep in water.

In Shibayama the problem the airport poses is not land acquisition so much as noise pollution and changes in the shape of the land caused by road, dam, overpass, and railway line construction. Commercial buildings, pipelines, and underground cables have affected the water table (which in turn affects the balance of flooding and draining necessary for rice cultivation), and have resulted in the depletion of woods and the removal of natural fertilizers, thus increasing the farmers' dependence on expensive chemical fertilizers. Population changes too have had negative consequences for farmers: suburbanization has set in and village priorities have changed. Indeed, the farmers in the Shibayama area have many reasons for opposing the airport, so much so that today the bulk of the Hantai Dōmei membership is from Shibayama.

The town itself is still a bit sleepy and rural. There are lots of old-

style houses, many with thatched roofs. Down the road and toward
the sea is the home of Kasé Tsutomu, one of the founders of the original Hantai Dōmei and an important early influence on the movement, although technically not a member. Kasé is a writer, poet, and
professional organizer for the Japan Farmers' Union. A moderate
radical with roots first in the Japan Communist Party and then in
the Japan Socialist Party, he lives surrounded by books, including
the complete works of Lenin and Mao, in a small room at the top of
his parents' farmhouse. The room is austere and simple. On the wall
is a photograph of Kasé being received by Chou En-lai.

Kasé's involvement in the airport protest began with the Tomisato Hantai Dōmei. However, his interest in popular rural movements extends back much further, to the days of peasant rebellions
in which his family, poor tenants, took part. The war interrupted his
education and he was unable to complete secondary school. A vora-
cious reader, he became interested in Marx and also was influenced
by a contemporary radical agrarian theorist, Yamaguchi Bushū,
who, offering a modern version of populism, was an advocate of rural
reform through radical transformation. Yamaguchi had been a
member of the Japan Communist Party for many years before strik-
ing out on his own version of radical populism and was one of the few
theorists of Japanese agricultural movements to become involved in
the Sanrizuka struggle, trying but not succeeding to become its intellectual mentor. Kasé was influenced by Yamaguchi's thought and
explored the history of peasant rebellions in the area, particularly
those occurring in the first decade of the twentieth century. He also
became an expert on village organization, both in his own hamlet,
Tako, and other local hamlets. Shibayama includes some of the oldest and most important Hantai Dōmei villages like Heta and
Higashi.

If you continue along the road past Tako hamlet, eventually you
come to the sea. It is a favorite spot for militants and farmers and
occasionally stray American servicemen, who sit on the beach or dig
for clams and bathe in the water. The sand is a coarse gray. Near the
beach are small roads with abandoned farm buildings as well as new
plastic houses built in the Japanese style. There are new factories as
well, reflecting the Japanese government's desire to decentralize industry and provide alternative occupations to farmers close at hand.
There is much unplanned development. However, nothing has happened that is comparable to what occurred along the eastern
beaches of Tokyo Bay. There, the shallow water, the nutritive salts

carried by rivers flowing into the bay, and the Japanese current had together resulted in one of Japan's richest fishing grounds. In 1951 it was decided that the first major land reclamation project in Chiba should be undertaken there. The Kawasaki Steel Corporation built a steel factory. Today there are about one thousand companies on the reclaimed land representing steel, power, oil storage and refining, and other enterprises. Tankers and coastal vessels have crowded out the fishing boats. Pollution of sea and air are major problems.

What happened to the fishermen is very much on the minds of the Shibayama farmers. For them the airport is the equivalent of the Kawasaki Steel Company, the first step in the process of irreversible change and a permanent disaster in terms of their way of life. Nevertheless, change has come about, and not all of it has proved to be objectionable. New consumer products and increased material benefits are important to hardworking farmers. Moreover, the gradual transition from rural life has been accompanied by greater individual choice and opportunities for new forms of social exchange.

One can see the changes best in Narita City. A center for the Japan National Railways and the hub for a network of buses branching out in all directions, Narita City is a provincial town making the transition to a large city. People are still familiar to one another but there is a marked decline in both courtesy and intimacy. There are, however, lots of small and pleasant encounters. Especially in the older parts of town, the narrow streets, small shops, and many restaurants facilitate chance conversations. There one will also find the Narita Temple complex of shrines, a few old buildings, and many large and new ones. One can also catch a glimpse of old and mysterious hidden gardens, or, in narrow lanes, a small shrine or a traditional open shop selling cereals or spices or woven bamboo.

All this is vulnerable to development. The bus stop where one boards for Sanrizuka with its forest of bicycles represents just such a cleared space. It is adjacent to the railway station and most conveniently located. The buses are a bit old-fashioned and provincial, but they are clean, well cared for, and extremely punctual. Their chromium fittings are polished and the little lavender lights with buttons that tell the driver where to stop all work properly. Drivers wear white gloves and salute smartly as they pass each other on the road. In the morning the buses fill up with young people en route to school, the girls wearing pleated navy skirts and white blouses, and the boys, hair closely cropped, wearing dark tapered trousers and white shirts. Later in the day, housewives constitute the main traffic.

Occasionally a farmer's wife will board, carrying a huge basket pack loaded with vegetables and wearing the peaked straw hat that one sees dotting the rice fields and vegetable gardens. She will struggle on and off the bus with her heavy load, attended by small children or perhaps her husband in his soft black boots with the divided toe. Still later one sees old ladies going visiting or, if dressed in black, en route to a funeral.

Narita City is still a considerable distance from Chiba City, the capital of the prefecture. The distance is measurable not only in kilometers but also in terms of social character and purpose. Chiba City, once a rural center, is today a vast complex of office buildings, factories, and business and commercial facilities. Its buildings are made of glass, concrete, and brick, with no pretension to architectural style; planners were concerned mainly with packing the most people into the least space. There are a few broad avenues and parking areas, but these inevitably lead to severe traffic congestion. A huge complex of buildings not far from the station, connected by motor arcades, is the site of the Chiba local government. Outside are car parks for official pool cars with drivers for important people. The governor has his office there. Prefectural governors are important politically and administratively. Caught between the demands of the national government and the needs of the local population, not a few of them have become "radical" and favor their constituents over national considerations. The governor of Chiba tried to mediate between the Hantai Dōmei and the Airport Authority during the early days of the conflict, but his efforts were largely unsuccessful.

In Chiba City are also the offices of the Airport Authority police and the Chiba Prefecture police, who share responsibility for protecting the airport. In the same government complex are housed the branch organs of the mass media, including Nippon Broadcasting Corporation and newspapers such as *Asahi Shimbun*. Anything that happens in Chiba is immediately communicated to the news media. Anything that happens in Sanrizuka will bring knowledgeable reporters and television crews racing to the spot. *Asahi Shimbun* also keeps a full-time reporter in Narita City, one who knows the Sanrizuka situation intimately. *Mainichi Shimbun* keeps a young reporter posted at the airport.

Chiba City and Sakura City have become part of metropolitan Tokyo, partly because of the same industrialization policy that led to the decision to build an airport in Chiba Prefecture. Not very long ago, though, Chiba City, Narita City, and Sakura City were rural centers. Sakura City and Narita City still retain certain historical associations that are part of current tradition. Some Hantai Dōmei farmers love to link up Sanrizuka's struggle with earlier ones in Chiba Prefecture, especially if they have had a bit of sake and want to entertain a visitor.

One story they tell is about Sakura, the site of Sakura castle. Once it was the seat of the Hotta family, which furnished many statesmen to the *Rōjū* (the chief council of the Tokugawa shoguns). In 1654, a band of village elders under the leadership of Sōgorō went to Edo in order to protest the tyranny of the Lord of Sakura. In those days to protest was a capital offense; an inferior's duty was to acquiesce in the mandates of his superiors. Despite the justice of his claims, Sōgorō was put to death. His wife was crucified with him. Their four male children were decapitated before their eyes. One son, seven years old, was butchered as he ate sweets thrown to him by compassionate spectators. Today incense is kept burning on Sōgorō's grave. "We are the descendents of Sōgorō," says an old Hantai Dōmei farmer.

The temple complex at Narita City is another source of inspiration for Hantai Dōmei storytellers. Once a flourishing center of Buddhism, its proper title is *Narita-san Shingo Shinshoji*, the Divinely Protected Temple of Recent Victory on Mount Narita. With the name goes a story that reaches back many centuries, to the time when Buddhism was founded in Japan and an Indian sculptor named Bishukatsuma carved a wonder-working image of Fudō. The image was taken to China, where it came into the possession of a priest named Keikwa Ajari. Kōbō Daishi, a Japanese saint, visited China in A.D. 804 in order to gain instruction in certain Buddhist mysteries. He became the disciple of this priest. Bringing the image home, he enshrined it in a temple near Kyoto with some figures he himself had carved. About a century and a half later, a certain Masakado, a courtier of noble birth, taking offense at not being appointed to an embassy in China, rebelled against the sovereign, Shujaku Tennō. He usurped the title of Mikado and built a miniature court that reproduced the place names of Kyoto. In the ensuing war, the legitimate ruler carried Kōbō Daishi's image of Fudō into battle. A loyalist placed it on a rock near the rebel capital and, performing prayers and incantations in front of it for three weeks, kept a fire burning on the altar. The upstart was defeated. The successful army left for home. When the abbot tried to lift the image in order to return it to its proper place he discovered it had become as heavy as a huge rock. Since it could not be moved, a huge temple complex was built on the site. There it stands today. So too, the Hantai Dōmei storyteller concludes, the movement will stand like a rock.

WHEN YOU VISIT Sanrizuka, it will be worth your while to linger for a time, chat, and—over a glass of sake, perhaps—listen to such tales. In Sanrizuka and beyond the inhabitants are friendly, as in most rural places, but they are also suspicious. Visiting is one thing; prying is another. Yet they are proud of their fight, and despite their vulnerability they will take a stranger in and share their concerns. For that you must offer something in return. A sense of understanding is perhaps enough, and a feeling that outsiders too have a stake in what is going on. They do not ask you to take sides. They only ask that you be fair.

Getting to know the militants may be more difficult. In some ways they are less articulate than the farmers. The farmers have learned how to put their grievances very well and with dramatic effect. The militants, especially the younger ones, are not in love with words. Language, especially the ceremonial, hierarchical language of Japan, is for them a form of tyranny. It is part of what they oppose. You have to live with them to see them as individuals rather than categories, and to lose the sense of unease that simply the word "sect" tends to generate.

Neither the farmers nor the militants are exactly thrilled by the prospect of greater modernity. Indeed, the Sanrizuka movement, along with others, may mark a turning point in Japan's romance with development. As in Europe and the United States, the ideologies of growth have gone a bit sour. Certainly the Sanrizuka movement is a protest against, among other things, rampant urbanization and industrialization, both of which are so evident in contemporary Japan. But for militants the context is also one of protest against capitalism and the bureaucratic state, even though a quick glance at socialist societies should quickly disabuse them of easy solutions.

Whatever their own differences, for militants the state is represented by the bureaucrats, a view that you are inclined to share if you have been followed by the police and observed by binoculars as you enter the no-man's-land, the homes of Hantai Dōmei farmers, or the fortresses of militant sects. Members of the movement will deny that the government too has a case. But for senior government officials the airport is a symbol of growth, without which Japan cannot survive as a democracy. For them planning and development are part of that architecture of mind and spirit, concept and action, work and imagination, which, despite headaches and political consequences, is the triumph of man over nature.

All the contenders are looking for solutions. Each group finds it easier to be opposed to what another side proposes than to be in favor of something. No solution is likely to be accepted. Moreover, the bureaucrats have difficulty with the politicians, and the politicians are frustrated by the power of the bureaucrats. Such relations keep the government from being more sensitive and responsive to the diversity of needs that development generates. Although one cannot live without development, living with it is increasingly difficult.

Such matters are not simply academic. Even though farmers may not put the problem in abstract terms, it is of direct concern to all the farmers in Sanrizuka. Two of them have articulated the problems of information, obligation, and political responsiveness very well, Shimamura Ryōsuke and Ogawa Gen. When they were young they were soldiers of the emperor. Like their fellow members of the Hantai Dōmei who fought the Chinese in Manchuria, they came home from the war disillusioned with a system they no longer believed in and embarrassed at what they had done, so unthinkingly, on behalf of the emperor. They are right to be suspicious of state power, of authority, and of appeals to their loyalty. They believe they have demonstrated loyalty many times. They fought to save the state in the war and in the struggle against hunger that followed the war. They believe they have now become victims. No one should doubt their sincerity.

Nor should one cast the militants into the villain's role, as government officials tend to do. Theirs is not some strange or aberrant form of behavior. The militants belong to an authentic radical tradition in Japan, as we will try to show. Most turn out to be serious, intelligent young men and women trying to find an appropriate way to reconcile the principles they believe in with the life they lead. Less hypocritical than most armchair radicals, probably less informed, and certainly less intellectual, they are at once more modest and more presumptuous.

As for the senior bureaucrats, they have of course been the direct targets of confrontation. They have been at various times flexible, tough, devious, manipulative; many other words would no doubt apply equally well. But on closer inspection, in the context of time and place and again history (always history), they are less pompous and more human, more intelligent, and more understanding than virtually anyone, including the politicians, gives them credit for. But they are also more clannish, protective, and reclusive within their jurisdictions than their affable appearance suggests. They are there to protect the state. They know how essential it is to have power. But they are also aware that at the very center power is a more fragile and collective phenomenon than it appears from the outside. They are right to be cautious.

2
Hamlets
and
Households

TODAY THERE ARE two Hantai Dōmei organizations, each hostile to the other. The farmers of both live mostly in hamlets outside Sanrizuka (within the larger administrative area of Narita City) and outside Shibayama Town. The hamlet (*buraku*) has no official status in the structure of government today; it is the village (*mura*), generally composed of five or more hamlets, that is the smallest official rural local government unit. Village, town, and city differ from one another in size and in degree of importance, both economic and administrative. The Western term "local government" properly applies to the prefecture. Cities of less than a million inhabitants, towns, and villages within each prefecture lack the jurisdictional power and political scope of their Western counterparts.

In the Sanrizuka-Shibayama area the typical hamlet has from five to twenty households. The hamlet's main purpose today is to discuss government policies and decisions and to deal informally with the community's immediate problems. Each person within the hamlet has intimate knowledge of the lives and circumstances of all the others, and each recognizes that it is the household as a whole that must be taken into account when considering its situation. Joining, remaining with, or leaving the Hantai Dōmei, for example, is invariably a family affair.

Two Crossroads

The importance of the hamlet has fluctuated in Japan as a whole. In the prewar period the hamlet was more significant than it is today. It tended to be romanticized as a collective body with roots extending back into Tokugawa times and before.[1] After the war the romanticism evaporated, and emphasis was shifted to the village. The shift was in part deliberate: the hamlet was seen as a remnant of the imperial system. The village, unlike the hamlet, is a practical administrative unit. A hamlet has a headman or chief (similar to a ward chief in a town); a village, on the other hand, has a mayor, village officials who deal with tax, burial, birth, and other records, and police and postal facilities.

Sanrizuka, although a rapidly growing entity, is not a hamlet or a village or a town or a city. It began as a crossroads at the imperial estate, a small commercial cluster catering mainly to those with business on the estate itself, and it grew in importance as the interest in agricultural experimentation and innovation increased, especially in the Meiji period (1868–1912). In its own way it was a functional response to societal needs rather than an organic community, just as the airport is today. In this it differs from the surrounding hamlets and villages, which are organic communities dating from different periods.

The airport itself occupies ground administratively divided between Narita City and Shibayama Town, both of whose boundaries incorporate a variety of hamlets with somewhat different traditions as well as different agricultural specialties. The movement against the airport has been called the Sanrizuka movement because much of the main runway and many of the buildings have been constructed on lands within or immediately adjacent to the old Sanrizuka crossroads, and also because Tomura and Kitahara lived in Sanrizuka. Actually, however, most Hantai Dōmei members now come from hamlets in Shibayama.

In the typical farm family in the Sanrizuka-Shibayama area, three generations live together in the same compound. To a remarkable degree social relations are marked by a respect for age and for a hierarchy in which the male head of the household has authority and the eldest son a privileged place. Within the family there are well-defined rules of mutual obligation and an exceptionally high degree of civility and discretion. The household head has power, but there are strict rules about its exercise: he must be just in supporting the needs of family members, for instance, and he should not make decisions without taking their wishes into consideration.

Similar obligations of respect prevail between families in a hamlet. No matter how much interests may differ from one family to another, the common ground should outweigh the differences until it becomes self-evident that family interests must prevail. It is essential, therefore, for the Hantai Dōmei to provide sufficient common ground to prevent family responsibility from constantly taking precedence over hamlet responsibility. In turn, hamlet responsibility must harmonize with the overall policies and objectives of the Hantai Dōmei. Mutualism and local solidarity, then, are the main principles regulating hamlet life; they constitute both the strength and the weakness of the Hantai Dōmei. They are a strength insofar as commitment is not singular but multiple, through both household and hamlet, which enables the Hantai Dōmei to exist even when its top leaders die or resign. They are a weakness in that few organizational initiatives can be taken without very solid support and then only after prolonged discussion.

THREE HAMLETS were obliterated in the first stage of airport construction, and others are threatened by the second stage. If and when the airport is completed, about 360 households will have been displaced. Of hamlets considered to be in a dangerous area (that is, subject to takeover), Yokobori, a Meiji hamlet, has four households left; Heta, which goes back at least to Tokugawa times, has twenty households, as does Nakago, also very old. All the households in these hamlets are said to be members of the Hantai Dōmei, but some households are inactive and others may effectively have dropped out.

For another twenty or so hamlets around the site, the problems of noise pollution and ecological imbalance remain important. Whether they support the one Hantai Dōmei or the other, many of the households in these hamlets are less concerned with eliminating the airport itself or restoring the land to its original condition than with forcing the government to recognize obligations to farmers in the affected area, and to farmers generally. That is, they are concerned not with reversing the government's decision on industrial priorities, which it is far too late to do and in any case would be impossible given the government's success, but rather with preserving and improving the farming conditions in these hamlets. This the government is increasingly willing to do.

The hamlets that concern us here—those that lie just inside or outside the site for the second part of the airport or within the wider noise pollution area—date from at least three distinct periods. One group of hamlets goes back to Tokugawa times. Others are "descended" from the older ones and remain linked to them by kinship ties; such "descended" hamlets were for the most part settled by second and third sons excluded from the original patrimonies by primogeniture.[2] "New" hamlets, the third group, consist mainly of the families of servicemen given holdings after World War II. Other residents of the "new" hamlets are ex-tenants who became proprietors as a result of land reforms made under American occupation authorities.

The three kinds of hamlets differ markedly. In general, the older the hamlet, the more conservative its orientation. The traditionally powerful families in the older hamlets still exercise moral and political authority and influence. Kinship and social prestige go together and still carry great weight. There is much deference, ceremony, and ritual. In the newer ones there is greater equality; manners are a bit rougher and people are more direct.

The houses differ as well. In the older hamlets the houses are large, with thatched or tile roofs. In the new ones houses are smaller, often made with plastic and concrete materials as well as wood. The "pioneers" who had to clear the land and cut down bamboo forests originally lived in huts until their incomes rose above subsistence and they could afford better housing.

Between hamlets there are residual tensions. Some people remember where others came from, both socially and geographically, and whether they were former landlords or tenants. Such distinctions persist despite the land reforms of the immediate postwar period, although they are less important in those hamlets that are pro–Hantai Dōmei.

The hamlets have responded somewhat differently to pressure from the Airport Authority, which wanted to acquire land for the first stage of the airport construction as quickly as possible. Some pioneers, the poorer and weaker ones, were among the first to sell their land. But among the toughest, most militant Hantai Dōmei members today are pioneers who are good farmers. Some of the most militant old hamlets in the first-stage area, on whose land fortresses and solidarity huts and steel towers were built to fight against surveying and land acquisition, caved in to government pressure en masse, a function of the hierarchy and deference that prevailed in their hamlets. When the most prestigious former landlord or powerful boss decided it was time to give up, everyone followed suit.

The pioneers are tougher. Most spent their youth in the army. When they were in their late thirties they began to be rewarded.with good crops. Aided by favorable government loan policies, resettlement programs, and a variety of agricultural marketing arrangements, by the time they were in their early forties they could look forward with some security to the years ahead. They had perhaps five good years, 1955 to 1960. Then in 1960 the government embarked on its famous income-doubling scheme, a policy which forced smaller farmers off the land. Once again they were the victims rather than the beneficiaries of government.

Even before 1960 all was not well on the farm. Farmers were often bewildered by sudden and apparently arbitrary changes in government policy. Changes that seemed quite sensible from the top looked whimsical from below. In one instance, the government announced a scheme to promote the growing of mulberry trees and the raising of silkworms. Just as farmers began to respond, the policy shifted so that it favored something else. Such a shift could result in inconsistent decisions on loans. Local officials responsible for handling loans and other financial matters interpreted rules and regulations in their own way, which led to favoritism, party factionalism, and disputes. Programs associated with the mechanization of agriculture and the use of chemical fertilizers were alleged to be administered in unfair and unethical ways. Officials who were members of the Liberal Democratic Party might, for example, discriminate against farmers who were members of the Japan Socialist Party. It was a situation in which local bosses had a great deal of power.

Until 1960 it was widely accepted that Japanese farmers were among the world's most efficient. The government, however, decided that farming was the inefficient sector of the Japanese economy. Although farm incomes continued to rise after the industrialization policy went into effect, other incomes went up faster. Among farmers, it was said, smaller farmers were the least efficient of all. While there was merit in this argument, by no means could it have been said that Sanrizuka farmers were poor.

Perhaps the best summary of government policy toward farmers has been provided by Ronald Dore:

> The settlement pattern in clustered villages, the crucial dependence on rice agriculture with its shared irrigation systems involving collective village control of water and who could use it, the juxtaposition around each village of tiny

plots whose use or misuse could affect the plots of a neighbor, the intricate patterns of labor exchange between households—all created a pattern in which the use of land was a right and a responsibility shared between the individual household and the village community. It was on these foundations that nineteenth-century governments built agricultural associations as means of diffusing new seeds and chanelling new methods, interlaced with appropriate moral exhortation, to the villagers. At first, like the villages themselves, the asssociations tended to be dominated by landlords. State paternalism and the paternalism of the village interfused in a relation of mutual support. But in the twenties new kinds of more democratically controlled co-operatives emerged; their functions were widened to include credit operations and marketing on a wider scale. During the war they came into their own as the channel through which agricultural materials were rationed and agricultural produce compulsorily requisitioned. These functions they retained for many years of shortage after the war, though in structure they were revamped (but again under state initiative, by close legislative prescription) as democratic organizations.

By the fifties they had grown into a formidable structure. They had a virtual monopoly over the rice market which they retained even after the loosening of government controls was a major source of their strength, but so also was the integrated multi-purpose nature of their operation. They would supply fertilizer on credit, market the crops, pay the proceeds into the farmer's savings account and debit that account for all his purchases of the wide range of goods on sale in the co-operative shop without his ever having to handle cash. The local co-operatives were further strengthened by their links with superstructural organizations—prefectural and national federations with specialized functions, culminating in a National Marketing Federation, a Consumer Supply Federation and a National Co-operative Bank (which by the late fifties had deposits in the immediate post-harvest months of such magnitude that it had a predominant effect on short-call interest rates).[3]

There were other benefits in the 1950s—a Farm Implement Modernization Fund; a Repair and Improvement of Farm Roads Fund;

an Owner-Farmer Establishment Fund, which helped efficient full-time farmers to purchase land; a Farm Successor's Fund, which provided funding for the modernization of farms taken over by a younger generation. There were Home Improvement Loan Schemes and Daily Life Improvement Schemes to ease the life of the housewife in the kitchen, Car Purchase Loans, and many others. In all these the cooperative organizations played an important part. Farmers became intermeshed with an elaborate credit and marketing structure. The rural household gained rather than declined in importance. And as the small farmer was assisted, his way of life strengthened. The government ideal was full-time farming. As Dore puts it, "Part-time farming—*unserious* farming, and hence *poor* farming—was to be thoroughly discouraged."

When government policy dramatically reversed itself and agriculture was downgraded in favor of industrialization, the matter was serious. Despite farmers' adaptiveness, increases in rural labor productivity had not kept pace with the general economic growth of the nation. The rate of Japanese farm labor productivity was equal to that of the United States and Europe, but it had not increased as fast as in other Japanese industries. This difference in labor productivity, the core of the government's shift in policy, was called the "gap theory." The government was concerned that the gap between agriculture and industry in terms of labor productivity was widening and that the rise in the standard of living for the Japanese people as a whole was not matched by a rise in farm family income. So the Basic Agricultural Law passed in 1961 was intended to push smaller farmers out of full-time farming and consolidate small land holdings into larger ones. The percentage of farmers engaged in supplementary occupations—that is, with concurrent employment in industry—rose from 66 percent in 1960 to 84 percent in 1970. In the government's view it was necessary to put an end to the overproduction of rice and to government rice subsidies. Japan's future would lie in "internationalism."

This policy has had an impact on both village and hamlet. In a 1970 survey of villages it was found that of eighty-one households in one farming community, only 7 percent were engaged solely in agriculture, 39 percent were engaged in concurrent occupations, and 54 percent were not engaged in farming at all.[4] Today, of the 5.4 million people in the labor force engaged in farming, only a small portion are full-time farmers. The government's policy is not only a reversal; it threatens to wipe out small-scale full-time farming almost completely and to transform the basic structural units of Japanese life—rural household, hamlet, and village.

IN THE Sanrizuka struggle much more is at stake than an airport. The movement is fighting to preserve full-time farming despite the costs. Neither a struggle of "traditionals" against "modernizers," nor a class struggle between "peasants" and "capitalists," it is, rather, a struggle of farm households and hamlets and villages against a state policy that threatens their survival. And because that struggle has so many historical and cultural aspects as well as political ones, it has struck a wider and more responsive core than anyone, including the farmers themselves, anticipated.

Different villages have responded differently to government pressure. In Sanrizuka, a dry-farming area, the older villages (which tend, as we have said, to act as units) were originally favorable to the Liberal Democratic Party. The picture was more blurred in Shibayama, a wet-farming area, where a history of peasant rebellions, rice riots, and tenant uprising had left an inheritance of involvement with the Japan Socialist Party and the Japan Communist Party.[5]

In some hamlets deep divisions appeared between pro- and anti–Hantai Dōmei groups. Attempts at mediation failed. Sometimes it was difficult to conduct hamlet meetings as a result. Even in small hamlets, which are important not as administrative jurisdictions but as consultative and informational units acting on behalf of larger units, discussions became difficult. Sometimes separate meetings had to be held for each group. Even the most commonplace issues were affected, like installing an automatic telephone system to replace the community phone, or paving the roads, or constructing distribution centers.

Some of the old hamlets that supported the original Hantai Dōmei—Komaino and Tokkō, for example—suddenly, after secret meetings, dropped out of it. In newer villages such as Tenjinmine, Tennami, Tōhō, and Kinone, each household had its own opinion and acted accordingly. In some school districts (Iwayama, for instance), several hamlets and villages reinforced their mutual opposition to the airport. The school district is in general a rather important jurisdiction: for a cluster of hamlets around a primary or secondary school, the school itself serves as the district community center and meeting place. When there are protests, or when the governor of the prefecture wants to address an audience larger than a village, the likely location will be the district school.

Even in areas outside Hantai Dōmei influence, many hamlets consider themselves semi-autonomous, and if not independent at least self-reliant. At the same time, however, they are linked to the rest of society through functional organizations, which can serve as a basis for a horizontal network of defensive associations throughout the area. Firefighters, for instance, are not only members of the firemen's brigade in their own hamlet but also associate with such brigades in other villages nearby. The equipment they use for signaling a fire alert can be used to warn of other dangers as well. The "early warning system" used by the Hantai Dōmei to sound the alarm against the police is, in fact, simply an extension of the firefighting brigades system.

The nuclei of the original Hantai Dōmei consisted of hamlet assemblies that met once a month in each hamlet in the Shibayama-Sanrizuka area (although when there was a crisis they met much more often). Although each hamlet had a headman who had nominal authority, there was no real leader. Indeed, the headman has always tended to be self-deprecating about power and regards his position more as a rather onerous responsibility. The assembly itself consisted of a representative from each household (usually the farmer himself, but not always). The internal division was according to functional groups, including women's, men's, and elders' "corps."

In structuring their organization around the system of "corps," the Hantai Dōmei was deliberately reviving old practices. In villages or hamlets in the old days, as Kazuko Tsurumi has written, "children from seven to sixteen belonged to the *kodomo gumi* (children's group); all boys from fifteen or sixteen until they married entered the *wakamono gumi* (young men's group); all young women of the same age joined the *musume gumi* (young women's group). Such co-equal relationships cut across differences in their parents' status."[6] Through these bodies individuals were trained for the various functional organizations in which they would later participate. Membership in the *gumi* (or *kumi*) formed the basis for solidarity within the women's, men's, and elders' organizations (*kō*) that the children would join as adults.

Just as *kumi* and *kō* created bonds based on age, sex, and function, involving the immediate membership of all people in the community on an intimate basis and reinforcing kinship ties, so it is with today's corps. They have their work cut out for them. One group might study the impact of pollution, or the impact of irrigation on the regime. Another is concerned with the effect of proposed changes in textbooks on children's education. The views of the corps are taken into account at village assemblies. The original Hantai Dōmei thus created a participant democracy in which "the coequality of the members of the sub-system count against the hierarchical structure."[7] It combined a radical belief in class struggle against the state with an organic view of society based on the small community. Behind the slogans of the Hantai Dōmei there was indeed a more complicated "deep structure" of earlier principles and obligations.

Of course hamlets are neither independent nor aloof from national politics, or for that matter from the local politics of Narita City and Shibayama Town. The functional organizations in each hamlet— men's organizations, women's organizations, the fire brigade, and so on—continue to carry out national responsibilities. At the same time each organization at the hamlet level has its own unique solidarity as a social body. The firefighters, for example, go on outings and picnics together in addition to practicing fire drills by running up and down the tall, Victorian-like towers, beating the fire drums, and learning to fight back flames. Their social events are occasions of merriment and camaraderie.

Perhaps the most important affiliation for farmers, other than hamlet and village connections, is membership in cooperatives. Not only do cooperatives link up farm interests all over the country, they serve as a kind of political party. Like political parties they adhere to fairly well defined ideologies.[8] The first main effort to build a farmers' cooperative (the All-Japan Farmers' Movement), around the turn of the century, was associated with anti-bourgeois feeling. In the postwar period the National Association of Agricultural Cooperatives, Nōkyō, has become a mammoth organization closely associated with the LDP. It participates in a government price support system that can and sometimes does peg the price of rice at four times its market value. Just prior to the 1960 shift in government policy, 90 percent of Japan's farmers were engaged in rice production, so the cooperation between the LDP government and Nōkyō in pricing rice virtually ensured the farmers' overwhelming support of the LDP. Rural overrepresentation in parliament adds to the importance of rural Dietmen. Farmers had, in effect, double access to participation—the cooperatives and the political parties.

There was also a more radical combination of cooperative and party. In Sanrizuka and Shibayama, the All-Japan Federation of Farmers' Union (Zennihon Nōmin Kumiai Rengōkai) was closely allied with the Japan Socialist Party. When the JSP split in 1960,

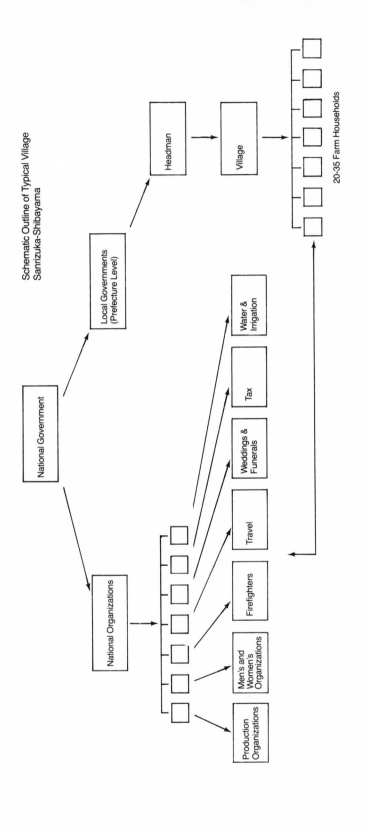

Schematic Outline of Typical Village
Sanrizuka-Shibayama

the Democratic Socialist Party (a social democratic party, in contrast to the more Marxist JSP) formed a rival farm organization of more moderate socialists, the National Farmers' Alliance (Zenkoku Nōmin Dōmei). This is a much smaller body that has had a very small role to play in the area. Nor does the All-Japan Reclamation Federation (Zennihon Kaitakusha Renmei), a national organization of farmers settled on land reclaimed for agricultural purposes, have much power. The LDP and the JSP, especially the LDP, have had the greatest involvement in the daily conduct of agricultural business in Sanrizuka, Shibayama, and elsewhere in Japan.[9]

Meetings, petitions and protests have all been as much a part of the inheritance of farms as planting and harvesting. All farm families participate in activities ranging from agricultural associations to party politics. In most farmers' organizations such as cooperatives that are associated with one political party or another, the LDP predominates. Farmers were generally shaken by the original industrialization policy decided upon by the Ikeda cabinet in 1960. But it was not until the crucial decision was made in 1962 to construct a new airport, followed by the New Airport Authority Act of 1965 which specified the original Tomisato site, that the LDP became anathema in the Sanrizuka-Shibayama area. Nor was the LDP the only party to be so regarded. The Japan Communist Party was believed to have "betrayed" the Hantai Dōmei, a view much intensified when the sects joined the struggle since they were all bitterly anti-JCP. Indeed parliamentary government in general has become an object of contempt with perhaps the only reasonably acceptable party remaining the Japan Socialist Party and only the Chiba branch, which has not only a considerable history in Shibayama, as we have seen, but is also associated with farmers' organizations and the struggle in Tomisato.

In Chiba, hamlets have always tended to be more autonomous than in other prefectures, a tradition based in part on organization and in part on ideology. Among the organizational grounds is the minimal residue of feudalism, especially the feudalism of the large domain; among the ideological is *Nōhon-Shugi,* the tradition of the "peasant-warrior," which we will discuss in Chapter 3.[10] As far back as the Edo period (1615–1868), the area was governed by small daimyos and bureaucrats. (The one exception was the Hotta of Sakura, a daimyo with a very large holding.) Independent village life was perhaps greater in this prefecture than any other. Chiba Prefecture itself was formed in several stages during the Meiji restoration. It involved the breaking up and reconsolidation of three feudal do-

mains, Omigawa, Tako, and Takaoka, which were formed into Niihari Prefecture. Four others, including Sakura and Katsushika, became Imba Prefecture, and four were formed into Kisarazu
Prefecture. In 1875 Imba and Kisarazu were combined into Chiba
Prefecture, and in 1877 three counties from Niihari were added in.
Hence, compared with some others the pattern was more pluralistic,
lacking in historical unity, susceptible to urbanization and modernization because of proximity to Tokyo. Local samurai and landlords
had considerable latitude to experiment with farming, education,
and social projects. There was also a history of tax wars, rice riots,
and landlord tenant rebellions—that is, a tradition of hamlet resistance to centralized authority.

Today, each hamlet in Chiba is typically composed of three kinds
of internal structures: functional organizations (for example, those
associated with water and tax and production); kinship organizations
having to do with age and sex, which also have national counterparts
(a women's organization, for instance, would include affiliation with
campaigns for prenatal care, breast feeding of infants, and so on);
and political organizations such as cooperatives and parties. Sanrizuka itself is unique among Hantai Dōmei communities since it is
part of Narita City. It elects members to the Narita City Assembly,
where its records of birth, death, and taxes are kept. Most Hantai
Dōmei hamlets are associated with Shibayama Town and hence
elect representatives to the Shibayama Town Council. Some hamlets have been so attenuated that they have joined with others, the
original Hantai Dōmei serving as a substitute village in and of itself.
For hamlets most affected by the airport, the Hantai Dōmei is in a
sense a village that is also a political party.

ANY DESCRIPTION of the structure of hamlets runs the risk
of ignoring, indeed obliterating, the actual life within them. We will
look, then, at a typical day on one of the small vegetable farms in the
Sanrizuka area.

Even on a summer morning the family does not rise terribly early.
Unless they have poultry it is not the crowing of a cock that signifies
the dawn; rather, it is the farmer's wife—or, better, their *yomé*
(daughter-in-law)—who gets up first and bangs open the outside
sliding shutters that cover the *shoji* screens. For Hagiwara Susumu
of Yokobori village, the day begins when his wife busies herself in
the kitchen. A modern refrigerator, propane stove, and sink stand
near an old brick-and-tile woodburning stove that is no longer used.
Hagiwara gets up and puts on his long underwear, even in summer.

He wears high socks with a divided toe inside the ubiquitous high-button, forked-toe, soft work shoes. Around his waist he wears a flannel stomacher. Almost the first thing he does is to light up a cigarette; like most other farmers, he smokes heavily. He washes up at faucets in the yard. His wife gives him tea and bean paste made with egg yolk, and perhaps some vegetables and a thin soup. She does not eat with her husband, by and large, but serves him. His teabowl is larger than those of other family members and is distinguished by some mark or design.

After breakfast and another cigarette, and after the children have been sent off to school, the farmer and his wife go out to the compound. Depending on the weather and season, Mr. Hagiwara makes plans to plant, weed, cultivate, or load. For certain kinds of crops weeding is partly a machine job, but in Sanrizuka most weeding is done by women, by hand. Many of the old women who have spent much of their lives weeding, or planting rice by hand, are permanently bent over.

In the compound Hagiwara tinkers with his machinery. His tractor is a fourteen-horsepower, two-wheeled affair with a sloping nose, power hitches front and back, deep-treaded rubber wheels, and large handlebars rather than a steering wheel. It hitches to a two-wheeled rack. His wife climbs on the rack for the trip out to the fields; she sits side-saddle, as it were, with one foot folded under her and the other draped over the edge. The fields are larger than a garden plot, but not too large for a husband-and-wife team. They work together almost every day: the man uses the machines, sprays, cuts weeds with a long-poled cutter; and the woman does the handwork, unless it is too heavy.

At noon they go back to the house for lunch, which consists mainly of vegetables. They eat together, but the farmer's wife hops up and down to serve. (At dinner she will again, as at breakfast, eat separately.) Hagiwara drinks beer or tea. Water for the tea is poured from thermos flasks, which keep the water temperature at about 68° C, into the small clay pots in which the tea steeps. (There are also, of course, tea breaks during both morning and afternoon.) After lunch the two return to the fields.

The schedule varies somewhat from household to household; it tends to be more flexible on farms with no livestock. In the afternoon, a farmer will often drive off to visit a friend or go to a village meeting, sometimes staying for dinner and then drinking sake until quite late at night. If there is a grandmother, she will look after the children. She may dress carelessly if she is very old. In summer when it is very hot her withered breasts may be exposed. This is not a lack of modesty so much as a sense of the organic, an identification with the decay of natural objects, a kind of earthiness that suggests a comfortable, slow slide into the earth itself.

Stock or dairy farmers rise early in the morning. Their barns are much closer to the house than is the case with a New England farm, and they have little grazing land. Their farms, miniaturized "milk factories," have up-to-date equipment. The cows are tended very carefully. Awards won in the many competitions—brass tablets, figures on pedestals, or blue, red, and yellow ribbons testifying to success in breeding or milk production—are placed near the shrine in the house. Chicken farmers have a different schedule: they must pick up eggs two or three times a day, candling and boxing them. Some have established their own cooperatives and sell directly to consumers in their own trucks.

Of the twelve Hantai Dōmei farmers still living in the second-stage airport site in 1982, all are of the Taishō period—that is, born between 1912 and 1926. In Toyomi village only two households are left. Iwasawa Shigeru, a chicken farmer aged fifty-five, owns three *chō* of land (a *chō* is a hectare or about 2.5 acres) and has a son, fifteen, in high school. The other remaining villager, seventy-seven, is ill; his twenty-nine-year-old son is not now engaged in farming.

Tenjinmine village is where Ishibashi Masaji lives. He owns only one *chō* of land, but he farms airport land as well, using a large four-wheeled tractor for plowing and cultivation. He is fifty-nine. His son, who works with him, is thirty-five. The former acting president of the Hantai Dōmei, Ishibashi Masaji is widely regarded as a good farmer. He has been deeply involved in the movement from the start. Ishibashi's mother, now in her nineties, was arrested for fighting with the airport police and pouring buckets of human excrement on them. The family's house is inside a large and comfortable compound with carefully cultivated trees placed among the rocks in the best Japanese garden style. Ishibashi often carries his granddaughter in a small sling on his back when he runs his tractor or works in the fields. His house is neat and comfortable. On the walls are two paintings of Tomura's, shown with pride to visitors. If one is lucky enough to be invited for dinner, the hospitality is lavish. Ishibashi likes to compare the Hantai Dōmei with the properties of Japanese sake—smooth, supple, and hospitable to those who respect it. He tells a story of being visited by representatives of the Black Panthers. On being introduced to sake in the quantities that farmers drink it on festive occasion—that is, in water tumblers rather than the thimblefuls normally served in restaurants—to a man the Panthers passed out on the floor.

Across the road lives Ogawa Kakichi, one of many Ogawas in this area. He is fifty-eight, has about five *chō* of land, and farms some airport land as well. In marked contrast to the very small Ishibashi, Ogawa Kakichi is very tall. He is one of the richest farmers in the area. His father was a tenant on the imperial estate. Able to accumulate some funds, he bought land before the war and developed it over many years, gradually buying up more property. Ishibashi has given up stock farming because his son does not like to care for animals, but Ogawa is a very successful stock farmer.

Ogawa's interest in the movement is somewhat different from others'. He is less anti-government than most Hantai Dōmei members. Rather, he wants the government to live up to its principles, to be more democratic, responsible, and accountable. He sees the crucial weakness of Japan's democracy (and the underlying meaning of the Sanrizuka struggle) as a lack of due process. He also believes that the farmers of the Sanrizuka movement represent the backbone of society. The government should have paid attention to their wishes and needs. To prevent such government arbitrariness, citizens must be able to make full use of the law to protect their rights. He sees participation in the struggle not as a revolutionary would see it but as the moral obligation of a virtuous and responsible citizen. When not busy with farming, Ogawa collects relevant documents for legal proceedings against the government. These, carefully filed, are being brought together methodically in order to prove the violation of due process by the government. In the countryside, where lawyers are conspicuous by their absence, Ogawa is creating the role. Even his manner is deliberate and judicious.

Ogawa's house and yard reflect his patience and sobriety. The house is spacious, with carefully tended outbuildings around it. He has a large truck. His farm equipment is neatly arranged and well cared for. Inside the house is an ancestral shrine made of carefully selected grained wood brought to a high polish. The arrangement of flowers and pots is precise and tasteful. On the wall is a picture of Mount Fuji. Next to it is a group photograph showing Ogawa meeting with Premier Chou En-lai on a visit to China.

Up the road a short distance is the house of Shitō Tōichi. His holding is very small, under one *chō*. Shitō is very active in the movement, despite his sixty-seven years; he frequently goes to rallies and makes speeches all over the country. A short, dynamic man, he was a soldier in Manchuria before the war and learned to speak some English. His very traditional, small Japanese farmhouse has curved center beams made of logs, a thatched roof, and mud-and-wattle walls that are beginning to crumble. Shitō's father was a not very successful fisherman who came to the area to open a small provisions shop along the road adjacent to the imperial estate. The tiny house was enlarged to include a shop area. Its shelves, now twisted and empty, bear mute testimony to what happened: when the emperor sold off some of the land nearby, commercial traffic along the lane was diverted to the Sanrizuka crossroads and the shop failed. At an early age Shitō enlisted in the army.

His life has not been easy. His wife went mad. But despite such hardships, Shitō has lost none of his toughness or vivacity. When we interviewed him he seemed to be having difficulty in replying to questions. Then with a grin he revealed why. A few days before, he had gone to Kita-Fuji to visit the "mother movement" of the Sanrizuka struggle, a movement of women in opposition to a military base on Mount Fuji. (Their struggle has been going on since 1947 and developed tactics later adopted by the Hantai Dōmei.) Shitō, enjoying himself, drank too much sake and left his false teeth on the bus when he returned. In any case, a day later he was in Tokyo as one of the four principal speakers from Sanrizuka on the platform of a huge public rally organized by Chūkaku-ha.

Also living in Tenjinmine village is Ogawa Kihei, the brother of Ogawa Kakichi. He is fifty-three. He has about two *chō* of land and also farms airport land. His uncle, Katō Kiyoshi, is fifty-seven. He too has about two *chō* of land; his son is a truck driver. Ishige Tsunekichi, one of the most important members of the Hantai Dōmei, is sixty-four and has a son, thirty-five, who works with him. He has about two *chō*. Ishige was in charge of liaison with sects until his resignation in 1982 and is one of the most courageous and militant of the farmers. He is a long-time member of the Japan Socialist Party, a founder of the local cooperative, and a fairly large dairy farmer.

In Tōhō village the only Hantai Dōmei member is Shimamura Ryōsuke. He has a little more than two *chō*, farms airport land, and is extremely successful as a very large chicken farmer. His second son, aged thirty-five, is also a farmer and works with him. His first son lives and works in Narita City. Shimamura is one of the main stalwarts of the Hantai Dōmei and much of its future depends on him. He is clear-headed and articulate, and he understands very well the larger principles at issue. A number of militants help him with farming. His compound is large and has the somewhat scruffy look of chicken farms everywhere.

In Kinone village the most important figure is Ogawa Gen, aged sixty-seven. Nearby lives his nephew, thirty-seven. Ogawa Gen's son helps him farm. Their holding is a little over two *chō* of land, and because they live very close to the airport fence they can farm quite a bit of airport land. The nephew works a one or two *chō* holding. Ogawa Gen is one of the toughest and best farmers in the Hantai Dōmei. Militants do not care to work for him because he drives them very hard. A striking-looking figure, he and his wife were pioneers who suffered severe privations before making their farm pay. Among his specialty products is pickled red ginger, which he bottles and sells locally.

All these farmers depend on the assistance of one or more militants from nearby fortresses and solidarity huts. Some are regulars who have virtually become members of the family. They help with weeding, plowing, planting, harvesting, and the many other chores a farm imposes. By doing so they not only enable farmers to survive economically (and indeed prosper) but also free the farmers to attend meetings and rallies and plan strategies for the long pull. The more permanent cadres in the huts and fortresses, the leaders of the various sects, also help to organize activities ranging from joint outings at the beach, some twenty-five miles away, to confrontations with the authorities—always subject to the general approval of the Hantai Dōmei itself. As close relationships developed between militants and farmers, some of those militants who dropped out of Japanese society at one level found their way back at another.

In addition to the twelve Hantai Dōmei families, there are several others who live in the airport site as well. Two farmers have already sold their land but still live in the site. One owns a small shop there; another, Shima Kansei, farms but does not own land; and one farmer, Koizumi Hidemasa, is the adopted son of Ōki Yone. Shima and Koizumi are members of the One-Pack Movement, which collectively rents land but does not own any. Also connected with the airport site is a carpenter who owns a small piece of land but does not live on it.

It is rare for a woman to be the head of a household. In this predominantly male system, each farmer sits foursquare on his patrimony, a little less easily if he married into it than if he got it as a first son from his father, a little more self-confidently if he created it out of scrub. Each farmer values his individuality. He expects it to be understood both by his family and by outsiders. In turn, he is expected to understand the totality of the family unit, the needs of and pressures on the women and the children. The farmer represents his household in the village council. As we have said, he and other family members also belong to certain functional groups that are organized within the hamlet but have national affiliations. If the farmer is looked up to as the head of the household, it is a role less patriarchal than political. A strong woman may well dominate her husband but many men try to escape from such women by having hostesses at places where they go regularly to drink. The men tend to go about in groups, especially in the evening.

Even among the Hantai Dōmei families, children are not very likely to want to continue in farming, despite their fathers' renewed commitment to it as a way of life. The new comforts of the kitchen have not made enough of a difference for women; many of them still find the life too hard. There is money to be made outside of farming, money for which one does not need to give up the farm altogether. But only full-time farming is regarded as appropriate if one is to be considered a good farmer. And only good farmers are members of the Hantai Dōmei.

EACH FARMER, then, has a "political" role in the family; as head of the household he has a political role in the hamlet. In turn, the hamlet has its own rules. Old hamlets tend to have a pattern of deference toward former landlords, who retain a somewhat privileged place, look after the hamlet shrines and the graves of ancestors, and exercise a kind of residual authority. A hamlet that is composed of the second or third sons of the families from an older hamlet who bought land and built houses still look to the older one as the main hamlet. New hamlets composed of "pioneers"—mainly ex-soldiers who at the end of the war received land that was marginal, forested, or pasture and had a difficult time making it properly arable—have more of a frontier spirit; the pioneers are less deferential. It would be unwise, though, to make too much of these distinctions.

In any description of life in the hamlets of the Sanrizuka-Shibayama area there are two terms that do not apply. One is the

word "traditional." Despite residual familial, patriarchal, and patrimonial features of hamlet life, neither religiosity nor the immemori-
ality that goes with it survive. Hamlets that look picturesque and
unchanging, with their thatched-roof houses and terraced fields, are
continuously adaptive (and a growing portion of the old houses are
owned by non-farmers). The other term that does not apply is "peasant." Well before the land reforms of 1946 and 1947, farmers became
rural entrepreneurs, oriented to production for a market. They make
calculations and decisions about capital, investment, and price.
They consider the commercial aspects of their occupation as crucial
facts of life.[11] No matter what their ideology, they remain rural capitalists, independent, difficult to deal with. Each one tends to nurture
his differences and individuality.

Nor have they ignored national politics—quite the contrary.
Sanrizuka farmers, and indeed farmers throughout Japan, have
probably been more involved in politics than those who live in cities.
As Joji Watanuki suggests, Japan differs markedly from other countries in this regard. Whereas in most countries it is economic growth
plus urbanization and the emergence of larger upper and middle
classes with higher levels of education and a greater sense of political
efficacy that lead to increases in participation, in Japan the effective
mobilization of the population in rural settings is greater than in
urban areas. This is not simply because village life has a communal
character; that is true elsewhere. Rather, as suffrage was extended
progressively in rural areas from 1890 onward, along with it grew
neighborhood associations congruent to village social structure, resulting in a high voter turnout.[12] In effect, it is not traditional hamlet
life that makes for participation but rather the mobilization and organization of the hamlet as it has evolved, including the responsibilities imposed upon it since the days of the Meiji state and the efforts
to democratize its structure through land reform, the organization of
cooperatives, and the formation of neighborhood associations. Participation in the *methods* of democracy is important to bear in mind
when we begin to examine the activities of the Hantai Dōmei, both
because farmers know what participation means and because the
prevailing forms of participation could not lead to the desired results. When farmers sought different and more radical solutions,
they had some ideological precedents.[13]

3

Past
and
Present

IN CERTAIN Japanese films and plays—Nō drama, for example—the action is deliberately drawn out, enabling the audience to focus not only on the actions and emotions of the actors but on their moral qualities as well. Slowly the audience becomes aware of how the actors are wrestling with circumstance and predicament beyond script and plot. Caught in an ensemble of collective assignments that are more and more difficult to resolve, each actor portrays the private anguish imposed by external causes, particularly when the resulting obligations conflict. Masked, the actor is a surrogate for larger forces. Hidden behind the mask is an acting individual whose private discipline in a field of public obligations instructs his audience on the nuances of appropriate behavior. Nuance is far more important than gaining one's object or losing it, since these are circumstances over which the actor has, after all, no control. What is important is whether he achieves discipline, and sometimes harmony, by sheer will. The actor triumphs over the inevitable by the way he behaves.

The audience plays a crucial part. As in real life, it can share most in what it can best anticipate. It knows the drama and the script by heart. Because the audience knows the outcome prior to the conclusion, the plot itself becomes the least important part. It is the performance that counts and the way the character of each actor reveals itself slowly in that combination of role, persona, and individual that makes each performance unique. For the audience, participation means to be engaged in a moral event.

In the drama of the two crossroads—Sanrizuka and the Narita airport, society and the state—the outcome is inevitable. The audience knows it. Those who continue to watch the drama do so to see the performances of individual actors. Their masks have been thrown off now. One can peer into the real faces themselves as they wrestle with imposed circumstances, trying to maintain their dignity and to instruct. The airport has been functioning since 1978, and the Hantai Dōmei, a remnant of its former self, is divided. But for those who continue to watch, however, the moral drama goes on. Over time new qualities appear among the participants. For each group of participants and for each individual a code of conduct applies, and within each code of conduct individuals play out their roles. Now, in the second act of the play, the main surprises occur in their personal performances. Certain personalities emerge as very strong, austere, imposing order upon turmoil. So it is with Ogawa Gen and Shimamura. Others crack; Ishibashi, Uchida, and Shima were forced to resign from their offices in the Hantai Dōmei but they remain on the site, cast out but never outcasts.

Today there is declining support and a smaller audience for the Hantai Dōmei struggle. Interest in the moral character of the struggle, the central concern of such dramas, is now better served elsewhere. But for a long time what was shared between actor and audience, the Hantai Dōmei and the public, was the power of moral instruction. The frame, the script, and the terrain enabled the actors to engage in a unique process of retrievals and projections in which—as in Nō drama—memory and a sense of the appropriate were crucial. Events and the revealed qualities of the individuals themselves worked on public opinion in such a way as to retrieve previous struggles, some legendary and some within living memory. A pool of previous events and old ideologies was stirred by the confrontations. Old principles were revived in a context of present performances.[1] For when the conflict over the airport first broke out in 1965 in Tomisato, most Japanese were at best only two generations away from their rural origins. Today they are a good deal further away in every sense.

What were some of the memories retrieved and some of the ideologies projected? We will indicate several before discussing the actual events of violence. Perhaps the most important thing to bear in mind is the rapid decline in Japan's rural population after World War II, a decline carrying with it a sense of obligation to the remaining farmers. Farmers were the "peasant-warriors" of the past and the backbone of Japanese society for as far back as anyone could remember. They were as well a symbol of the past sufferings of the Japanese people, associated with difficult times. In the Meiji period, for instance, landlords grew desperate for money because a modernizing and militarizing government was placing heavier and heavier taxes upon them. To survive, landlords shifted the burdens to their tenants, taking half of their produce, or more. The struggle for survival then involved physical power as much as the weather or the market. Many tenants rebelled. While some landlords became rich, others were ruined. The term "rural class struggle" was real enough.[2]

One set of symbols evokes another. Behind the memories of the Meiji period is a layer of legend from an earlier time, when peasants revolted against feudal lords in the days of the Tokugawa. In those conflicts the autonomy of the hamlet and the peasant-warrior eroded. The conflicts are legendary but not imaginary; their consequences are recorded in a series of peasant revolts, rice rebellions, and other uprisings. The inheritance of struggle is as much the Japanese farmer's patrimony as the inheritance of land.

Nor did it take the Sanrizuka affair to resuscitate such memories. They were ingredients in the formation of explicit ideologies—some right, some left—long before this movement, and they helped legitimize many revolutionary projects. In the part of Chiba Prefecture with which we are concerned, resentments from the old days of imperial rule still smoldered. People recalled the discipline required of every rural household and the militarism imposed. If in old hamlets people preferred to remember the plight of the landlords, in more recently settled ones they remembered the plight of the tenants.

Although Chiba never experienced the large-scale farmers' uprisings that characterized Ibaragi Prefecture, adjacent to Chiba, radical movements did become noticeable in the early 1930s. Two leaders, Jitsukawa Kiyoshi from Chiyoda and Horiuchi Akira from Futagawa, were both JCP members. In 1966 there were about sixty JSP members in Shibayama, including Uchida Kanichi and Seri Makoto, both of whom were founding members of the Hantai Dōmei. Certainly by the 1930s there was great unrest which leaders of both parties tried to capitalize upon, but the actual numbers of people involved was small. In Shibayama Town, for example, there were at the time roughly six or seven landlords and fifty-seven tenant households, the latter including a number of former landlords who had become so indebted that they had lost their lands. Descendants of some of these households consider the airport conflict to be part of a continuing class struggle. They see Meiji modernization replaced by parliamentary methods which accelerate both the erosion of rural life and the march of enterprises into the countryside.[3] Those who had actually been involved in JCP or JSP activities also knew all the tricks of clandestine organization (until the end of World War II the JCP was an outlawed party) and all the nuances of ideology.

From the first, then, the confrontation at Sanrizuka reminded farmers of their radical inheritance. The history of landlord-tenant struggle and before that the peasant revolts was never lost. It is not coincidental that in this area people emphasize that the Japan Farmers' Union was founded originally under JCP auspices and that when it came under the control of the JCP it continued to be well supported. And it was not without symbolic significance that they say that one of the main headquarters of this union was established at Sakura City, where the struggle of Sōgorō occurred, at the center of Lord Sakura's domain.

THE HANTAI DŌMEI, then, has an inheritance of anti-capitalist and anti-bourgeois struggles. The part of the past which is recognized today is radical, sometimes communist, more often socialist. But there is another part which, although it has virtually disappeared, was at one time more pervasive. It too was anti-capitalist and anti-bourgeois, but it was also romantic, organismic, and rightwing—indeed some might call it fascist. It too played a part in the early ideological formation of the people of the area. Where the radical tradition emphasized class struggle, the other was committed to precisely an opposite view—to the unity and solidarity of the household and hamlet communities that represented the rural way of life.

This right-wing radical tradition was never very well defined. Nor did it require a specific membership. The tradition was based on a belief in the ideal of the peasant-warrior. In this ideal, the peasant household is complete, a universe of its own; and the hamlet, composed of these households, is also complete. In this notion egalitarianism should prevail within the hamlet and its families—an idea that was always provocative, given the strict hierarchies in the Japan of the old days. The doctrine, or rather the bundle of doctrines, that represented the ideology of such independence was called *Nōhon-Shugi*. Its main emphasis—local solidarity and the unity of landlord and tenant against higher authorities—was based on an original myth of the peasant-warrior of pre-shogunate times who lost his autonomy and became a serf under the Tokugawa.

Nostalgia for this mythic peasant-warrior was first expressed in the writings of Kumazawa Bansan (1619–1691). It continued well into the eighteenth century, especially in the writings of Ogyū Sorai, who in effect established it as a tradition. Revived again by Fujita Tōko (1806–1855), it waxed and waned periodically throughout the late nineteenth century and in the 1920s and 1930s. At each revival its emphasis changed somewhat, but what remained at the core was the ideal of the stalwart and independent peasant-soldier, the head of his patrimony and his household, a yeoman who not only represented the essential qualities of the Japanese but whose personal loyalty to his lord and to the emperor was the foundation of the imperial system.

The movement itself began when the samurai became a class and a distinction was made for the first time between the peasant and the warrior. The ideology opposed what quickly became a landlord-warrior class (*nōhei*), a class that evolved out of wars between the Taira and Minamoto clans and became the backbone of the Tokugawa system. The doctrine, in turn, came to serve the landlord-warriors in Tokugawa times when they began to recruit peasant armies to overthrow the Tokugawa. During the Meiji Restoration the more rustic samurai or *gōshi*, a kind of squirearchy of officials who had lost their titles but retained their land, used the doctrine to oppose the Meiji. Later the Meiji government, following the example of the landlord-warriors, employed it as the official ideology of a conscript army, elevating again the ideal of the peasant-soldier in order to overcome rural resistance to conscription.[4]

Nōhon-Shugi was a doctrine of protest before it became an ideology of power. Its revivals during the Meiji period coincided with oppressive events—for example, when feudal levies of rice were eliminated and replaced with heavy taxes in cash, and when landlords were freed from feudal overlords but lost the security of their occupancies. Revivals occurred when tenants became more dependent on the paternalism of the landlord. Not surprisingly, between 1868 and 1877, during the first impact of the agricultural reforms of the Meiji period, there were over 190 peasant uprisings in Japan. In part they were aimed at eradicating remnants of feudal privilege, and in part they were reactions by conservative peasants against governmental innovations. As the Meiji government embarked on a policy of building an industrial base, taxes reached a level of between 60 and 70 percent of produce. In 1876 the tax burden was eased, but there remained great bitterness in the rural areas.[5]

Later versions of *Nōhon-Shugi* were aimed at restoring the solidarity of the village against the state. In trying to prevent class conflict between tenant and landlord, *Nōhon-Shugi* was in direct contrast to socialism and communism, both of which aimed at intensifying rural class conflict. In Chiba Prefecture, *Nōhon-Shugi* represented itself as a kind of populist agrarianism, a doctrine described as "agriculture-as-the-essence-ism." Its proponents, known as the *Nōhonshugisha*, "were diverse critics and theorists who used farming as the basis for this vision of an ideal Japanese social and political order."[6] It kept alive the earlier ideals of the Tokugawa. Its nineteenth-century proponents made it specifically anti-capitalist. Later, as an official ideology it stood for the spirit of the "nation," including a "faith in agricultural economics, an affirmation of rural communalism, and a conviction that farming was indispensable to those qualities which made the nation unique."[7]

Versions of *Nōhon-Shugi* can be grouped in several categories. One type, sponsored by bureaucrats concerned with the virtues of rural discipline, appealed to small landowners, particularly those being attacked by tenants. Many of these landowners had plots of land of only two to five hectares themselves. They bore the brunt of tenant animosity, as for example in the rice riots of 1918 and subsequent tenant disputes. Those of them most vigorously anti-capitalist in their views became followers of Shinagawa Yajiro (1843–1900). A later version of *Nōhon-Shugi*, this one more popular with tenants, was espoused by Gondō Seikyō (1868–1937) and Tachibana Kōzaburō (b. 1893). Both of them "denounced centralized government, industrial capitalism, foreign culture and the same national bureaucrats who a scant generation earlier had been the main advocates of *Nōhon Shugi*."[8]

There were many other versions of the doctrine. We cite them in part to indicate both their diversity and the tenacity of their hold. There was Kawakami Hajime's doctrine of "farming without capitalism," which considered the village as necessary to a sound army and emphasized the old Tokugawa ideal of the peasant-soldier. There were Yokota Hideo (1889–1926), who said that farmers should be classless, above class, and that capitalism causes rural decline, and who favored the economic autonomy of the village, and Ya-mazaki Nobukichi (1873–1954), who believed that inroads by government on village self-rule causes rural decline, and stressed "household thought" (*ie no shisō*), emphasizing household harmony and the unity of the farmer's way and the warrior's, sometimes known as rural *bushidō*. There was the "imperial" interpretation of Hirata Tōsuke: he believed in the emperor as the "father of society and the state as a family (*Kazoku kokka*)." It was he who gave *Nōhon-Shugi* its most official flavor. The emperor "unified the people in his role as chief priest of Shinto and intercession with the gods on behalf of all Japanese,"[9] Hirata Tōsuke believed.

In Chiba perhaps the two most important figures were Gondō Sei-kyō (1868–1937) and Tachibana Kōzaburō, twenty-five years his junior. Gondō had great influence on rural extremists and army officers. (In 1932 a group of them assassinated two of Japan's financial leaders and attempted a coup.) Gondō, a rural romantic and agrarian nationalist, was, prior to 1900, a Confucian scholar living in a temple and studying texts. He favored Japanese imperialism and colonialism, but on a basis of local self-rule. Tachibana, who was attracted to violence and terrorism and spent eight years in jail, believed in land and community as the origin and foundation of human history. In his view land blunts materialism, individualism, egocentrism, selfishness, and capitalism. Capitalism has let greed triumph over virtue.

These ideas were more pervasive than any specific version of the doctrine itself. But today if one asks farmers in the Sanrizuka-Shibayama area about the influence of *Nōhon-Shugi* on them or on the Hantai Dōmei hamlets, one is likely to be met by blank stares. Even among those who remember Gondō or Tachibana, none were drawn into their movements. Nevertheless their generation was exposed to some version of its principal beliefs, and many still recognize it as an explicit alternative doctrine to socialism—that is, as a "radical" ideology of anti-class struggle. Indeed, the doctrine, representing what Ronald Dore called "the last dying kick of Japanese feudalism," was not fully discredited until the end of World War II, when people came to think of it as a fascist doctrine favored by Japanese militarists during the 1920s and 1930s. But it was also an authentic expression of anti-commercial, anti-bourgeois, and anti-capitalist principles. Combining devotion to the village as the basis of the imperial system of *Tennō,* it appealed to those anxious to prevent intense conflicts between landlord and tenant, squirearchy and peasant. It provided a language for expressing the commonality of Japanese rural life at the hamlet level, some elements of which remain embedded in the language to this day.[10]

In the 1920s and 1930s, the period of Japanese militarism that led to the discrediting of *Nōhon-Shugi,* the authorities used the doctrine to impose central authority "in the name of a system in which the Imperial Household is the Main Family from which all families have branched out."[11] When, in the 1930s, *Nōhon-Shugi* became an official policy defining the desired relationship between hamlet and village and government and an ideology twisting the original relationship out of shape, the hamlet headman no longer had real power. He was not even the coordinator of the various functional organizations of village society; indeed, he became an ideological figurehead. It was the resident law officer in the village who came to represent the peacekeeping authority, and the school principal the discipline of the school, which was responsible for instilling proper values and habits in the young. Not least important was a figure who represented the state religion, the Shinto priest. (It is not an accident that the nursery school in Sanrizuka is also the site of the Shinto Shrine as well as a building for the elders.) Village head, law officers, principal, and priest were the powers of the *hamlet.* But the real power was the person who represented the central government, the bureaucracy in Tokyo, and the imperial household itself: the Boss, *Oyakata,* an important landlord. Although *Nōhon-Shugi* could still serve as the ideology of rural anti-capitalism, in this context, as a form of national ideology and state control it was in reality a form of fascism.

Not surprisingly, the doctrine disappeared after World War II and left a radical space that could be filled by the left—not immediately, of course. Land reform, the evolution of rural cooperatives, participation in the factional politics of the LDP, and involvement in the JSP (and more occasionally in JSP party politics) replaced the romantic themes of *Nōhon-Shugi* with the harder considerations of the market. The warrior-peasant became the rural businessman.

But the anti-capitalist and anti-bureaucratic part of the *Nōhon-Shugi* ideology and the conservatism of its radical expression of protest were important ingredients of Hantai Dōmei ideology. The connection was not explicit, of course; Hantai Dōmei ideology made no specific reference to so thoroughly discredited a doctrine. At best, the *Nōhon-Shugi* tradition enables contemporary radicalism to contain meanings that would otherwise not be there, most particularly the sheer "historicity" of localism and its traditions of hamlet autonomy. It also helps to explain the curious militarism of the original Hantai Dōmei, for despite their bitter opposition to the airport and the state as militaristic, and their anger at the remilitarization policies of the present government, the Hantai Dōmei farmers were also old soldiers in the tradition of the autonomous yeomanry, with each household a nucleus within the hamlet, and with both hamlet and household defending themselves against outside interventions.[12] The explicit revival of old hamlet principles, the organization of the traditional associations, the emphasis on horizontal rather than vertical authority, the romanticization of village life, and the anti-bourgeois and anti-capitalist character of the movement itself cannot be understood purely in terms of the radical left ideologies that have come to predominate.[13]

THE FARMERS, of course, are only part of the story of Hantai Dōmei ideology. There is also the influence of the militants, several generations of them. The first wave that went to Sanrizuka grew up in grimness, poverty, and individual hardship. That generation, "AMPO 1960," knew the past as shame and hunger. Today its members are known for their austerity both in principle and in practice. It and the succeeding "AMPO 1970" generation, which directed the explosions in the universities, have provoked crucial questioning on large issues of principle and made political demands for due process and greater citizen and community participation. They attacked not only the direction of government policy but also the way government policy was made, arguing that the factionalism and corruption of the Liberal Democratic Party, the legalism and bureaucratism of the Japan Communist Party, and the ineffectualism of the Japan Socialist Party meant that parliamentary government was no good. They rejected too the highly structured network of prevailing institutions. So total was their critique that the militants became marginals in their own society. Walking out of established institutional networks and showing contempt for the legal and social practices that they represented, they voted with their feet. Some dropped out of the educational system. Women walked out of arranged marriages. Many men and women left their jobs. Those who first came to live in sects organized around radical principles represented the first New Left, a phenomenon that appeared in other countries later than in Japan.

The militants' attack on the state is far more sweeping than the farmers'. They see Japanese capitalism as sustained by three basic institutions: family, education, and government. Through the Sanrizuka struggle they set out to attack all three. They regard the household as the building block of the state, with education serving as the link between household and state because education involves socialization as well as allocation of roles.

In contrast to Hantai Dōmei farmers, many militants want to change the household and the nature of marriage in Japan, particularly the role of women within the family. Few are against marriage as such, but they want to make women equal partners. A "radical" family should not devote so much of its energies to the pre-training of children or orienting them to do well in school. However, most militants recognize that for some time to come the family must continue to be a social welfare institution, and they have not tried to change the farmers in this regard. They also recognize the obligation to care for aged parents. For the time being, then, the family is accepted as an economic unit in which husbands and wives must share more equally in work and responsibilities. Both should have co-equal freedoms.

The militants' views have found considerable acceptance among the women of the Hantai Dōmei, particularly among the yomé, the traditional daughters-in-law, whose role requires absolute subservience to their husband's household. They have been particularly influenced by the young militant women who left the universities to come live in the solidarity huts and fortresses. In turn, farm women, veterans of confrontation, have gone all over Japan, dressed in their baggy field pants and wearing straw hats and bandannas with violent slogans printed on them. They tell their audiences that in the Sanrizuka struggle the women fought harder than men. They have learned equality by becoming equals.

Preaching equality is one thing, practice is another. Militants can oppose the state much more easily than they can the family or the educational system. The latter two are intimately connected. Indeed, a key inhibition against too drastic a change in family relationships is the responsibility the family retains in preparing the young for school. In a system in which recruitment to a job involves more or less lifetime tenure, everything depends on the educational system. Individuals are ranked and graded from the start. (So are educational institutions.) What the family offers to the child in preschool education, nurture, and guidance is crucial. The problem with such a system, from a militant's perspective, is that for such a system to work compliant behavior must be inculcated at every stage, and that it reproduces hierarchy and inequality.

Performance in primary school is crucial in determining which secondary school one will attend. Performance and the rank of the secondary school will determine the university one attends or what profession or job one goes into. A university is a less pressured academic environment than secondary school but it is a critical arbiter of one's future. At the top of the rank is Tokyo University, which supplies most of the higher civil service. (In this airport case, the majority of the senior officials at the Ministry of Transportation and the Airport Authority graduated from the University of Tokyo Department of Law.) Militants who dropped out of these institutions because they found hierarchy oppressive or the atmosphere stifling found it difficult to locate themselves anywhere else in society, and they went the whole way in an opposite direction to live in the forts and solidarity huts at Sanrizuka.

As they did so, farmers welcomed them in a parental embrace and thus kept them from becoming refugees, from becoming entirely lost, and also in a sense from becoming terrorists. Indeed, among those students who are militants, few consider themselves professional revolutionaries. Within the fortresses some have passed the age (usually thirty) for suitable positions outside and have lost their social citizenship. As they turned their backs on the institutional structure of society, society turned its back on them. Although farmers and militants have in common the loss of both their place and their function in society because of changes in the political economy and their own responses to those changes, in the end it is the militants who are the more vulnerable.

In the fortresses and solidarity huts militants live like medieval anchorites. They use their marginality to claim the need for a redeeming, transforming, and disjunctive event. The sects, as the last, seek to be first, by overcoming the entire institutional network of family, school, university, business, and capitalism; for them that is the meaning of the Sanrizuka struggle. On this basis sects receive support from radical trade unionists and occasionally a radical trade union like the Chiba branch of the locomotive union, as well as other radical groups and individual members from the teachers' union or the postal workers, where strong JCP influences prevail.

The militants' ideology goes something like this. The airport is a symbol of Japanese imperialism, created by the needs of Japanese expansionist capitalism and the remilitarization that goes with it.

Farmers are being driven off the land to create an industrial reserve army of highly qualified and proficient workers. Industrialization is encouraging a new world role for Japan. There is renewed penetration of Southeast Asia, which is increasingly subservient to Japan. Southeast Asia provides Japan with food and raw materials, serves as a market for Japanese finished products, and provides a cheap labor force for multinational Japanese firms. In association with banks and other monopolistic forces, the multinationals exert pressure for the remilitarization of Japan. Pressure from U.S. capitalists escalates the remilitarization process.

Such a summary of what is inevitably a more complex process is serviceable for those militants less concerned with theory than action. Most authorized versions of ideology derive from a vulgarized Leninist text, principally from *Imperialism, the Highest Stage of Capitalism.* But to dismiss the radical movement in terms of the weaknesses of its ideology would be as wrong as dismissing the farmers' movement because of its historical romanticism. The very looseness of the ideology allows very diverse groups to join forces. In this sense, Hantai Dōmei ideology is a function of its coalitions. Within these ideological texts, the roles are played by crucial individuals, survivors, many of them quite remarkable. The "survivors of the survivors" are the tiny band of households still left in the designated second-stage area and the cadres in the fortresses. Both have the mentality of survivors. They are tough, prideful, quick to take offense, and in addition they believe that they are the last "fundamental" Japanese. If in fighting the parliamentary state they have become "radicalized," behind their radicalization is a deep devotion to their society. It is the word "state" that does not exist for them. It never did.

Among the militant survivors are a few who have been in the fortresses and solidarity huts almost from the beginning. They have seen thousands come and go. Their views of Japanese society remain unchanged by facts of economic accomplishment, the growing public shift to the right, and the lack of effective trade union support. As the line taken by the General Council of Trade Unions of Japan (Sōhyō) has become more conservative, the militants are only confirmed in their belief that they themselves are the only authentic representatives of the working class.

For farmers and militants the immediate enemy is the government, especially its surrogate, the Airport Authority Corporation, which has the main responsibility for construction. Those officials originally involved have retired to other jobs, the most important of them nonetheless remaining in positions closely associated with the airport and retaining considerable influence. Today a younger group has taken over. Not bound by the past, this new group is anxious to explore new possibilities to prevent a repetition of the violence that characterized the first phase. Where the first generation of civil servants was concerned with the technical problems of building the airport—finances, crosswinds and weather, support facilities, access roads and pipelines, projections of use, impact studies, design, and so on—today's generation recognizes Narita as a political problem that must be handled by the Cabinet, the Ministry of Transportation, and the Airport Authority.

But the administration also has a collective bureaucratic memory. Moreover, this is reinforced by relatively fixed patterns of consultation and jurisdiction. Officials may be familiar with the lives and problems of each farmer and each household. Indeed, some senior officials may know more about the lives of farmers than of their own families. But how flexible they can be with regard to the second stage of construction is not clear even to themselves. Sanrizuka as a political problem is more delicate than as a technical one. The one group most knowledgeable about the entire struggle consists of journalists with offices in the Ministry, in the Airport Authority, and in Chiba City and Narita City. They have built up an immense fund of expertise about the movement, and they have a clear picture of the state of play in the game between administrators, farmers, and militants. They and the more radical journalists—some independent, some associated with *Labor Information* and other such bodies, some associated with the larger sects and publishing houses—have seen the drama as it has unfolded better than anyone else, often as participants and go-betweens.

THE VIEWS of the journalists are crucial, for they represent the link between the drama and the spectators, the players and the audience. Public opinion is a critical factor in any democracy, for it limits the rules of the game for all sides. It is because of public opinion rather than principle that farmers have ruled out terrorist tactics entirely. There have been no attempts to attack planes or passengers or to seriously interfere with the activities of the airport. To use guns, for example, would be to make all those in the movement social outcasts and outlaws. Eschewing such weapons has made it possible for journalists, writers, professors, and intellectuals generally to cast their protective cloak around the movement. In addition to verbal support the Hantai Dōmei receives free help from lawyers in defending militants, some of them standing trial for offenses committed years ago. Public opinion limits police violence, too. Authorities have not gone about knocking down solidarity huts and fortresses with tanks or bulldozers at will. No matter how violent some of the events in the Sanrizuka struggle are, the boundaries of the situation are clearly defined.

This brings us back to the *Nō* drama and to the audience that participates. Public opinion is crucial for all those engaged in this movement, for or against. But public opinion is not simply a set of attitudes toward an airport; it is also a set of feelings about the nation as a whole. Today public opinion is shifting away from the Hantai Dōmei. But when the movement began the context was different. What could be described as post–World War II attitudes of the Japanese (about themselves, their democracy, their role in the world, their changing values) still prevailed at the time the movement began. There was a great deal of political ambivalence. On one hand there was much admiration for American ways of doing things and a desire to emulate, but on the other hand there was confusion about the war and its aftermath. Some of these ambiguities can be seen in the surveys conducted by the Office of the Prime Minister. Let us look at the survey of November 1967, when the first important confrontation between the Hantai Dōmei and the government occurred, for it reveals something of the public mood at the time.

The survey was designed to ascertain the degree of public confidence in Japan and particularly Japan's position in the world at large. Virtually all the responses are hesitant and somewhat blurred. This may be in part due to a certain natural reticence and a preference for the understated that generally characterizes the Japanese. Too, there was at the time a more deferential attitude toward the United States and some other Western European powers than obtains today. When asked "What do you think of when you hear the term 'National Power of Japan'?" the most widespread response was not industrial accomplishment, or innovation, or productivity, or an improved or competitive economic position, but "having a population of one hundred million." Yet all Japanese would agree that there are countries with larger populations and less "national power."

Perhaps more interesting was the range of replies to the question "Why do you think Japan is an advanced country?" Forty-six percent, the same proportion as on the item mentioned above, gave "popularization of education" as the main response. Education was on everyone's mind, not only because the universities were beginning to be torn apart by student violence but mainly because everyone was well aware of the crucial connection between education and social hierarchies. Behind the response is the murmur of voices in even the smallest village, where, if you happen to be strolling on a hot summer Sunday when families are together, you will hear through open doors and windows mothers priming their small children for their fall classes.

Above all, however, the survey shows widespread concern about the moral quality of Japanese life in relation to Japan's role in the world. It also suggests the ambiguity of the role itself. For example, to the question "Do you think Japan is considered important or unimportant in the world?" only 15.9 percent said "very important" while 63.6 percent said "rather important" and 16.9 percent said "rather unimportant." Ambiguous too (but symptomatic of the debate over the airport itself) were responses to two questions: "What do you think is the most important thing for Japan to do in international society?" and whether or not Japan "should become a strong economic power." To the first, 33.4 percent replied, "play a leading role in Asia," a position that seems to favor government policy. But did this include economic domination and penetration? One does not know. In answering the second question, although 27.7 percent favored Japan's becoming a stronger economic power, a larger response (34.0 percent) was that Japan should "become a country aiming persistently at independence and peace."

To the question "What are you most dissatisfied with in the present Japanese society?" 44.3 percent cited "lack of or degeneration of public spirit," and 49.3 percent said "degeneration of politics." As causes of this "lack" 51.4 percent mentioned juvenile delinquency, and 26.5 percent mentioned a tendency toward egoism. Most of the farmers and militants would also have agreed with this general dissatisfaction but would have put the degeneration of public spirit down to a degeneration of politics, not to speak of the egoism in high places. To the question "Like what country do you think Japan should become in the future?" 19.4 mentioned Switzerland while 35.0 percent said the United States. There was no suggestion that Japan might be a model for others.

Of course, it is difficult to interpret such responses in today's context. The national mood in those days was exceptionally complex.

Two Crossroads

Surveys today show a much higher degree of self-confidence. Japan's "second industrial revolution" has paid off handsomely. Most of the dislocating changes originally produced have now largely been absorbed, particularly those pertaining to agriculture. In the early sixties, shortly after the change in policy from agricultural to industrial priorities, the percentage of the labor force engaged in agriculture dropped from 24.7 percent in 1962 to 18 percent in 1968. (In the preceding period the decline was even more dramatic.) There was also a marked decline in the proportion of school graduates going into agriculture. By January 1969, of the remaining 16,730,000 farm families in Japan, only about 1,170,000 were engaged chiefly in farming. There was chronic overproduction of rice. By 1969, 4,380,000 commuted from farm households to industries for work. From 1960 to 1973 the agrarian population living in villages dropped from 34,410,-000 to 24,380,000. It continues to drop.[14]

If today the general mood in the country is again uncertain, this time it is not about Japan's role in the world. There is less soul searching and more concern with specific economic problems and international relations.[15] Despite the intense factionalism of the Liberal Democratic Party and the need for money by each faction, and despite the favoritism and corruption this has led to, the widespread desire for an identifiable public interest has become less pressing. Perhaps, too, the concern over the behavior of the militants has declined. Student violence became, after all, a universal phenomenon. The events of May 1968 in Paris took the heat off Japan.

II

The Sanrizuka Movement

In Kyoto you occasionally see memorial candles lit in the stone lanterns and water basins of courtyard gardens. Should you ask why, you will be told it is "because of the war." Surprisingly, this does not mean World War II. Instead, people are thinking of such confrontations as the Hamaguri Gomon Uprising of 1864 and the Tobafushimi Battle of 1868. Or, in cases where the historical records have been destroyed by fire, the candles may even date back as far as the Ōnin War of 1467.

Kanto Shigemori, *The Japanese Courtyard Garden*

4

Fields
and
Fortresses

IN A WORLD of households, farms, and other small-scale enterprises, the construction of any large facility intrudes. Social space
is violated; livelihoods are affected. But most people learn to live
with such intrusions and accept as necessary even those that, like
the airport, seem so out of scale. Why, then, did the Sanrizuka
project serve as the venue for a conflict that would challenge both
government policy and the power of the state to define the public interest?

Part of the answer is violence, or, better, that violence which becomes symbolically illumined within a frame of extra-institutional
protest. But as well the very intimacy of the circumstances helped to
enlarge the sense of outrage. The events of confrontation occurred in
a context in which strands of intimacy and familiarity were shared
by virtually all the participants, including those who came from outside Sanrizuka.

The farmers, students, senior government officials, Dietmen, prefectural authorities, police, and others drawn into the struggle did
not come from different universes or separate worlds but rather from
similar networks of school and family. Leaders of sects were sometimes from the same families or had attended the same universities
as government officials. Some students were the children of teachers

or government officials; others had grown up on farms. The police came mostly from farming or working class families. Even the acting president of the original Hantai Dōmei had a niece who was married to an Airport Authority official.

Intimacy can also limit violence. No matter how angry the actual confrontations were, a certain sense of the appropriate prevailed. Despite the anger of embattled farmers and the extremism of the militants in their red or blue or white helmets, few threw themselves into battle without regard for consequence. Indeed, for a long time the Hantai Dōmei tried to avoid open violence and eschewed guerrilla tactics, but after the Airport Authority used police to protect surveyors in what became known as the outer-rim land survey confrontation, people began to get a clearer idea of what they were up against. Increasingly farmers were prepared for physical violence.

Tools as weapons were emphasized from the start. The 1968 outer-rim land survey was undertaken during the busiest time for farmers. In their rush to resist the encroaching survey parties and police, farmers grabbed whatever farming implements they had— sickles and forks used for harvesting and treating compost, bamboo sticks used for carrying rice grass. Tomura told them that agricultural tools were the farmers' symbol and would provide the necessary spirit.

But this emphasis on weapons and violence had a special place within the Hantai Dōmei code of conduct. A certain politeness and formality prevailed among members and extended to the world outside. Farmers are hardly rustic philosophers, any more than their comrades in the sects are radical theoreticians, yet they have always been acutely aware of the symbolic implications of their acts, and the action of their symbols. They defended their interests in a context of principle in which each episode became an expression of more fundamental and widely understood feelings. Each stage of the struggle legitimized the farmers' position against the state. In an atmosphere of intimacy each was understood as both a symbol and a sign of the larger implications of the struggle. Hence it became possible to transform Sanrizuka from a social terrain into a mobilization space by ritualizing the violence, even as violence escalated with each succeeding confrontation.

The first confrontations occurred in 1967; between 1971 and 1977 pitched battles were fought at various interludes. The farmers and militants built forts, towers, underground bunkers, and tunnels to obstruct the clearing of land, the leveling of houses, the obliteration of grave sites, and the construction of roads and facilities. Major violence ended in 1978 with a final large-scale confrontation. Just as the first stage of the airport was about to open, militants stormed the control tower, cut the main cables, and destroyed valuable electronic equipment. When the airport actually opened two months later, the government promised that the second stage of the airport project would be pursued by peaceful means and negotiation.

To the militants Sanrizuka was important not for the attempt to preserve a way of life or for the land itself. Rather, Sanrizuka seemed a good place to reproduce AMPO 1960 on a larger scale, one involving broad sectors of Japanese society. The government's industrialization policy would, the militants believed, create both an authentic proletariat and an industrial reserve army. Forcing the farmers off the land was part of the process of world capitalism, a form of primitive accumulation. Experience elsewhere in the world indicated that a permanent revolution was under way. China's cultural revolution showed a course for rural radicalization, and Vietnam suggested the power of a peasant-based rebellion.

Sanrizuka seemed ideal as a point of mobilization. Two imperialisms, those of the United States and of Japan, were pitted against the interests of farmers and workers. If the public could be polarized and the trade unions radicalized, then each confrontation would reveal more fundamental antagonisms. The scope of conflict was broadened by shifting from universities, which in the last analysis remained only universities, to Sanrizuka, where the militants brought into play a dynamic of class, power, state, and society.

This was not the first time that farmers and outsiders had fought together. One early case was Kita-Fuji, the "mother movement," which began in 1947. In that struggle women played a critical role. The transfer of a military base on the slopes of Mount Fuji from Japanese to United States control was opposed for several reasons, among them the loss of privileged access to government forest and the loss of land taken for firing ranges. The women, wearing baggy farm trousers and headbands as a kind of uniform, were angry as well that their daughters were becoming bar girls and prostitutes, that their lives were being corrupted by the Americans and their livelihoods destroyed. The women were the first to build a fort inside of the perimeter of a United States artillery range; they kept three-woman teams on watch there twenty-four hours a day. Students later made heroines of them. The Hantai Dōmei was visited very early by representatives from Kita-Fuji and learned some of its tactics. Solidarity huts at Sanrizuka in which militants lived were barricaded and thus converted into fortresses. The Hantai Dōmei began twenty-four-hour watches from inside them, one of which lasted for five hundred days.[1]

If Kita-Fuji was extremely instructive for the Hantai Dōmei, so was the "father movement," a similar case at Sunagawa involving the expansion of a United States military base. At first the expansion was opposed by the people in the affected area with the support of Sōhyō and other labor unions. After 1956 students from Zengakuren, the All-Japan Student Association, joined in the struggle. The protest was successful, and the government gave way.[2] Both cases, Kita-Fuji and Sunagawa, were models of protest by farmers' groups against military bases. Their principles were reincorporated in an even more elaborate form at the New Tokyo International Airport, which was regarded as being primarily for military use in a rearmed Japan, its civilian commerce representing capitalism and imperialism.

In the government's view, of course, building a new Tokyo metropolitan airport seemed a prudent move in the early 1960s. The airport construction was considered as a part of a long-range consolidation plan for the Tokyo area at a time when supersonic transport, freeway construction, urban expansion, and the spread of industrial facilities were more or less unquestioned indicators of a successful industrial society.

To the government, the issues raised by the farmers and militants were simply irrelevant. The plan itself called for a metropolitan airport within one hundred kilometers of central Tokyo, or roughly one hour's travel time. Comparisons were made with Chicago's O'Hare Airport and Washington's Dulles Airport. Construction was to begin in 1964 and end by 1971. Five runways (two 4,000-meter, one 3,000-meter, and two 2,500-meter) were planned at an estimated cost of 135 billion yen. After the Tomisato struggle in 1965 the government scaled down its plan to roughly half of what was originally intended. The airport opened in May 1978, seven years after the planned opening date.

BEFORE THE Cabinet's decision to shift the site of the airport from Tomisato to Sanrizuka had officially been announced, the word spread and there was immediate and spontaneous protest. On June 28, 1966, more than twelve hundred residents of Sanrizuka gathered at the Tōyama Junior High School in the Tōyama school

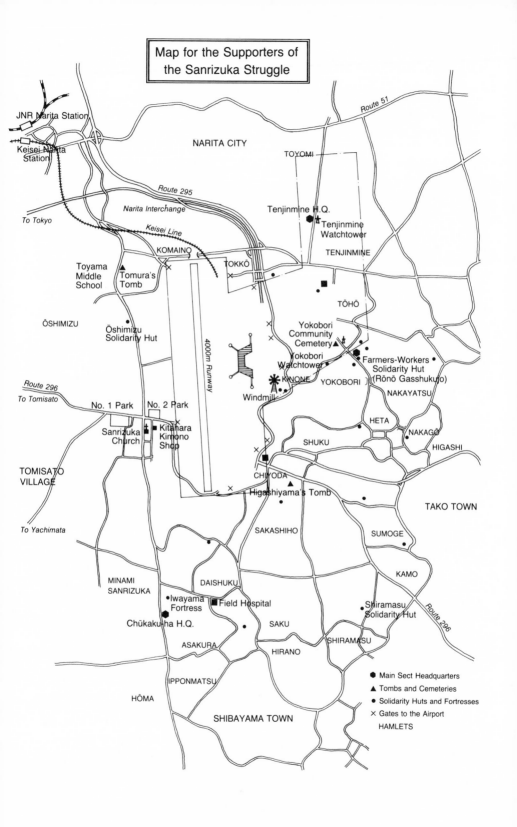

district to form the Sanrizuka Anti-Airport League, or Hantai
Dōmei, and chose Tomura Issaku as president. The Hantai Dōmei
adopted the following declaration:

> To forcibly deprive us farmers of our land permeated with
> our sweat and blood;
> To destroy our agriculture;
> Further, by means of noise and other pollution, to force the
> whole agrarian population of the Hokuso District into a
> situation where they cannot make a living by agriculture;
> And the livelihood and education of residents in the vast
> neighboring area is disrupted;
> This is a blatant policy of disregard for our human rights
> which we can never accept!
> We participants in today's rally declare that we will reso-
> lutely fight the Sato government and the prefectural au-
> thority until they abandon their plan to build the
> Sanrizuka Airport.[3]

The next day the newly formed Hantai Dōmei sent representatives to the prefectural government to protest the airport decision.
They asked the mayor of Narita City, Takeo Fujikura, to reconsider
the airport plan as well. A day later another rally was held, sponsored by the Shibayama Farmers' Cooperative. About one thousand
people, calling themselves the All-Member Convention to Stop the
Construction of the Airport, gathered from Narita, Yachimata, Tomisato, and Sanrizuka. On July 4, when the government officially
announced its airport plan, approximately eight hundred people
from Shibayama and Tako protested at the governor's office and the
prefectural headquarters of the LDP. The Prefectural Assembly
adopted a Sanrizuka Airport Construction Promotion resolution favoring the airport. The Narita City Assembly voted against it and
decided to protest. On July 7 the Ministry of Transportation opened
a branch office of the Aviation Bureau in Narita City. Two days later
sixty residents of the three villages on the site, Tōhō, Komaino, and
Tokkō, went to Vice-Governor Takahashi, who was also the director
of the Airport Survey Office, and presented him with a petition containing nineteen hundred signatures.

Shortly after these events the Sanrizuka and Shibayama Hantai
Dōmei organizations merged to form what we refer to as the original
Sanrizuka-Shibayama Hantai Dōmei with the support of about fif-
teen hundred households. It is this body with which we are con-

cerned in the present analysis. It lasted intact from its foundation until 1983, when it split into two organizations.

The newly merged Hantai Dōmei engaged in many forms of peaceful protest. Its officers were well versed in conventional political techniques. Dietmen were contacted. Prefecture assemblymen and local officials were asked for support. Since the farmers had friends among local bosses or were indeed bosses themselves, and since they had influence in cooperatives, the JSP, and the LDP, they expected that their pleading, public meetings, petitioning, and remonstrating would provide grounds for a renewed debate. But all attempts failed; the authorities held firm. The Airport Authority began to engage in extensive negotiations for the farmers' land. They tried to convince village councils that it was in their interest to accept government compensation terms. On October 10, 1967, under the protection of two thousand riot police, the government and the Airport Authority forcibly carried out what was the first outer-rim land survey. When the Hantai Dōmei blocked all the roads, a direct clash between police and farmers was inevitable.

The farmers hoped that, confronted with violence, the government would withdraw. Once it became apparent that construction would continue, the Hantai Dōmei began to organize more seriously. It adopted the hamlet system as its model; hamlets became its nuclei. Hamlets were linked by a network of Hantai Dōmei "corps" of elders, youth, women, and children. The farmers themselves were organized as an Action Corps. Each group had a "commander." All, even the Children's Corps, were equipped with helmets and sticks. They were intially supported by members of the Japan Communist Party and the Japan Socialist Party, and soon other outside supporters joined in, including people who came to observe the confrontations and became involved. The first solidarity huts were built by farmers for supporters who could not be housed by the farmers themselves. Some were built with watchtowers, heavily barricaded; these became the first fortresses.

A major turning point came in November 1967, when the All-Japan Student Association (Zengakuren) sent the first students to Sanrizuka to help the farmers. Living in the huts and fortresses, the more committed supporters began to help with farming as well as with fighting. On February 26, 1968, at a Hantai Dōmei–Zengakuren joint rally, a major clash with the police resulted in the arrest of 249 students and injuries to 1,380 others. The government took the involvement of students in the struggle very seriously; for them it changed the rules of the game. The policy of confrontation and containment was matched by growing outside support. By the end of March the Hantai Dōmei and Zengakuren were able to mobilize about ten thousand demonstrators in a series of rallies. At the most important of these, a march on the Narita office of the Airport Authority, many farmers and militants were injured and about five hundred arrested as they forced they way past armed riot police. A long series of conflicts followed. In November 1969, when the Airport Authority began building roads in the site, pitched battles were fought with those trying to survey the land. After the arrest of thirteen Hantai Dōmei members the battles began to resemble a real war.

From February 22 to March 6, 1971, the "first expropriation" struggle resulted in 461 arrested and 1,400 injured. The September 16 "second expropriation," involving 3,200 Hantai Dōmei members and militants who clashed with 5,300 police, resulted in the deaths of three policemen. In March 1972, the combined opposition constructed a huge steel tower at Iwayama village, just prior to the construction that was to begin on the 4,000-meter runway. Conflict over forts and towers continued during the next few years, and public concern mounted. As construction was delayed and the airport thrown completely off schedule, the number of outside supporters increased. On April 17, 1977, an immense rally was held involving 280 different organizations and 23,000 participants from all over Japan. When, three weeks later, on May 6, 1977, the steel tower erected at Iwayama was forcibly removed, the violence was intense. A militant student, Higashiyama Kaoru, was shot and died at a field hospital some distance away. His death was followed by massive "guerrilla" attacks. Despite all these conflicts, work on the airport continued and more farmers dropped out. Increasingly the movement depended on a hard core of Hantai Dōmei members, militants, and outside supporters. The airport opened in May 1978. Tomura, the president of the Hantai Dōmei, died on November 2, 1979.

Such a brief recounting of events necessarily leaves out the character of the events themselves. But several points should be stressed. Lack of legal redress and due process, the failures of public petitioning, and the inability to gain much of a hearing at an early stage enraged the farmers. The movement only attracted public notice when direct-action tactics began to be used, such as women chaining themselves to trees that were to be cut down, or people throwing themselves in front of bulldozers. The Boys' Brigade or "Children's

Action Corps" also brought the Hantai Dōmei great publicity for a while. Fitted out with helmets and taught to march out to confront the police, children were brought into the fortresses, solidarity huts, and underground tunnels and caves containing food, medical equipment, clothing, lights, and sharpened bamboo spears. Some of these children were injured by the police.

A variety of other tactics were employed to arouse public support. A farmers' broadcasting tower had been constructed, bearing at the top a Japanese flag framed in black with the inscription "We Oppose Land Confiscation in the Name of the Japanese Peasantry." It was used for surveillance of police activities and for the broadcasting of encouragement and warnings to the farmers. A symbol of defiance, of "speaking to the nation" as well as to each other, it was torn down on September 16, 1971, by police using cranes and bulldozers. In the summer of 1967, when the Hantai Dōmei was trying to prevent technicians from carrying out soil surveys, the Old People's Brigade, sometimes known as the Meiji or Elders' Corps, began dousing riot police with human excrement brought in plastic bags and fired by means of long-handled wooden dippers. When the enraged police arrested the old people, the Women's Corps took up the same action.

Despite such tactics, however, the government's negotiations with farmers over the sale of land met with mounting success. The government used a spy system to penetrate both the Hantai Dōmei and the sects. To protect themselves against those selling their lands to the airport, Hantai Dōmei members speeded up the purchase of tiny parcels of land by supporters who pooled their funds not only to show their support of the Hantai Dōmei but to complicate the process of land acquisition (called the "one-*tsubo* movement"—a *tsubo* is about four square yards). At one time some 140 Japan Socialist Party Dietmen, as well as many others, were involved in this action.

It was in this context of symbolic tactics that Tomura Issaku became a critical figure and his role crucial. Standing above factions, able to sustain the support of the sects despite their wide differences of views, Tomura with remarkable skill translated farmers' interests into principles reminiscent of radical Christianity. He used early Christian symbols and parables as his guide and the Bible as a source for many of his ideas. He endowed the movement with dignity. The humbleness of the farmers became, in his vision, a restatement of the virtues of traditional Japanese life. Tools and implements for farming became weapons for an assault on political conventionality. He retrieved old themes of peasant rebellion and the old ideal of the radical peasant-warrior, but, stripped of earlier nationalist overtones, his vision of a new and more communitarian society was not very different from the thinking of early Christian utopians and perhaps Tolstoy, whom Tomura had read.

The ideas were crude, and they were not well understood by Hantai Dōmei members. But they were powerful all the same. There was, as well, a certain artfulness of presentation, for Tomura was a fine artist and sculptor as well as a lay preacher and true believer in the Church. Just as he worked with scrap iron and old engine parts to weld them into powerfully abstract forms, so for him the movement had to be put together from its immediate bits and pieces, from the social life of households and hamlets, which in his mind the government regarded as "scrap." He tried to convert each incident, arrest, trial, or confrontation into an occasion for moral judgment against the government. The government was on trial. No matter who won or lost specific court cases arising from the conflict, even if prosecutors won their convictions, the government lost in a moral sense. If Tomura had an overall strategy, it was to prevent the government from convincing the public that farmers were simply defending their own self-interest against the larger public interest of society.

The government's power and strength became a symbol of the autocracy of the state. The size of the airport project, the largest single project ever undertaken by the Japanese government, dwarfed the farmers and their holdings. It emphasized how puny their citizenship was. Tomura insisted that the opposition and the government could negotiate only from parity, as equals, a condition the government would not accept. He published letters to Prime Minister Fukuda, Transportation Minister Fukunaga, and Chief Secretary Ōhira in major national newspapers. In a letter to Ōhira he pointed out that while the government made much of Narita as a big national project in which the national dignity was involved, the prime minister had never visited the site nor asked for cooperation.

Hence, while the movement might have been simplistic, it was not simple-minded. Its activities gained considerable popular support. Even elderly and retired persons who would have been expected to be conservative wrote letters supporting the Hantai Dōmei to editors of influential newspapers. Letter-writers complained about the lack of fair play by the government. Some letters compared government actions in Sanrizuka to the notorious Maintenance of Public

Peace and Order Bill of prewar days. In one of his last acts, Tomura wrote in an open letter to the prime minister, "Prime Minister Fukuda called the attack on the control tower a challenge to democracy; however, I think now is the time for the government itself to practice democracy." He went on to denounce the special legal measures adopted by the government, and the use of riot police.

Of the various episodes of violence, perhaps five stand out as most significant. The first major confrontation was the second outer-rim land survey, in 1968. When the land surveyors came to Yokobori hamlet three to four hundred people a day were organized to build wooden blockades. The farmers placed barrels filled with human feces and urine along the roads so that they could spray the police. Leaving their watermelons in the fields to rot and allowing their carefully tended vegetable fields to be overrun by weeds, they laid down iron wire to trap the police and surveyors and hid bamboo spears in the bushes. It took sixteen hundred men from the Airport Authority and ten thousand riot police to complete the land survey. In the three-month ordeal (ending on July 18, 1968), six people were wounded and more than three hundred arrested. It was during these early confrontations that the Hantai Dōmei developed both its internal solidarity and its bitter hostility toward police and other authorities.

For both farmers and militants the outer-rim land survey came to stand for the rape of the community by the officials of the government. In turn these officials were seen as the representatives of state capitalism. The meaning of the outer-rim land survey, to farmers and militants, was the violation of local and private space. In this context individual exploits came to stand for a great deal. Seventy-eight-year-old Sugasawa Kazutoshi, for example, a local boss who had served as Chiyoda village assemblyman and chairman of the local Election Management Committee, was arrested for throwing plastic bags of feces and urine at the entrance of the Chiyoda Farmers' Cooperative. When arrested he announced that he did not need a lawyer because he was fighting a just war, and promptly went on a hunger strike. The police, at a loss, simply set him free. He remained the commander of the Old People's Corps until his death. Even more startling were militant old women like Ishibashi's mother. She was close to ninety years at the time. Militant students of Zengakuren built their first headquarters and a huge watchtower on her son's farm. When the police attacked the headquarters she poured human excrement and urine on them with dippers. She told the police when they arrested her that she had raised eight children by herself after she was widowed at age forty and was not going to let them take away the land she had cared for with her own sweat and tears.

The women were an important part of the struggle. Instead of acting like deferential farm housewives subservient to representatives of authority, they surprised and shocked the police with their militancy. Hasegawa Take, a former schoolteacher who became the commander of the Women's Corps, appeared in farm clothes with another woman, Yanagawa Hatsue, in front of the riot police as the land was being surveyed. Both shouted epithets at the bewildered police. The latter, mostly young, were themselves from farm or ex-farm families. Aghast at such behavior among elderly women, they fell back in disarray. Mrs. Yanagawa, a large woman, became known as "the heavy woman with acrimony." But the Hantai Dōmei called her *Yanagawa no Okkaa,* Mama Yanagawa, and regarded her as "the symbol of fighting mothers."

ONE OF THE REASONS why the government had chosen Sanrizuka as the airport site after the Tomisato protests was the availability of land from the imperial estate. This was particularly painful for Tomura Issaku. For him the imperial estate represented many things. The estate was in fact the main reason why the Tomura family had come to the area in the first place: Tomura's grandfather had moved to Sanrizuka to work for the experimental farms. For Tomura, then, the takeover of the estate was a desecration of imperial property, a lese majesty that would once, he reminded his public, have invoked the death penalty. (The allusion upset militants who believed he was "protecting the emperor.")

Perhaps most of all, however, the estate simply appealed to Tomura as an artist. For years he had tried to express the charms of Sanrizuka in watercolors and more elaborate works of art. People came from all over Japan to see the ten thousand cherry trees of the imperial meadow in blossom. Artists came to the area to paint, much as they did at Barbizon, which was about as far from Paris as Sanrizuka was from Tokyo. As a child Tomura would sometimes skip school to go to the meadow to watch the artists at work, and eventually he too became a painter. The prospect of seeing the meadow converted into a wasteland of concrete and steel was more than he could bear. When the time came for the estate to be turned over to the Airport Authority in a special closing ceremony, Tomura was passionately involved.

The event was all the more shattering for Tomura because of what had happened earlier, when the airport decision had first been announced. Tomura had gone immediately with his cousin, Tomura Shōsuke, to meet with an officer of the Imperial Household Agency. The officer had assured them that although the agency could not object to a government decision to take the estate, it would certainly not encourage the government to do so. Tomura took this as a commitment that the estate would be safe. Since the estate was in fact the first land to be conveyed to the government, Tomura believed he had been deliberately deceived.

For Sugasawa Kazutoshi, the seventy-nine-year-old commander of the Old People's Corps, the taking of the estate was also painful. He had worshiped the Meiji emperor, and like Tomura he loved the meadow. The Shimofusa Imperial Ranch on the estate represented to Sugasawa the innovative farming of an earlier time. The ranch had been used for raising sheep and for breeding livestock under the Meiji government's policy of "rich nation and strong army." The Meiji minister of the interior, Ōkubo Toshimitsu, had introduced new technology using the Shimofusa sheep meadow and Tokkō livestock farm in demonstration projects in 1875. Sheep raising was considered important, and the government had sponsored a domestic wool industry, bringing four thousand sheep from the United States along with an American engineer named Jones to take charge of operations. Arabian horses were bred on the Tokkō livestock farm, and Dutch cows were imported. The first domestic cheese had been made at the estate and the first veterinarians trained. Students from Komaba Agricultural School (now the Faculty of Agriculture of Tokyo University) had used the estate as a field station.

At any rate, Tomura was invited to the closing ceremonies along with senior dignitaries of the government such as Imai Yoshifumi, the president of the Airport Authority, and a host of others, including the vice-governor of the prefecture and the deputy director of the Imperial Household Agency. The estate officials feared that the presence of riot police would spoil the dignity of the occasion and irritate people, so, despite advice to the contrary, no riot police were on hand. When the Hantai Dōmei attacked, two hundred strong, there was no one to stop them. Removing a bamboo barrier, they dashed into the building where the Self-Defense Force brass band was tuning up. They grabbed the microphones, overturned tables with food laid out for the guests, and pulled down a curtain over the stage. Tomura spoke into a microphone, saying, "Are you of the Imperial Household Agency going to run away? We want you to stay here." For the farmers the "running away" of the agency was a serious blow. Of the estate's 430 hectares, 300 were to be allocated to the airport directly or used as alternative lands for resettlement of displaced farmers; most of the rest was to be used for mass housing for government employees. Only a small piece was intended to be kept as a park, the Sanrizuka Memorial Park.

Sugasawa and Tomura represented the older generation in the protest at the ceremonies. There was also a third leader, Hagiwara Susumu, who represented a younger generation; he was the commander of the Youth Corps. A serious and thoughtful farmer from Yokobori village, he represented the concerns of the young people over the future of farming in the area. After the abrupt termination of the ceremonies, the police decided that they could hardly arrest Sugasawa, an old man, or Tomura, who was too influential, so they went after Hagiwara. On the grounds of breaking and entering and the destruction of property, a warrant was issued for the arrest of Hagiwara Susumu and two other Youth Corps leaders, Shima Kansei and Ishii Shinji. The police went to Hagiwara's house, but he wasn't there. As luck would have it, the night before the warrant was issued, people had gathered for a meeting at Hagiwara's house, and Ishibashi had gotten so drunk that Hagiwara had had to take him home. Because it was late, Hagiwara had spent the night at Ishibashi's house. When the police came the next day and found Hagiwara's futon laid out but no sign of the man himself, they assumed that he had escaped, so they went to Ishibashi's house and arrested his son Takeji instead. Actually Hagiwara was sleeping next to Takeji, but the police thought he was a student and left him alone.

After the estate had been turned over to the government no time was wasted. The cutting down of cherry trees—including some big ones that had been planted in Tokugawa times—began immediately. Tomura went to the company that had the contract to do the cutting and pleaded with them to stop. The company refused, saying that if they didn't cut down the trees someone else would. The Youth Corps broke into the lumber company's office and caused damage, but the cutting continued. Then Tomura remembered how difficult it is to cut wood with chainsaws where there are nails in the trees. Youth Corps members went to Tokyo and bought five barrels of five-inch nails. Dressed in black, they went to the meadow in the night and hammered nails into the trees. It took them several nights to do the job. But the nails didn't stop the chainsaws, and gradually the area for the main runway was cleared.

Then one morning Sugasawa came to visit Tomura on foot from Hishida, some miles away. He brought a collection of signatures with him, signatures of people who had decided to kill themselves under the trees. They had already prepared the white garments of the dead. Tomura agreed and asked to join them. The Hantai Dōmei, however, objected, and refused to allow the old people to die. The Hantai Dōmei pointed out that the act would be interpreted as nothing more than a protest directed at the lumber company, and moreover, they reasoned, the company was actually pro–Hantai Dōmei and had made secret contributions to its treasury. The point angered Tomura, who regarded it as a weak argument. It enraged Sugasawa. His relations with the Hantai Dōmei were never the same again.

For the Hantai Dōmei the transfer of the imperial estate to the Airport Authority came to have very particular meanings. First, it constituted betrayal, most particularly the government's betrayal of the older generation and Tomura. For the militants the event stood for primitive accumulation, something like the Japanese equivalent to the Enclosure Acts in England. For both the episode represented illegitimate conveyance; it helped establish the rightness of their own cause, when that cause was seen in contrast to the recklessness of government officials.

DESPITE SUCH PROTESTS and the increasingly effective mobilization of outsider supporters, farmers began dropping out of the movement in large numbers. By 1969 the Airport Authority had succeeded in purchasing 670 hectares of privately owned land. Added to the imperial estate only 82 hectares remained in private hands. Despite resistance the land survey was soon completed, the police simply resorting to survey helicopters when the fighting became too intense. The government seemed likely to have its way, and even very active Hantai Dōmei members began dropping out. It became clear to Tomura and others that a more vigorous defense would have to be mounted.

The government was having problems of its own, however. As it reached the point where it would have to acquire land by force, it clashed head-on with the small group of farmers refusing all proposals to negotiate the sale of their land. The provisions of the Land Acquisition Act specified that if all efforts to compromise failed, the government could forcibly take land and offer no compensation. This was the government's ultimate weapon, but it was not used because the prefectural government, which had been given the main responsibility for land acquisition, was reluctant to use it. Governor Tomonō of Chiba Prefecture preferred negotiation. Differences of opinion over how best to proceed mounted. The Airport Authority saw the events as a challenge to the government and favored a hard line. But the governor, feeling closer to the problem and to the people of the prefecture, continued to resist such pressure despite difficulties with his own staff and with other governmental agencies. (For example, the governor and his vice-governor did not always agree.) The governor's views prevailed for quite a while; even though it meant protracted proceedings and delays in construction, negotiation seemed the best course. When a real stalemate occurred and remaining farmers refused to compromise, the governor was finally persuaded that force would be necessary. In the first expropriations of February and March 1971 and the second expropriations later in the same year, the government decided to take all steps necessary to clear the first-stage airport area.

We have described the violence prior to the first expropriation. At that time violence was neither a strategy nor deliberate on either side. What changed during the first expropriation were the attitudes on both sides toward violence as a strategy. Each side came to favor it, the Hantai Dōmei because they were getting desperate and the Airport Authority and the governor because more peaceful means had been exhausted. For the Hantai Dōmei violence meant a last-ditch stand, in the literal sense of the term. The prospect for them was that the Airport Authority would otherwise pick off the last few diehards by force and leave them victims without compensation under the terms of the Land Acquisition Act. Indeed, it was threat of force and expropriation that Hantai Dōmei farmers believed had been decisive for those within the first-stage area, where all families except one sold out. The one exception, an old woman, Ōki Yone, became a symbol of the resistance. Poverty stricken, with virtually no land and a tiny house, she refused to move.

Hantai Dōmei farmers outside the first-stage area never knew the state of negotiations between the government and a member inside the site. No farmer would indicate to the Hantai Dōmei that he was thinking of selling. Land inside, where three solidarity huts and fortresses had been erected, was secretly sold by the owners to the government. In the case of the Tennami fort, Tomura went with the Hantai Dōmei lawyer, Onagai Ryōzō, to plead with the owner of the land on which the fort had been built not to sell. But the owner said that the Hantai Dōmei could not win and asked whether the Hantai Dōmei would compensate him for the loss of his lands. The question was rhetorical, for the Hantai Dōmei had no money. The owner of the land on which the Kinone fort stood asked the Hantai Dōmei to remove it. It was relocated onto adjacent land belonging to Ogawa Meiji. The land on which the Komaino fort had been built was owned not by a Hantai Dōmei member but rather by a sympathizer who did not live on the site. He had let the Hantai Dōmei use the land, but now, although he was opposed to the airport, he too negotiated the sale of his land.

How to treat dropouts—farmers within the site who sold their land—was a problem the Hantai Dōmei never resolved. No dropout ever rejoined. But many had fought hard for the organization, and in fact the farmers who dropped out had little choice in the matter. Either they negotiated for the sale of their land or they risked losing everything under the Land Acquisition Act. Tomura, hoping to stop the outflow, believed that as a matter of principle the dropouts should be publicly punished or humiliated. Most farmers disagreed, however, saying that those who had fought in the Hantai Dōmei, or had been wounded, deserved respect and even remained entitled to certain courtesies associated with hamlet and village life. Hence, while Tomura treated the dropouts as betrayers, Hantai Dōmei farmers were sympathetic to the needs and circumstances of individual households. Tomura finally had to give way as farmers continued to provide help to those who had sold out—aiding them in moving their possessions, holding farewell parties for them, and so on. The links of kinship and association are far too durable to be quickly or ruthlessly broken. But Tomura's attitude made him even more of an outsider. Slowly he moved closer to the militants, among whom he found more support for his views.

It was at a New Year's meeting at the beginning of 1971 that a new strategy was decided on. Ogawa Meiji, an ex-navy officer, suggested that military tactics be adopted. His idea was to dig holes in the ground from which farmers and militants could defend themselves, as in foxholes during the war. His tactic, which had actually already been used at the Kinone fort, was accepted. But it soon became apparent that more than foxholes would be required. The Hantai Dōmei decided to follow the example of the Vietcong and construct underground bunkers connected by tunnels so that the defenders could not be routed. On January 6, 1971, the Hantai Dōmei authorized digging in the pine and cedar forests in the six main areas to be expropriated. Each hamlet—Heta, Hishida, Sanrizuka, Chiyoda, and Iwayama—was assigned a hole to dig; the Youth Corps had a hole of its own. It became a form of hamlet competition to complete these as quickly as possible. In two weeks, forty to fifty meters were dug in all six areas. Tomura called them catacombs, for they reminded him of the underground cemeteries of ancient Rome where the Christians found sanctuary from persecution. The main tool was the shovel. The farmers had experience in building underground storage facilities for vegetables, and so they were highly skilled diggers. Vice-President Ogawa Meiji, an expert on yam digging, gave advice on how best to loosen the soil. Another farmer who knew how to build wells taught the farmers how to reinforce the walls. Underground rooms were connected by tunnels 1.2 meters high and a meter wide and buttressed by wooden pillars. The tunnels curved to avoid rocks. At wet places, pine needles were distributed. No matter how cold it was outside, the underground rooms remained warm, about 15° C. Each tunnel was given a number. The Youth Corps completed its tunnel first, the no. 2 tunnel. Thirty meters from the entrance a 3 × 3 meter room was built 2 meters in height. Green bamboo forced through the ground provided ventilation. Double-decker beds were built. A similar construction at the no. 6 tunnel in Iwayama included electricity from the Komaino solidarity hut. Even a telephone and a T.V. set were installed. An ex-miner who came to visit was surprised by the professionalism of the job.

The rooms and tunnels were put in a state of siege. Relatives of the farmers, even some opposed to the Hantai Dōmei, donated food and equipment. The tunnels were stocked with food, sake, cigarettes, futons, and so on. The farmers found them reminiscent of the bunkers in which they had fought during the war. (Many said they smelled the same.) For the farmers these bunkers became monuments to Ogawa Meiji, whose idea they had been and who died after work on them began.

Ogawa had been a well-known figure in the area. After the war he returned to Shibayama, his home town, as an activist. He organized a movement to open the imperial meadow to farmers. He bought one hectare in Kinone and lived in a makeshift hut (until 1953 lacking even electricity) with his wife and seven children. Not until 1967 was he able to build a decent house. He had just doubled the size of his land to two hectares when the airport issue began. Although deeply conservative, he was so angry at the government over the airport that he even opposed the Hantai Dōmei's decision to expel the Japan Communist Party from the site. The enemy of an enemy, he

reasoned, is a friend: "We should not forget our duty [*giri*] so easily."
While instructing some students on how to dig tunnels he felt a
pain in his stomach. Three days later, attending a gathering at a restaurant of alumni of his elementary school, he suffered a heart attack. Before he died in the Narita City Red Cross Hospital, he told
his family never to sell their land. The name he chose at his death,
Tōkon Hisshō Koji, means a man of fighting spirit and ultimate victory; its symbolism is elaborate. Among the characters of a death
name, at least one usually contains the given name or an image of
the person. Ogawa excluded any reference to his given name precisely to show that he was not only ready to die for the movement
but that he would remain a nonconformist even in death. Tomura,
two years older, felt the loss of Ogawa deeply.

While the tunnels were being built Governor Tomonō sent out a
letter of warning. This only increased the determination of the Hantai Dōmei members; they extended the tunnels. The longest tunnel,
no. 6, was increased to 95 meters in length. The construction lasted
seventy-eight days and involved 11,600 people. The work was done
by two groups, one aboveground and the other below. Eight vertical
holes were dug. The underground group consisted of about ten people at a time. One person held a flashlight, another dug the soil, and
the rest passed the soil out in buckets. Since the work was monoto-
nous they sang songs. The ventilation was bad, and farting was a
particular problem. Narrow spots were made in the tunnel to prevent police in full riot regalia from being able to pass. Lattice doors
were put in as traps. Three restrooms were built. The living quarters
were constructed in the shape of an H, with a wooden floor and double-decker beds for eight people. The aboveground group, using tri-
pods and pulleys to deliver the materials needed for construction,
prepared cement and constructed pillars. Plastic tubes 10 centi-
meters in diameter were used for air, and the tunnel was connected
to an old unused well that belonged to a pro-airport farmer (not for
water but for air, in case the police pulled up the tubes). A "death
squad" was selected to occupy the room.

During this construction Governor Tomonō asked Tomura if they
could meet. Tomura thought the governor would be afraid of undertaking the expropriation, the first in Japan's history on such a large
scale. Although a majority of Hantai Dōmei members did not want
the meeting to take place, Tomura said that it would be an occasion
for the governor to apologize. On January 23, 1971, the governor
went to the office of the imperial estate and met with Tomura, Seri
Makoto (a vice-president who later "betrayed" the movement),

Ishibashi, Uchida, Kitahara, and the prefectural assemblyman (and, at the time, a JSP Dietman) Ogawa Kunihiko. The widow of Ogawa Meiji, carrying a picture of her late husband in a black frame, was also present. The governor bowed deeply to her and said he was very sorry.

Tomura asked why the governor had initiated the meeting. The Hantai Dōmei was not afraid of the expropriation, Tomura said, and he wondered whether the governor had a plan to make scapegoats of the farmers. The governor replied that as governor he had to help the citizens who were being made to suffer and hoped that the meeting would be only the first in a series of negotiating sessions. Mrs. Ogawa then asked the governor to pray for her husband, and he did. Ishibashi broke the spell by saying tartly that bowing and scraping would not solve the situation and that if the expropriation were to take place the farmers would be hurt. The governor suggested that half the blame would be on the Hantai Dōmei. Ogawa Kunihiko pointed out that the governor had the ultimate authority in regard to expropriation; the governor then replied that he could not stop the expropriation but that fighting in tunnels was surely not the only way. The meeting terminated with the governor saying he was satisfied. But after that the Hantai Dōmei decided on total confrontation and total mobilization involving farmers, sects, women, and children.

The question of whether or not to use children aroused great controversy. On February 11, 1971, Tomura made a speech to a hundred elementary and middle-school pupils gathered together in the plaza in front of the Airport Authority branch office. This would be an exciting time, he told them; they would not go to school for months so that they could help their mothers and fathers win the war. "To stay home to fight is different from just not going to school," Tomura said. "It is an act of protest against the compulsory education system. The anti-airport struggle which your parents have been involved in is an act of protest; it is impossible to change Japan. What you are doing is a wonderful thing. There are land thieves called the Airport Authority. Probably they are not bad people but they are told by a villain named Sato Eisaku to rob.[4] You should go there and teach them to repent and stop doing bad things." The children then went to the branch office, shouting, "Go home, go home." Riot police came out to stop them; it was the first confrontation between police and children.

A few days later one hundred Boys' Corps members occupied Shibayama Middle School. At around 8:00 A.M. about forty middle-school pupils, some from Tōyama Middle School, began marching in the school athletic field, saying, "Stop the expropriation" and "Stop the airport." They went into the gymnasium with their shoes on, a gesture of extreme rudeness, and shouted, "Denounce the principal and teachers who pay no attention to our struggle." About forty students led by "antiwar" teachers besieged the principal in his room, asking him questions like, "What do you think will happen when the airport is built?" Another fifty marched through the school to occupy the broadcasting room. One began to broadcast, asking, "How can you live in the same town while ignoring the hardships of our parents?" At 11:00 A.M. a bargaining session was arranged in the gym, with several hundred non–Boys' Corps pupils looking on. The Boys' Corps had prepared a list of "Questions from the Fortress" addressed to teachers, questions such as, "What would you do if you were in our situation?" and "Do you want to teach in sound-proofed classrooms?" Someone took out a hand siren and said, "Once the jumbo jets begin flying the noise will be nothing compared to this." The session went on until 3:30 in the afternoon.

Governor Tomonō continued to hope that the airport matter could, in the end, be settled by negotiation. But he operated under increasing constraints. When he had first consulted with the secretary general of the Cabinet, Hori, he was told that the construction of the airport had already been rescheduled for completion by the end of 1971. Hori stipulated that the governor should now proceed with expropriation as soon as possible. When Tomonō requested a second meeting with the Hantai Dōmei at the imperial meadow, Tomura refused to see him. Tomonō then held a press conference, saying that he had tried his best to settle the case by negotiation but that the Hantai Dōmei had refused his offer. He pointed out that the airport construction had become a national "emergency" project, to be completed by early 1972 at the latest. He now had no choice, he said, but to approve the expropriation of land. Tomura found out from the next day's newspapers what the governor had said and regarded the speech as an open declaration of war.

On the morning of February 21, 1971, with Ishibashi, Kitahara, Yamaguchi, and representatives of supporting sects, Tomura settled into Komaino fort, two hundred meters away from the site of the expropriation. Members of the Hantai Dōmei took up their posts in the six tunnels. Point no. 1 in the Hishida area was led by Hantai Dōmei Vice-President Seri Makoto (who later dropped out), with Chūkaku-ha as the main supporting sect. The tunnel in the Yokobori-Heta area, point no. 2, was led by the deputy commander of the

The Sanrizuka Movement

Action Corps of the Hantai Dōmei, Atsuta Hajime (who in 1982 became Action Corps commander), with Chūkaku-ha as the supporting sect. Vice-President Ishibashi Masaji and Secretary General Kitahara Kōji of the Hantai Dōmei were the leaders at point no. 3 (in the Chiyoda area) and point no. 4 (in Sanrizuka), respectively; the supporting sect in both tunnels was Kaihō-ha (Liberation). Point no. 5 in the Saki and Asakura areas was led by Town Assemblyman Sannomiya Gorō and supported by a non-sect group. Finally, point no. 6 in the Iwayama area was led by the commander of the Action Corps of the Hantai Dōmei, Uchida Kanichi, and supported by the Fourth International.

Each tunnel was well fortified. The barricades surrounding point no. 1 were two meters high, made of logs tied together with barbed wire. There were three huts and fortresses with a lookout. Point 2 was similarly defended with a fifty-meter moat constructed in front. At point 3 a bamboo mechanism had been placed inside the barricade to trap intruders; a marsh and a rice field were in front. At point 4 ditches one meter deep and one meter wide were constructed and filled with human feces and urine. At point 5 there were wooden barricades with a watchtower on top of two tall pine trees, and at point 6 two ditches one meter wide and one meter deep were built around the barricade while inside were bamboo spear entrapments. In addition to these facilities there were a field hospital with twenty beds and a farmers' broadcasting tower.

On February 24, the third day of the expropriation struggle, government forces were divided into three groups. Protected by private guards hired for the occasion, they approached points 2, 4, and 6 and were attacked by militant students carrying bamboo spears and throwing stones. The guards carried shields and wore helmets, but they were not used to such confrontations; many of them were injured. The Children's Corps then entered the fight. About fifty boys wearing black helmets and masks attacked the expropriators who were proceeding to point 6. Later about one hundred Children's Corps members confronted the guards along with militant students. Seven children were injured. Dietmen and prefecture assemblymen from the Japan Socialist Party immediately protested at the Airport Authority branch office. Surrounded by guards, the politicians got into a fist-fight with the police. The governor, attempting to avoid injuries, then called for a temporary halt to the expropriation.

But the following day hostilities were renewed. As Tomura was giving a speech to two hundred militants, Komaino fort was attacked by riot police armed with sticks and shields. In the afternoon of the same day points 3 and 4 were attacked. The police arrested 141 students (on the grounds that the students had used weapons) but no farmers. On the following day the underground bunker at point no. 4 caved in. The farmers were buried but all managed to get out, most without serious injury. Tomonō then issued orders to the police not to use sticks. Concerned that farmers might die, again he temporarily stopped the expropriation proceedings. Tomura made a speech at the site telling the crowd not to forget the violence of the riot police and warning that the police "will shoot gas guns into the tunnels and put sticks into the Women's Corps members' bodies." "They will do anything," he said. He wore a huge sash with "The truth shall make you free" written on it. He believed that the government was afraid that if farmers died this would be a political disaster of such magnitude that the entire project would have to be called off. Not only were there Hantai Dōmei members ready to die in confrontations, but the Old People's Corps publicly announced their willingness to die. Each hamlet had bought chains with huge locks with which to tie people (mainly women and old men) to the barricades, to keep the police from pulling them off. From the broadcasting tower, speeches exhorting courage were punctuated by revolutionary songs. An effigy of a policeman was hung on the tower with a sign saying, "I killed myself because I was sorry to treat the farmers so badly." In the fields old tires were burned, the black smoke interfering with the patrolling helicopters.

Three weeks had been allocated for the expropriation. The violence lasted for two. A contemporary account of the events tells the story well:

> The Opposition League (Hantai Dōmei) had shut themselves in trenches behind barricades at six points in the small valley of Komaino, which contained the . . . land to be expropriated. Lying on the floor of the valley were the first four fortresses, the fifth lay on the valley slope, and the sixth was situated on a small hill looking down on the valley. The four fortresses in the valley proper were defended mainly by farmers, the other two mainly by students. Nothing hindered the view . . . a desolate landscape of bare, red soil, which had already been surveyed for construction. The only thing reflecting the warmth and throbbing of human life was the log barricades, and the black and white

smoke trailing off into the dark blue sky from the fires by which the farmers and students were warming themselves. In the still wind there waved dozens of flags and banners: the sun flag of Japan, the red flags of the students, the straw flags of the farmers. On them were written the militant messages of the League: "Keep to the land until death"; "We defend life, heart, and family"; "The spirit of the farmer"; "We will defend the trenches to the death"; "We won't give away this land, cultivated with the soul of the Japanese farmers"; "The destiny of Japan depends on this battle"; "Each member will fight to the end!"

On March 5, the 12th day after the beginning of the land expropriation, the Airport Corporation became irritated with the fruitless negotiations and took control over the proceedings from the Chiba prefectural government. It brought in 3,500 riot police, placed the area around Komaino under its control, and shut off traffic to and from the area, fearing the thousands who were crowding in to confront the state power. From early in the morning the government forces were busy making ready to take the land, taking every possible measure to keep the situation under their control.

At around five in the morning the writer and some supporting students entered one of the fortresses. Everyone was working hard to repair the barricade which had been destroyed twice in the fighting the day before. Small children and old people, men and women, farmers and students, all were joined in the work, bringing in stones and logs of fir and pine, lashing them up to form barricades in the faint morning light. At the top of one tall uncut pine was a small wooden lookout hut, like a bird's nest. Below, two youths had chained themselves to the trunk. The heavy fragrance of the fir trees spread throughout the barricade. Finally the barricade was finished ... green and brown, as if it had grown up out of the earth. Another flag was raised against the sky of deepening blue: "Be ready for bloodshed, riot police! ... Youth Action Brigade."

Around six o'clock the barricade was surrounded completely by riot police. Timid officials of the Airport Corporation were pushed forward, and they announced the beginning of expropriation. As they approached the barricade rocks were thrown and bamboo spears thrust out to hinder their progress.

After repeatedly being repelled by stones, the attackers brought out a bulldozer which moved forward under the cover of a police armored truck with a water cannon. However, the bulldozer was quickly disabled by a Molotov cocktail.

The attack was escalated. Two more water-cannon trucks were brought forward to cover a power shovel sent in to dig out the barricade. The water from the water cannons made it hard for us to open our eyes. A rainbow, long and thin, appeared momentarily in the mist, and then was gone.

How powerful was the machinery! The shovel thrust once, twice . . . and the barricade was broken with a crush. The Airport Corporation officials were shouting arrogantly, "Come out of the barricade to avoid danger, leave this land and do not interfere with us in the execution of our duty." At last they announced that all people inside the barricade were under arrest for interfering with them in the execution of their duty and for assembling weapons.

Next a big truck was brought forward loaded with sandbags, which were used to fill in the lower ditch. At this point, the Opposition League farmers told the students to leave the barricade, saying that they alone would form the last lines of resistance, and prevent physically the entry of the riot police and the Airport Corporation officials.[5]

In one of the last acts of the first appropriation struggle the Hantai Dōmei held a Buddhist service for Ogawa Meiji. A tomb of concrete was built on the site of the runway. His last will and testament was read. "I will fight in Sanrizuka and take my last sleep in Sanrizuka," Meiji had written. "I will keep fighting even after I am dead."[6]

THE FIRST land expropriation was widely understood as a metaphor for violence. To the militants it was a clear example of the class struggle. Not only did the conflict involve the oppressors and the oppressed, it also represented the polarization of Japan into two increasingly hostile parts, society and state.

The second land expropriation only deepened these convictions. Indeed, the second expropriation, which took place in September 1971, was even more bloody and intense than the first. The police had learned a good deal about tactics from the way the first expropriation had been fought. They evolved a "three-ring plan" to prevent outsider supporters and militants from going to Komaino fort, where a fifteen-meter steel tower had been built in the land acquisition site. In one ring, the outer perimeter where militants got off the trains and buses (particularly at the stations in Narita City), the police monitored the flow of traffic and prevented supporters from going to Sanrizuka. The second ring was the general Sanrizuka-Shibayama area, containing the fortresses and solidarity huts and the hamlets and households of the farmers. The third ring was around each fortress. The police blocked all roads leading to them. Tomura was able to get to his fortress by leaving his home at 4:00 A.M., but after that time the only way to get to the fort was by fighting the police.

The fighting began when a group of police checking people at the Sanrizuka and Shimizu intersections were attacked by sect members—some wearing the white helmets of Chūkaku-ha, others the red of the Fourth International, and others the blue of Liberation—who were brandishing bamboo spears. At the Tōhō intersection only 1.2 kilometers from Komaino fort the situation was particularly bad; a police troop was attacked by five hundred militants. As the militants mobilized their numbers mounted. In collaboration with the Youth Corps of the Hantai Dōmei they began to attack the police at many different points. In one of these attacks by three hundred militants, three policemen were killed: Fukushima Seiichi, forty-seven, commander of the sub-unit; Morii Nobuyuki, twenty-four; and Kashimura Shinji, thirty-five, a police chief. The news surprised Tomura—he had anticipated the death of Hantai Dōmei members and militants, but that police might also be killed had not occurred to him.

In the second expropriation four places were to be taken by the police. These included three areas, Komaino, Tennami, and Kinone, where the forts had been rebuilt and underground bunkers reconstructed. At Fort Komaino, where militants had used 150 tons of concrete seven meters below the ground to build walls one meter thick, Tomura believed the defense would be impregnable. But then a disaster had come. Late in the evening of September 7, well before the second expropriation action began, a typhoon had hit the area with torrential rains. The bunker quickly filled up with water, and no amount of pumping could get rid of it. The bunker became useless.

The second appropriation began on September 16. The police attack was powerful and efficient. Some 5,000 policemen and 130 pieces of earth-moving equipment, cranes, water cannons, and power shovels moved in on Fort Komaino. Using the crane they toppled the tower above the fort. Some 476 people were arrested.

Militant students then counterattacked. At Tennami village, where the fortresses had been heavily barricaded with beams that were reinforced by sandbags and barbed wire, the militants threw Molotov cocktails at the attackers from a large reinforced watchtower. Members of the Youth Corps joined the militants, faces swathed in towels to protect them against tear gas. Those in the tower were attacked by water cannons. In turn the government's earth-moving equipment was ignited by Molotov cocktails. The fortress fell eventually, after many casualties on both sides.

The heroine of the expropriation struggles was Ōki Yone, the old woman who had refused to give up her house after all the other farmers in the first-phase construction site had sold out to the government. The riot police made a surprise attack on her tiny house. She resisted. Three of her teeth were broken in the ensuing struggle. The riot police had to carry her off on the back of a shield. She rejected a house that the Airport Authority offered her and turned down compensation money that the government made available (although it did not have to). Until her death in December 1971 she remained an important symbol of the resistance, and her adopted children are an important part of the movement to this day.[7]

The Hantai Dōmei lost the two main battles over land acquisition but gained much in national prominence and outside support. Its resistance did not stop with the expropriation struggles. In 1972 two steel towers were built, one at the point where the 4,000-meter runway ended and another near the flight path. The towers were sixty and thirty meters in height, respectively. It was when these fortress towers were destroyed in a dawn police raid in May 1977 that another martyr in the struggle was created: Higashiyama Kaoru, a militant, was killed by a plastic gas grenade. In December 1977 the Hantai Dōmei erected two three-story reinforced concrete fortresses, the first on the site of the demolished towers and the second on farmland to be used for the second stage. In February 1978 the Hantai Dōmei erected a twenty-meter tower on top of the second fortress. Its total height of thirty meters was enough to be a danger to air traffic. The day after it was built it was surrounded by riot police and attacked with water cannons, tear gas, and a large crane. The forty-five farmers and militants inside again showered Molotov cocktails and stones on the police. By night the police broke in and arrested forty-one of the people inside, including Hasegawa Take, the sixty-nine-year-old commander of the Women's Corps. Four militants climbed to the top of the tower and held out for forty hours in a temperature that dropped to −7° C. When water cannons and tear gas were fired on them the water hoses froze. Two of the militants held out until the Hantai Dōmei leaders, fearful that they would die, appealed to them to come down. They did, and were arrested.

As with the other main episodes, the second expropriation struggle acquired very special meanings. For the farmers the deaths changed the entire character of the struggle. No one could any longer doubt their seriousness of purpose. Suddenly it was not only grave sites that were being desecrated but human life itself. For the militants the second expropriation stood for the extreme marginalization of the farmers, the government throwing into the discard those who had previously been the most central to the life of the community. They saw this as the systematic effort of government to create an industrial reserve army that would make available cheap and efficient labor and speed up the pace of effective industrialization at the expense of ordinary people.

POPULAR SUPPORT continued to mount. Christian groups formed a coalition called Christians Cherishing Life in Sanrizuka. But despite such efforts, the government proceeded with construction. When the opening date was finally at hand and dignitaries had been invited for the ceremonies, one last major confrontation occurred. During the week of March 26 to April 2, 1978, the Hantai Dōmei made a last-ditch effort to prevent the airport from opening on schedule and called on supporters to come from all over Japan. An attack on the main control tower was planned, mainly by the Fourth International, with Hantai Dōmei support. The heavily guarded control tower was, of course, the electronic and operational center of the airport. The airport itself seemed sealed. Fences and patrol areas were manned by riot police. There were barracks for reserves both inside and outside the barricades.

The leadership of the Fourth International obtained detailed plans of the airport showing the main cable lines and all the networks of conduits—sewers, electricity, and so on—both above and below ground. (Such information was quite easily available.) They studied the location of all the rooms and memorized the precise layout of the corridors, stairways, doors, and elevators in the main buildings. Of course they also had detailed maps showing the roads leading to the area, the airport's inside arrangements, and the location of the main police details.

The government mobilized some fourteen thousand riot police and put the airport under martial law, and the violence began. The Hantai Dōmei had reconstructed one of the destroyed fortresses, rebuilding its cement base and adding a sixteen-meter tower. About three thousand police were sent to attack it with water cannons and cranes. In fact, rebuilding the tower was a diversionary tactic by the Hantai Dōmei, intended to divide and draw off the police. Kitahara, the secretary general of the Hantai Dōmei, led a group of about fifty to the front of the tower. Stones and Molotov cocktails were thrown at the police. Giant slingshots and bows with steel arrows were employed. While the fighting continued other supporters were arriving from all over the country. Anti-pollution, anti-nuclear, Christian, and women's groups, some ten thousand strong, rallied in Sanrizuka Park, under the surveillance of helicopters and police. As yet another diversion, almost four thousand militants wearing red helmets (Fourth International) gathered near the second fortress. Breaking into smaller groups, they dispersed in several directions, police contingents following them. One group smashed through the main gate of the airport, using a fortified flatbed truck to break through the barricades. The truck carried steel drums filled with burning fuel. Hundreds of people followed the truck through the gate. Even gunfire from the police did not stop them.

The diversions were successful, for the main point of the attack went largely unnoticed. Some fourteen militants, almost all of them from the Fourth International, had eluded the guards and entered the airport through the sewer system the night before. When the diversionary attacks began, they emerged through a manhole near the control tower. Ten of them managed to get inside the control tower, despite being fired upon by police revolvers. Six made it to the sixteenth floor by elevator and into the control room, where they smashed the sophisticated electronic equipment with sledgehammers and dumped equipment and documents out the windows. They hung a huge red flag from the control tower as the Hantai Dōmei and militants broke into the airport in fourteen places. At the rally in Sanrizuka Park, a great shout arose.

For them the control tower takeover was an act of transcendence, the triumph of the revolution. It was an expression of the final legitimization of the struggle and the final separation of the movement from those favoring more peaceful mediation.

Each of the main events—the outer-rim land survey, the transfer of the imperial estate, the first and second land expropriations, and

Sanrizuka as a Semiotic Space

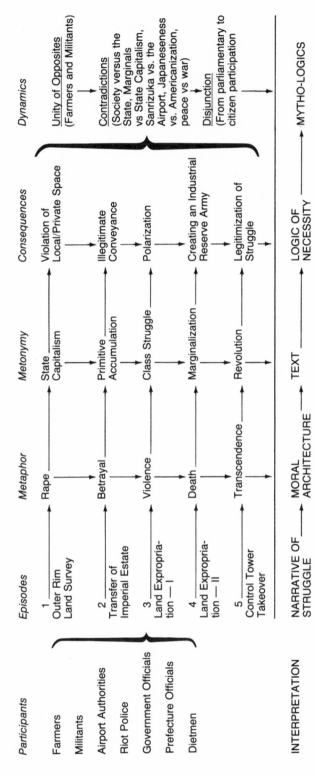

Participants	Episodes	Metaphor	Metonymy	Consequences	Dynamics
Farmers	1 Outer Rim Land Survey	Rape	State Capitalism	Violation of Local/Private Space	Unity of Opposites (Farmers and Militants)
Militants	2 Transfer of Imperial Estate	Betrayal	Primitive Accumulation	Illegitimate Conveyance	Contradictions (Society versus the State, Marginals vs State Capitalism, Sanrizuka vs. the Airport, Japaneseness vs. Americanization, peace vs war)
Airport Authorities	3 Land Expropriation—I	Violence	Class Struggle	Polarization	
Riot Police	4 Land Expropriation—II	Death	Marginalization	Creating an Industrial Reserve Army	
Government Officials	5 Control Tower Takeover	Transcendence	Revolution	Legitimization of Struggle	Disjunction (From parliamentary to citizen participation)
Prefecture Officials					
Dietmen					

INTERPRETATION → NARRATIVE OF STRUGGLE → MORAL ARCHITECTURE → TEXT → LOGIC OF NECESSITY → MYTHO-LOGICS

This diagram, derived in part from the work of Roland Barthes, Claude Lévi-Strauss, Edmund Leach, Paul Ricoeur, and Pierre Bourdieu, describes episodes of violence as they are interpreted by the participants themselves. The meanings given as metaphors and metonymies were derived from interviews and written descriptions of events provided by those deeply involved in the movement. Together they form a narrative of moral outrage and a radical text. They constitute both the moral force and logical integrity of the movement and make convincing, at least to followers, the idea that such a small group of participants can win such a big victory. The ingredients of the ideology represent what Lévi-Strauss has called a mytho-logics. Evidence is provided by the actual episodes. A complete and total system, the mytho-logics serves as an interior discipline of language and an ordering of signs. By the same token, what orders within is disordering without. It captures certain critical ambiguities of modern life in Japan, ambiguities which are widely felt but rarely articulated, the shock value of the incidents attracting outside clienteles.

the control tower takeover—formed a narrative that the participants relish recounting to this day. The fortresses in the fields, like the villages and hamlets around the airport, constituted a moral architecture surrounding and sealing off the "corruption" of the airport itself. Each event became part of a radical text. Violation of local and private space, illegitimate conveyance, polarization of society and the state, the creation of an industrial reserve army, and the legitimization of struggle together formed a logic of necessity—the necessity for extra-institutional struggle against the parliamentary state. So Sanrizuka became converted into a mobilization space, a surrogate for larger forces. It made the transition of the Sanrizuka crossroads complete. What once was a functional ecology became a moral architecture and as such a focus of attention both by the media and the public at large. Tomura, his figure rising above the rest of the participants, became not only the voice of the movement but a vehicle through which increasingly oracular visions could be broadcast to a wider and more attentive audience. As the lives and fortunes of the participants were more closely bound together, the airport itself became less the object and more the occasion for a revolution against the state.[8]

With the control tower takeover the movement scored its most resounding success. But despite the "victory," the government doggedly repaired the damage. Security at the airport was increased and plans went ahead for a new opening in May. This time the event went off without a hitch. One of the first planes to land at the New Tokyo International Airport at Narita was from the People's Republic of China.

1. Tomura Issaku speaking at a rally.

2. The church on Tomura's compound. The building on the left (now demolished) was the original church built by Tomura's grandfather; militants stayed there during confrontations.

3. Tomura's widow at the farm implements shop. Next to her are some of Tomura's sculptures.

4. Kitahara Kōji, secretary general of the original Hantai Dōmei and now the head of the Kitahara Hantai Dōmei.

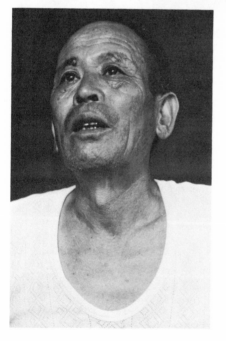

5. Ishibashi Masaji, the acting president of the Hantai Dōmei after Tomura's death, forced to resign in 1982 because of charges of collaboration with government officials.

6. The windmill, symbol of the Hantai Dōmei. Situated in Kinone hamlet, it abuts the airport fence and is used for irrigation of airport land being farmed by militants.

7. Farms and fields just outside Sanrizuka.

8. A farmer and his wife setting out for the fields. Virtually all farmers in the area use these snubnose tractors and hitches.

9. Police reinforcements at the Sanrizuka crossroads.

10. The fence around the airport with a police watchtower in the background.

11. A woman chained to a post during the first expropriation confrontation at Fort Komaino.

12. Chūkaku-ha militants in a protest march.

13. Sect members snake-dancing in the street during a rally.

16. A typical fortress near Yokobori hamlet.

On facing page

14. The watchtower and solidarity hut on Ishibashi's compound.

15. The Chūkaku-ha headquarters in East Sanrizuka.

17. A One-Pack Movement wife, a militant who married a member of the Youth Corps of the Hantai Dōmei.

18. Ogawa Gen, one of the most stalwart Hantai Dōmei farmers.

19. Atsuta Hajime, a former action commander of the original Hantai
Dōmei and now the leader of the Atsuta Hantai Dōmei.

5

New Left Sects and Their History

THE WORD "sect" refers to an organized group of militants separated from other groups by doctrinal differences. A sect can be on the left or the right. The term has other connotations, too: a high degree of commitment, a set of rules for social life, a network of mutual obligations that take precedence over others, and a discipline binding on the members. To be a member of a sect, then, implies a solemnity and seriousness of purpose often associated with religious groups. In Japan the history of Buddhist sects includes violence between one sect and another and betrayal, persecution, devotion, loyalty. These same qualities apply in varying degrees to the New Left sects under discussion.

New Left sects, together with the Hantai Dōmei and outside supporters, originally constituted "the movement." But there was no firm boundary around it; people entered and dropped out. And within the movement there were generational changes that affected relationships and attitudes. The first "generation" of sects, which we will call the AMPO generation, was characterized by great determination and moral perseverance. Broadly speaking, its concern was always United States imperialism. The second generation, AMPO 1970, was deeply involved in university struggles and in opposing the Vietnam war. The third generation, faced with the declining influence of the New Left generally, was concerned with a much altered international and domestic situation, particularly Japanese imperialism.

These broad characterizations of the generations of sects raise several important points. First, what Sanrizuka meant changed continually. The place of the movement in Japanese social life is very different today from what it was at the time of the first confrontations. Second, since the airport is a functioning facility, the movement has lost an important battle and the government has won. What remains is largely a struggle over unfinished business between farmers and the government. Third, as the New Left declines, Sanrizuka is for certain sects the last stand. For them the movement must go on, even if all the farmers drop out.[1] The balance at Sanrizuka is shifting: sects are playing a growing role in the movement and the farmers a declining one, one reason why the Hantai Dōmei divided. Finally, the New Left itself is changing, not only generationally, but also in terms of external conflicts and issues. Maoist or pro-Chinese sects, for example, have largely disappeared, and the issue of Vietnam is now an embarrassment because of Vietnam's invasion of Cambodia.

The New Left sects involved in Sanrizuka are not simply groups of militants who favor the farmers' cause. They are part of a complex radical history consisting of many different strands, each of which finds its contemporary outlet in the Sanrizuka movement. Indeed, the sects endow Sanrizuka with a tradition of struggle that, while not entirely separate from the farmers' struggle, is nonetheless very different.

To appreciate more fully what the sects represent, we will first need to describe briefly their origins, the particular evolution of student militancy, its special relationship to the Japan Communist Party, and the formation of the New Left sects, particularly after 1956. It is worth noting that the so-called New Left phenomenon began in Japan in a variety of protests. It started on university campuses but then moved outward to participate in struggles like the one in Sanrizuka. We will describe some of the doctrinal differences these activities produced among the most powerful sects, examine sects' relations with farmers, and conclude with a brief commentary on membership, authority, and the newspapers under their control.

THE FIRST NEW LEFT SECT to make a substantial impact was Zengakuren, or *Zen*-Nippon *Gaku*sei Jichikai Sō-*Rengō* (All-

Japan Student League), which was formed under the auspices of the Japan Communist Party in 1948. It broke away from the JCP because of disagreements over several concrete issues and principles, among them the Soviet invasion of Hungary in 1956 and the JCP's decision to become a legalist party and to renounce underground tactics and violent means. A militant organization from the start, Zengakuren fought a series of struggles and "spring offensives." Some of these made history: the Red Purge struggle of 1949–1952, the Sunagawa struggle, which was the "father movement" of Sanrizuka, the AMPO struggle of 1960, and the Nuclear Test struggle of 1961. The intense confrontations over these issues and the struggles that took place in universities, including the elite Tokyo and Kyoto universities, created cadres of leaders with great experience in physical combat against the authorities.

It was this experience that the sects brought to Sanrizuka. The new tactics of the New Left were combined with the tactics of farmers for whom "combat" meant wartime experience. The sects also brought problems to Sanrizuka. Each "offensive" tended to intensify ideological differences as well as to form coalitions. At each stage and within each generation there has been a continuous process of fission and fusion, coalition and conflict, between the sects. When they came to Sanrizuka, such differences had to be muted. Each sect was required to sign a pledge not to engage in activities that might be harmful to the Hantai Dōmei. In this way the farmers asserted their preeminence. Meiji and Taishō grandfathers brought up in the tradition of peasant-warriors joined with militants in an alliance of "grandsons and granddaughters," but each side maintained its separateness.[2]

Perhaps the relationship would not have been successful without Tomura Issaku, who had been responsible for inviting the first representative of Zengakuren to participate in the Sanrizuka struggle. He was also a key figure in expelling the JCP from the site. Tomura articulated a set of principles satisfactory both to the sects and to the Hantai Dōmei in universal, absolute, and passionate terms. The more passion, the more violence, and the more absolute the judgments. Tomura gave violence dignity and made dignity violent.

The history of the left in Japan, old and new, is associated with violence; so is the history of the area with its previous peasant and tenant rebellions. The government, too, is associated with violence—mainly, of course, because of the imperial system and the war. In Chapter 4 we saw how violence escalated in the Sanrizuka struggle. Does violence have special significance for the Japanese?

Some people would argue that despite elaborate codes of behavior, the mechanisms of mediation and accommodation that these codes imply, and the courtesy and deference in personal and family relationships that in Japan are more pronounced than anywhere else, and despite even the abhorrence of violence itself, "underneath" the Japanese are fundamentally more violent than most other people. A substantial literature exists that deals with the question of differences between Western notions of individual guilt (with Judeo-Christian origins) and Japanese notions of collective obligation, suggesting that the former is missing in Japanese moral life.[3]

There may be some merit to this argument when applied to Japanese decision-making, as we shall see when we discuss the bureaucracy. But such a formulation is inadequate in describing the militants of the Sanrizuka movement. Most of them, particularly those of the AMPO generation, appear to be deeply concerned with individual moral conduct and in particular with the question of how to live in a manner consistent with their moral principles. Members of even the most militant sects are preoccupied with this issue. In a sense, then, sect members are more individualistic than most Japanese and more prone to "individual" guilt and soul searching.

The issue of individual responsibility can be seen in the case of the militant who was killed in the 1977 razing of the two steel towers. Typical of many militants of the second AMPO generation, Higashiyama Kaoru, the son of a teacher, came to Sanrizuka in 1971 to help build a solidarity hut. After dropping out of the university he remained in Sanrizuka, living in the solidarity hut as an unaffiliated (non-sect) activist. For a while he made money by driving a taxi part-time. Deeply concerned about the degree of his own sincerity, he wrote an essay posing certain questions for himself. "What is my position in supporting the Opposition League?" he asked himself.

> First, we cannot remain aloof from the Sanrizuka struggle, because it is not the attempt of a particular region to jack up land prices, or of a particular community to get rid of an airport it would be happy to see somewhere else, but instead it is the Japanese people's most advanced struggle of absolute opposition at the present stage.
>
> Secondly, we are overcoming the weaknesses which existed in our contacts with the workers during our struggle on the university barricades in 1968 and after, as well as the weaknesses in our relations with the general society in the

1970 anti-Treaty struggle. We are doing this by learning from the strengths of the farmers, both as producers and in their daily lives, as we fight alongside them.[4]

The simplicity, the linking of Sanrizuka to past struggles, the idea of learning from the authenticity of farmers, the desire to connect with society on renegotiated terms, are not especially profound. But they are similar to the views of many others. When Higashiyama was killed, at age twenty-seven, Tomura spoke at his funeral and exhorted the members of the movement to "change your grief over this murder into anger."[5]

It was Tomura, a Christian, who best understood the link between Christianity and radicalism. The intimacy between Christianity and early socialism in Japan began with protest movements before the turn of the century. In the Ashio Copper Mine case, for example, workers in Tochigi Prefecture were being poisoned by mining wastes. Despite mounting concern, the company did nothing to prevent this. In 1901, about a thousand university students, along with Meiji Christians and socialists, came to the site to demonstrate. Figures such as Kōtoku Shūsui became identified with the fight against pollution and militarism and with the defense of rural interests.[6] Influenced by the Russian populist movement, he combined pacifism in principle with a vague attachment to terrorism in practice. He opposed war but accepted assassination as a way to get rid of reprehensible political leaders and attack the state power. His transformation from a pacifist to an advocate of violence against the state was closely paralleled, decades later, by the growing militancy of Tomura. Tomura was certainly not unaware of Kōtoku Shūsui, who, accused of conspiring to assassinate the Meiji emperor in 1910, was executed in 1911. At the time of his own death, Tomura had accepted the need for violent confrontation both as a method and as a discipline.

STUDENTS HAVE ALWAYS been involved in radical movements in Japan. Anti-militarist themes and social protest against the forced draft changes induced by the Meiji reforms were particularly attractive to students, and when the Japan Socialist Party was founded in 1906 there were many students among its members. Out of a total of some fourteen thousand socialists in Tokyo, about seventy-five hundred were students.[7]

A few of these early student radicals were influenced by Russian populism, and the relationship between Christian, anarchist, and early socialist radicalism was a close one. The influence of Tolstoy was particularly strong in the early days, especially among those who, like Kawakami Hajmine (1879–1946), came from a samurai background and sought an appropriate expression of aristocratic values and populism. Christianity and socialism seemed to offer the right combination. For many radical Japanese, particularly the intellectuals, there seemed to be a basic continuity between their own traditions and Western ideas. "The Meiji warrior, whose moral system was undercut by the destruction of the feudal system, turned to Christianity precisely because it offered a means of preserving those values—loyalty, single-mindedness of purpose, sincerity, etc.—that lay at the core of the former warrior ethos."[8]

Early Japanese radicalism expressed individual concern over the choice between obligations to self, to family, and to society, and showed a growing consciousness of the social meaning of such choices. Solutions were sought in the concrete setting of social conflict. The context of struggle was essential. It was relatively easy to take the next step—to go from Christianity to Marxism. Both involved an exegetical tradition. Both employed specific texts. Both were concerned with the translation of their meanings into direct action. Direct action in Japan involving industrial pollution, anti-militarism, and the preservation of traditional values paralleled the movement in Russia, which also went from an early Christian populism and anarchism to socialism and Marxism.[9]

Neither Japanese Christians nor Japanese Marxists saw any conflict between socialism or radicalism and Japanese values. As industrialization and militarism became more prominent in Japan, Marxism seemed even more relevant, since it denied absolutely the premises of the nationalist state and the possibility of realizing appropriate moral and civic traditions under the conditions of capitalism. Many, of course, were concerned about the direction of Japan's political economy, but Marxism provided the most sweeping analysis of why capitalism and liberal political institutions were absolutely corrupting. Marxism offered a formula for self-discipline and a reason to break with prevailing networks of obligation constituted by the imperial system.[10]

But despite the individualism of conscience, such a break could never be undertaken in a solitary way. In this respect Marxism offered not only a doctrine but a substitute social system. It constituted its own networks. At first there were socialist study groups that required discipline, obligation, and mutual regard. Not long afterward, in 1922, the first radical militant student groups were formed. In 1926 a group of student radicals in Shinjinkai with about 120 members divided into two groups, those who were activists and those with more scholarly interests. The first became union organizers; the others, particularly those interested in economic theory, formed into study groups. Both would come together in a communal lodging, the "solidarity house" (*gasshuku*). As Henry Dewitt Smith describes it,

> It was here that the study groups and endless arguments took place, here that the theory and tactics of the entire Japanese student movement were worked out, and here that contact with the whole spectrum of the Japanese left was maintained by frequent visits from labor leaders, radical politicians, progressive academicians, and left wing artists.
>
> The tone of radical student life was not such as to lure recruits for its comforts, for it was puritanical, physically demanding, and intensely serious. The *gasshuku* itself was plain and almost wholly undecorated. The boarders rarely drank, in a country where heavy student drinking was not only a tradition but at times a major social problem.[11]

This description would fit life today inside the fortresses and solidarity huts. In the *gasshuku* there was a passion for secrecy as well:

> Many of the students, especially those participating in off-campus agitation, went by aliases, some having perhaps two or three different names for underground work as well as a pen name or two for articles in left wing magazines. Few of the radical students in this era wore the traditional uniform, preferring working class clothing both as a camouflage and as a mark of solidarity with the proletariat. Plain-clothes detectives were on constant watch outside the Shinjinkai *gasshuku,* and the individual members themselves were often followed. Vigilance had to be paid against the possibilities of spies within the membership (one or two such cases were actually discovered) or of police attempts to bribe the less committed.[12]

The dress is a bit different today: the uniforms have given way to running trousers and striped jackets, and headbands have replaced hats. But the lack of heavy drinking, the rather circumspect character of sexual relationships, the seriousness—these all are true of the militants in solidarity huts and fortresses of Sanrizuka.

Fortress life has a peculiar chemistry. Cadres remain calm under continuous police harassment, but during a confrontation this calm, almost detached behavior fragments. It is within the smallest, most serious groups, those most devoted to the study of Marxism, that the most severe and intense splits occur. The small group is the focus of ambiguity, of commitment and betrayal. But such a group provides a sense of communal achievement, especially when personal autonomy and purity of motive are realized. This sort of individualism requires group affiliation; it cannot stand alone in the individual *qua* individual. Outside the group people tend to lose their radical commitments. Indeed, from the start the Japan Communist Party "depended very heavily on the coherence and sustaining power of the close group of comrades, the *dōshi* or 'like-minded.' When isolated from the group, the ideology which it had carried was deprived of much of its meaning, and the individual communist alone in a jail cell had little reason to sustain his allegiance."[13] The same holds true for sect members today.

In 1922, the first organization of students, with a combination of political and humanitarian goals, took up such issues as the recall of Japanese troops from Siberia, the recognition of the U.S.S.R., and Russian famine relief. Some of the leaders were lone wolves or anarchist-Bolsheviks like Ōsugi Sakae. Others were more prone to unity within a single federation. Smith describes the actual formation of the group as follows:

> These intermural contacts soon led to a plan for a radical federation, reviving the concept which had aborted three years earlier in the Youth Cultural League. This time, however, a far greater number of groups were involved, since rudimentary organizations had been set up for famine relief collection at many schools that had previously been organized. The majority of these groups were based on the debating clubs, the traditional birthplace of student radicals in Japan. Initial plans for the federation were drawn up in October, and the simple name of Student Federation (Gakusei Rengōkai), commonly known by the abbreviation of *"Gakuren"* was chosen. The founding meeting was held on November 7, 1922, the fifth anniversary of the October Revolution, on the Tokyo Imperial University campus.[14]

The Sanrizuka Movement

The main point of convergence was militant activism, and within this activism the most important single event was the Russian revolution. It was in support of that revolution that the first-generation student movement was formed.[15] Since the JCP was illegal, discipline was essential.

In the post–World War II period the JCP became a legal party, and the need for discipline declined. Concrete struggles, "spring offensives," led to the formation of various coalitions, fronts, rallies. Different groups of militants made common cause against authorities on a variety of issues, but as tactics of confrontation evolved, differences between groups arose, most particularly over the appropriate use of violence but also over the relationship with the Soviet Union and the role of the JCP. For a time the Chinese revolution, the Cultural Revolution, and the Vietnam war were also divisive issues. Two tendencies—the propensity to coalesce and the propensity to divide—have been equally important in the history of radical sects. The propensity to coalesce showed itself in the formation of common fronts to mobilize the masses to attain concrete goals. But within each coalition the propensity to divide appeared as groups competed with one another and some performed better than others. Both propensities can occur at more or less the same time. That is, a broad coalition like the student Zengakuren movement can give rise to sects while in turn sect division becomes a political process within Zengakuren itself.[16]

Perhaps the most important original source of the splits within Zengakuren was disagreement between two JCP factions over control of the organization. The weaker JCP faction, the so-called International Group, succeeded in taking control in 1950, losing power the following year. In 1957 a Revolutionary Communist League was organized out of the Japan Trotskyist League which was founded that same year, leading to the establishment of the Fourth International. In turn, a National Committee was formed in 1959 out of the Revolutionary Communist League, splitting into two groups, Kakumaru-ha and Chūkaku-ha, in 1963. In 1964, under Chūkaku-ha initiative, the Three Sects Zengakuren (Sampa-kei Zengakuren) was formed.

This latter group has been the main force in Sanrizuka. Its president at the time was Akiyama Katsuyuki. Two other sects in the Three Sects Zengakuren were the Socialist Student League and the Socialist Youth League. Among the reasons why these groups formed a coalition rather than establishing a more unified organization was that the members continued to differ in their evaluation of such issues as Stalin, party structure, the Chinese cultural revolution, and China's nuclear tests. One group, the Socialist Youth League (Kaihō-ha or Liberation), which was organized in 1965, was close to the Japan Socialist Party.

THE ORIGINAL Zengakuren was to the student movement what Sōhyō is to the trade union movement—a grand coalition. Just as Sōhyō is organized around unions but subject to the politics of different political parties and sects, so too with Zengakuren. (The parallel holds for Sōhyō as it is today. When it was originally organized, however, it was an anti-communist labor organization. Formed at the time of the "red purge" of 1950, it split off from the Japan Labor League, Nihon Rōdō Sō-Dōmei, which had been organized in 1919. Over the years Sōhyō has changed very much. Today it includes pro-JCP trade unions such as the teachers' union. It is more radical and more all-inclusive, even though it has moved more toward the right in recent years. It still commands the support of most Japanese trade unions.) There are certain structural similarities between Sōhyō and Zengakuren which are of significance mainly as a way of emphasizing the common ground between workers and militant students.

The primary unit of organization of the original Zengakuren was the student body of each university; within the university the students were grouped by department affiliation. All students automatically became members as they entered the university. Each member paid a fee, which gave him or her an equal right and an equal responsibility to participate in activities, to run for office, and to share in decision-making. There was a student convention in the university with all-member participation and a representatives' convention as well. Committee members could be elected by direct or indirect methods of voting. Daily activities were decided by representatives chosen by each class, according to the subdivisions of the faculty.

Each university student body was part of a prefectural *Gakuren* (student union), and the entire network formed the *Zengakuren*. The main decision-making body was the convention consisting of representatives sent from the student body of each university, the number of representatives dependent on the number of students enrolled. Between conventions Zengakuren was run by a central executive committee of thirty members chosen by the convention; in turn it appointed secretariats to carry on daily activities.[17]

The Sanrizuka Movement

Thus Zengakuren represented the widest possible coalition of students. Its general purpose was to organize students in Japan within a single body not only to improve student conditions but also to cooperate with democratic forces inside and outside Japan in trying to realize eternal peace, achieve internal detente and the independence of Japan, and protect democracy, academic freedom, and university autonomy. Zengakuren called for the development of cultural and scientific creativity as well as the protection of democratic education.

Zengakuren before and after AMPO 1960 were very different organizations. Before 1960, as we have indicated, there were no sects, and the JCP ruled. By 1960, it was ruled by an anti-JCP Communist League (really ex-JCP). Today there are three Zengakuren bodies: Kakumaru-ha Zengakuren, which is not part of the Sanrizuka struggle and to which the movement is opposed; Chūkaku-ha; and the Democratic Youth Zengakuren, which also remains outside of Sanrizuka and is part of the JCP.[18]

The biggest single event in the evolution of the New Left was AMPO 1960, when several million people were mobilized against U.S.-Japan Mutual Security Treaty Revision. The Sanrizuka struggle cannot be understood without some knowledge of it, for it was a turning point in Japanese protest movements. It kindled hope among militants that the power demonstrated there would grow, and it marked the entry of the New Left into serious Japanese politics. AMPO 1960 was a mass movement larger and better organized than anything Sōhyō, the General Council of Japan Trade Unions, had been able to muster. Many non-radical students were mobilized, including thousands from the five Christian universities in Tokyo. Intellectuals, many of whom had never before been engaged in politics, and university professors were involved; seventy-five percent of the faculty of Tokyo University signed petitions demanding the dissolution of the Diet and calling for new elections. Groups of housewives and actresses were organized. Sōhyō itself conducted a work stoppage involving five and a half million workers, the largest action of its type in the history of Japan.[19]

Also involved in AMPO 1960 were those who followed the line of armed struggle and rejected parliamentary politics. One group, the Bund, emphasized underground activity, armed struggle, mass struggle, and world revolution (although rejecting terrorism). The Bund, or Communist League, was founded in 1958 and then broke up into smaller groups because of differing positions on the issue of revolutionary tactics.[20]

Chūkaku-ha was the first of the New Left groups to enter Sanrizuka and remains the most important to this day.[21] But to one degree or another Sanrizuka became important for all the militant
groups who had mobilized for AMPO 1960. In Sanrizuka the state
(or its surrogate, the airport) could be attacked directly, and the
principle of class struggle against imperialism could be raised.
Forming a coalition of workers and peasants against the state became the first objective. It was hoped that the attack on Japanese
imperialism and militarism at Sanrizuka would lead to a new
AMPO, this one on a wider and more popular scale.

Not all sects accepted these views, of course. Kakumaru-ha completely rejected the idea that a real class struggle could be pursued
at Sanrizuka, preferring to concentrate on organizing factory workers. Both the farmers and the sects allied with them feel an intense
hostility toward Kakumaru-ha because of its attitude toward the
movement, and the Hantai Dōmei has expelled Kakumaru-ha from
the site on the grounds of spreading "malicious gossip." The general
aims of Kakumaru-ha (as stated by its chairman, Kuroda Kanichi)
are to realize world revolution through anti-imperialist and anti-
Stalinist tactics, to destroy state power in Japan as part of the proletarian world revolution, and to develop anti-Stalinism—aims that do
not seem to differ substantially from Chūkaku-ha's. The sects claim
to have different tactics, however. Chūkaku-ha considers Kakumaru-ha too much like the Communist Party, and more concerned
with its own survival than with the cause. In one infamous event at
Tokyo University known as the Fall of the Yasuda Auditorium, Kakumaru-ha allegedly fled in order to avoid a final confrontation with
the authorities. In turn, Kakumaru-ha has accused Chūkaku-ha of
blindly pursuing mobilized armed upheaval while avoiding physical
confrontation with the riot police.

The hostility between the sects has become a full-fledged war. To
many of the sects at Sanrizuka, the war with Kakumaru-ha is as
central a concern as the conflict with the Airport Authority. Kakumaru-ha members have killed Honda Nobuyoshi, the secretary general of Chūkaku-ha, and Kasahara Massayoshi, the leader of the sect
Kaihō (Liberation). By June 1980 Kaihō-ha had killed some twenty
Kakumaru-ha members.

Chūkaku-ha is one of the most powerful sects in Sanrizuka. The
Fourth International, too, has been important. Emphasizing mass
mobilization and a united front, it is opposed to the confrontations
between Chūkaku-ha and Kaihō and Kakumaru-ha. The Fourth International has been more attractive to the working class and has

more workers as members than the other sects, and it is the only New Left sect to be supported internationally. While insisting on its extreme radicalism, it has also been more open to association with other sects. In March 1978 it organized the takeover of the airport control tower.

Kaihō, the third largest sect in Sanrizuka, was derived from the Bund, breaking away in 1965. It received support from the Japan Socialist Party in an attempt by the JSP to rejuvenate the party after the 1960 AMPO riots. In 1971 Kaihō cut its ties with the Japan Socialist Party because it was too militant and violent for the JSP. The sect has been responsible for the deaths of over twenty Kakumaru-ha members.

Although these sects employ violence, they need to be distinguished from the groups using terrorist tactics and often loosely called "red army." The Communist League Red Army was established by militants from the Kansai area, mainly Osaka. Evaluating the "defeat" in the streetfighting and university struggles of 1968 and 1969, they decided that what was called for was the organization of an army willing to use guns and bombs. They declared that the third world war had begun and attacked police boxes with Molotov cocktails. In 1969, while practicing guerrilla warfare in Yamanashi Prefecture, the majority of them were arrested. Nine members hijacked a plane and fled to North Korea in March 1970. Most Red Army formations were eventually wiped out. There are two surviving sects of the Red Army, Proletarian Revolution and the Japan Committee.

The most significant alternative to the sects and the most important single group within the Japanese Red Army was the United Red Army (Rengō Sekigun), a coalition based on the principles of world revolution as advocated by the Bund and the leftists in the Japan Communist Party. Its main priority was war against the United States because it saw the United States as the main spearhead of imperialism. Its strategy was until recently called the PBM tactic. Tactic P was the kidnapping of famous people. Tactic B was bombing and building up bases for armed struggle. Tactic M was obtaining money. They established bases in the mountains and became the object of intensive police activity. Their main base was discovered in 1972. On capturing it, the police discovered that some fourteen members had been lynched and others died after torture and "self-criticism." One of its leaders, Mori Tsuneo, committed suicide after admitting "mistakes" in 1973. Other top leaders such as Nagata

Hiroko and Sakaguchi Hiroshi are in prison and have been sentenced to death.

What is left of the Red Army is mainly overseas. The leader, Shigenobu Fusako, was sent to Beirut as liaison officer between the Red Army and the Popular Front for the Liberation of Palestine (PFLP). Her group, the Arab Red Army, was involved in the Lod Airport incident in Tel Aviv in May 1972. The sole survivor of the attack is in jail in Israel and it is said that he has tried to convert to Judaism. Other members of the group hijacked a Japan Airlines jumbo jet in July 1973, attacked the Shell Oil Company in Singapore in February 1974, the Japanese Embassy in Kuwait in February 1974, and the French Embassy at the Hague in August 1975, and engaged in the Dacca hijacking in September 1977. Today the group has no formal ties with the Red Army in Japan and is quite different from the Red Army sect of the Communist League. There are about thirty members abroad and about one hundred supporters in Japan.

The Sanrizuka movement must be seen as completely separate from various terrorist groups such as the Red Army. Farmers and sects believe that the use of guns is counterproductive, and a set of rules for violence has emerged at Sanrizuka. The police also respect rules and have refrained from wiping out solidarity huts or directly attacking fortresses unless they stand on land already acquired by the Airport Authority or are put up in the path of construction.

For a time, some individuals, both in the original Hantai Dōmei and in the sects, fearing that the movement was losing ground, played with the idea of "internationalizing" the struggle—that is, making links with the Palestinian Liberation Organization and with other groups using violent methods. Indeed, in 1980 there were some conversations about this in Hawaii with PLO officials. Such activities were not supported by the Hantai Dōmei as a whole, however, even though Tomura, when visiting Beirut to participate in an exhibition of paintings and sculpture, had preliminary discussions with PLO representatives and had a generally pro-PLO and pro-PFLP outlook himself.

Among broad-based coalitions supporting Sanrizuka perhaps the most important has been Zenkoku Kyōtō Kaigi or Zenkyōtō (All-Student Joint Struggle Conference). A mass movement that evolved out of the university struggles of 1968–69, it was not specifically organized around sects (as is Zengakuren). Each university had its own branch; the Nihon University and Tokyo University branches became the best known. The movement was characterized by study groups, discussion, soul searching, and an absence of doctrinalism. In 1969 eight anti-JCP sects formed Zenkyōtō. The relatively open organization and the emphasis on diversity made it into a model movement for citizen participation.

Another organization that was important in the organization of wider supporting networks in Sanrizuka is Beheiren, a citizen protest movement organized specifically to oppose the Vietnam war. It too was broad-based and combined many forms of popular protest. The airport at Sanrizuka was considered by Beheiren to be an extension of U.S. military needs because of the Vietnam war. When air routes were made public and one of them, "Blue 14," was described as representing a basic line of flight from Sanrizuka to Southeast Asia, it convinced many people that there was an indisputable link between the Vietnam war and the construction of the airport. Beheiren, originally formed out of the "silent majority" groups organized more or less spontaneously at the time of the AMPO Diet demonstrations of 1960, first really asserted itself as an organization independent of all political groups in April 1965. Its first demonstration was a protest march over the February bombing of North Vietnam. Among its original members were several figures important in the AMPO demonstrations, particularly the well-known writer Oda Makoto. Other founders were Kaikō Ken, Hotta Yoshie, and Takahashi Kazumi, all writers; Shinoda Masahiro, a film director; and Sato Sampei, a cartoonist. These and other intellectuals, particularly journalists, were at different times very important in presenting the Sanrizuka movement to the public, and in their writings and rallies they helped mobilize support for militants who were standing trial.

Although it began as an organization of small citizen protest movements, Beheiren became part of the network providing support and sympathy both for militants and for the Hantai Dōmei itself. By 1969 it had moved sufficiently far to the left to be considered part of the New Left, its activities including peace rallies and anti-Vietnam war mobilizations. More incidentally, it helped American soldiers in Japan who were opposed to the war. Like Zenkyōtō it opposed restrictive controls by the sects, considering them to represent an incipient elitism; but the more it moved to the left, the more it lost its less political members and the more like a sect it became. It officially came to an end in February 1974.

The trade union movement has also provided support for Sanrizuka. Although trade unions are in general very far removed from the New Left (and in the last few years have moved even further from it), one group, Dōrō Chiba, the Chiba branch of the locomotive union, is very much involved with Chūkaku-ha and Sanrizuka. It could at any time shut the airport down by refusing to deliver fuel, all of which comes by rail. Another union that is small but has a number of locals sympathetic to the Hantai Dōmei is the All-Japan Metalworkers Union (Zenkin). Finally, the Japan Postal Workers Union, although it has never offered any specific assistance to the movement, has a very sympathetic membership.

Most New Left sects remain implacably hostile to parliamentary government. A few, however, have begun to contest elections. When the Bund (Communist League) split into more than ten sects, one of these, Kyōsan-Shugi No Hata (Flag of Communism), organized a nationwide study group called Zenkoku Shakai-Kagaku Kenkyukai (National Social Science Study Group). After changing its name to the Marxist Workers' League in 1972, the study group took as its main goal the organization of the public around the workers. It became critical of the Bund's strategy of armed struggle. Although its membership was small, about five hundred, it nominated ten candidates to the June 1980 House of Councillors election, one from a nationwide electoral district and nine from local districts. It received 200,000 votes in the 1980 elections and has become a recognized political organization.

THE SECTS were not originally the farmers' main source of support. The first groups to get involved at Sanrizuka were the Japan Communist Party and the Japan Socialist Party. An early Hantai Dōmei rally, held at the Narita Municipal Athletic Field on October 2, 1966, had over five thousand participants, among them representatives of women's and workers' organizations and JCP and JSP Dietmen. Two of the speakers were Amaya Shūzō, chairman of the JSP Special Committee on the Airport, and Hakamada Satomi, a Central Committee member of the JCP. In the months that followed there was a great deal of activity. In December 1966 the Hantai Dōmei constructed a base at Ishibashi Masaji's compound, including a thirty-three-meter wooden tower and a hut for a small permanent staff. By February 1967 Komaino fort was built and in April Kinone fort. It was not until the following September that Akiyama Katsuyuki, president of the Three Sects Zengakuren, visited Sanrizuka and attended meetings at Komaino fort. During these meetings he spoke to the defenders, emphasizing the relationship between the Sanrizuka struggle and the larger anti-war movement.

He recalled particularly the role students had played in the Suna-gawa struggle. In November, after a number of rallies, the Chiba Prefecture Anti-War Youth League Committee and the Prefecture Labor Union Representatives Conference held a rally linking the airport with the Vietnam war. Shortly thereafter, on November 28, 170 farmers from the Hantai Dōmei went to the governor of the pre-fecture to protest the prefecture's participation in land acquisition as well as police violence. The farmers were joined by JSP Prefectural Assemblymen and sixty students, among them the president of the Three Sects Zengakuren. The JCP withdrew from this rally, saying that Trotskyites were trying to destroy the movement. At a rally later that same evening, the JCP proposed to the JSP that the Three Sects Zengakuren be expelled, even though the students had been explicitly invited by Tomura. The JSP refused, and forty JCP members left the site with their flag. What was left was a coalition of the Hantai Dōmei, the JSP, the Three Sects Zengakuren, and the Anti-War Youth League. After that rallies were held regularly. Thousands came to participate. As more arrests were made and more people wounded, more Three Sects Zengakuren members came and stayed. By May 1968, approximately one hundred mem-bers were installed, organized into sects, and Chūkaku-ha had built its solidarity hut. Students also stayed in farmers' houses. The movement became increasingly militant. When a major rally was held in Sanrizuka Park in June 1968, the students wore helmets and armed themselves with spears and sickles. As they helped farmers, participated in confrontations, and recruited support from outside, militants gradually replaced both the JCP and the JSP as the main partner of the Hantai Dōmei.

The participation of the sects at Sanrizuka has thus lasted for al-most a whole generation. During that time a number of differences between sects and between generations of sects have arisen. The AMPO 1960 generation is considered to be stoic, to live up to its be-liefs. AMPO 1970 militants are regarded as less puritanical, less ideo-logically committed, not as dedicated to political activities; many of them see themselves as communists but live as capitalists. Militants born around 1940 can remember not having enough food. Those born in 1946 remember poverty. Those born in 1950 remember Viet-nam. The first AMPO generation experienced all three, the last only the Vietnam war. And there has been an erosion in the moral stature of both Vietnam and the People's Republic of China; Ho Chi Minh and Mao Tse-tung are no longer heroes.

Other factors as well enter into a militant's degree of commitment. Those who were in graduate schools in the late 1960s were less involved than those who were undergraduates during that time. Undergraduates were the main participants in student riots, university confrontations, and the culmination of these in the context of Vietnam and Cambodia from 1968 to 1971, turning their backs on the normalcy of Japanese life. Another factor was which university a student attended. In the more important ones, debates were intense; Zengakuren politics were all-important.

Chance and personal encounters were involved, too. Friends who joined the movement persuaded others. If an eldest brother joined, the younger members of the family almost invariably followed suit. Thus generational differences, principles and tactics, university affiliation, and friendship and kinship all played a role in determining which sect one joined and how sects divided.

Sect membership involves, above all, writing. Even rank and file members who are relatively inarticulate in their speech may be involved in writing and distributing leaflets, pamphlets, and other materials. Almost all important leaders spend a great deal of their time writing articles and making "studies." Writers and photographers in both Sanrizuka and Tokyo collaborate in these efforts. One of the members of Chūkaku-ha is an exceptionally gifted calligrapher.

All the major sects have newspapers. Chūkaku-ha's newspaper, *Zenshin,* has a circulation of fifteen thousand and sells for 300 yen. The sect itself has approximately five thousand members, of whom about half are activists. The Kakumaru-ha newspaper, *Kaihō,* has a circulation of about twelve thousand and is sold at the same price; the sect has about two thousand activists. Kaihō's newspaper, entitled *Kaihō* ("liberation") also, has a circulation of about eight thousand and it too is sold at 300 yen; the Kaihō sect has between seven and nine hundred activists. *World Revolution,* the journal of the Fourth International, sells for 250 yen and has a circulation of about seven thousand. The sect has about twelve hundred activists. Each journal or newspaper tends to be six or eight pages. The sect's solidarity hut or fortress in Sanrizuka is a distribution point for the newspaper. Sales constitute an important source of income for all sects.

In these written materials one finds a curious mixture of mobilizational, hortatory, and even evangelical qualities. The action of writing is important; the words themselves are evidence, on the printed page, that the revolution exists. They could be said to represent what J. L. Austin calls "performatives"—expressions that are not factually correct or incorrect but rather by being uttered are aimed at having a consequence.[22] But because these performatives are expressed in the context of descriptive statement of fact, of concrete situations, they take on the appearance of "constatives," truths or falsehoods. Most of what is written, then, is the performative in the guise of the constative. Saying things about the struggle, the farmers, or the state makes the things said true, and the actions of those involved are affected by the truths said. To make what is written consequential requires prior belief; to establish prior belief requires materials that are written. The system is above all a symbolic network of words and acts. Through written materials Sanrizuka becomes an important part of a larger dialogue, part of the wider world of radical politics.

6

The Sects at Sanrizuka

THERE ARE some seventeen militant radical sects with members living in and around Sanrizuka, mainly in thirty-three solidarity huts and fortresses. Three-fourths of the sects are "affiliated"—that is, linked to outside organizations. The unaffiliated one-fourth consist of small organizations with commemorative names like "November 30th Struggle Group." They have little or no outside support but work together with other sects and with farmers.

The majority of the solidarity huts and fortresses are manned by "cadres," which range in size from about five members to forty-five. The cadres are generally posted from central headquarters, particularly in the case of the larger sects. There are very few women, but in several of the most important sects a woman has had major responsibilities under a top male leader. She looks after relations with the farmers, farmers' wives and families, and visitors, and is responsible for general management and organization. These women tend to be exceptionally intelligent, with a long history of militant participation. Most are divorced or separated from their husbands.

Among the cadres are trade union activists, many ex-university students, and a few former junior civil servants (a very broad category that can include school teachers). They come from virtually all over Japan. In one solidarity hut, for example, cadres who had been on the site for more than two years came from such universities as Meiji, Yamagata, Nihon, Hōsei, Tokyo, and Kyoto. One older member had a degree in philosophy from Kyoto University. A quiet and thoughtful man, somewhat reserved, he was known as "Great Teacher" (*Daisensei*). The head of the solidarity hut was a graduate of Tokyo University with a degree in business administration. The key organization and liaison person with the farmers was a divorced woman in her thirties who was the daughter of a farmer from Kyushu, himself a member of the Communist Party. She lived in the solidarity hut but kept a small apartment in Tokyo.

There is no clear distinction between a solidarity hut and a fortress. A solidarity hut is essentially a dormitory that can house a large number of supporters who come to Sanrizuka either for a rally or when farmers need special assistance.[1] A fortress is a more formidable structure, usually commanding an area likely to be contested. Many have been built at strategic points (like the intersection of a road) and have high walls and watchtowers. Some are close to the airport fence, where they look into the police watchtowers. They were constructed to guard farmers holding out in partial isolation near land already purchased by the government. Some of the huts and fortresses are actually large tin shacks with plywood walls and floors, reinforced on the outside by tension cables crisscrossing the exterior walls. These are identical to other buildings in the Sanrizuka area used as warehouses, farm sheds, small factories, and lumberyards. All use lookouts and rely on telephone and radio communications with each other, and all have electricity and water and gas.

In both the solidarity huts and the fortresses live cadres who are always ready to respond to attacks by police. Police harassment is a routine matter. In full riot gear the police come by on foot, often at quick step, stopping in front of the hut or fortress to bang on the gates, peer over the barbed-wire enclosures, shout, observe the occupants through binoculars, make holes in the fences, and photograph those inside. They may stay for a few minutes or for an hour. Those inside pay little attention. The following and stopping of sect cars and trucks is also routine. Detectives or police will question drivers and occasionally conduct searches or ask for documents. An atmosphere of hostility is sustained even when nothing special is going on. Occasionally a hut or fortress will be entered by the police, something the farmers themselves almost never experience. Occasionally a militant will be roughed up in questioning or arrested.

After a major event there are numerous arrests. The trials, which are expensive and long, sometimes dragging on for years, cause families a certain amount of embarrassment. Among the consequences for the person arrested are loss of a job and expulsion from a trade union.

Important leaders of the two main sects, Chūkaku-ha and the Fourth International, have experienced confrontational events elsewhere. Most have been arrested several times and have been in jail. Some leaders represent themselves as professional revolutionaries. The top leaders live not in Sanrizuka but in main sect offices elsewhere. A major transition in generational leadership is under way: in Chūkaku-ha, for instance, out of eleven top leaders five are of the AMPO 1960 generation, three are of an "intermediate" generation corresponding to the Japan-Korea normalization struggles of 1965, and three are from AMPO 1970. The top leader of the Chūkaku-ha solidarity hut at Sanrizuka is AMPO 1960; his second in command is AMPO 1970.

Chūkaku-ha owns two new headquarters buildings, one in Tokyo and another in Osaka. For important events at Sanrizuka the leaders go out to the site. Most of them, even those who do not live there, have had firsthand experience in Sanrizuka. Of the sect members living more or less permanently in the solidarity huts and fortresses, some have been there for five, ten, or even fifteen years, assisting with farming chores and carrying on "ideological work." In a sense they are internal exiles from the age-graded networks of Japan's social hierarchies. The major "crises" they confront in their personal lives (particularly the men) come at around age thirty. In Japanese society this is the normal time to make a transition to family and job responsibilities. Most militants give up their active political phase then.[2]

Full-time cadres of major sects are supported from outside. Chūkaku-ha, with about forty cadre members in the main solidarity hut at Sanrizuka, has expenditures of several million yen a month. Funds come from workers and students in all parts of Japan, as well as from a few wealthy supporters. The sect spends half a million yen a month on gasoline alone for its twelve cars and twenty motorcycles. In addition to going out to help farmers, members are engaged in constant travel back and forth to Tokyo, distributing leaflets, preparing for meetings, and so on. The sect has about five hundred members who have no profession or means of earning a livelihood other than full-time organizational activities for Chūkaku-ha; they are supported by other members who have jobs. The required ratio is approximately ten supporters for each full-time member, which suggests that there are at least five thousand dues-paying members of Chūkaku-ha.[3]

LIFE INSIDE the solidarity huts is a bit like dormitory life in a university. There are large sleeping areas where people roll up on futons. There is little rigid discipline. And, as in a university, privacy is respected despite collective living; people do not surrender their personal points of view or priorities to the group. Dormitory life does not in fact mean communal living. There is little effort within the solidarity huts and fortresses to create a model of how revolutionary society should be structured; instead, the huts are organized on practical lines of how best to help the farmers. No matter how permanent life within them has become, it must be temporary. In this respect solidarity huts and fortresses are completely different from, say, monasteries or collective farms.

Men and women sleep in the same *tatami*-mat barracks room. One may be awakened in the morning by the sound of a poorly recorded taped version of the Internationale in several languages followed by more inspirational Hantai Dōmei war songs in the fashion of semi-folk popular music. People wake slowly, then wash in the kitchen or find an outdoor facility or faucet. Breakfast is more or less an individual matter, although rice, the basis for all collective eating, is available, hot, in a huge electric rice steamer. Cleaning up can be very casual indeed. Some solidarity huts seem almost deliberately dirty, unkempt, with food on the floor to be eaten by cats or dogs. Others are well maintained, clean, and well ventilated. Inside each hut and fortress, often scattered about, is a miscellany of equipment: projectors, tape recorders, radios, cameras, wiring equipment, pieces of motorcycles, helmets, travel bags, old suitcases, maps, posters. Presiding over the main room there is often a portrait of Tomura. A calendar with excellent line drawings by a sect artist shows aspects of the struggle or beautiful places in Sanrizuka that have been, or will be, obliterated. A good many of the paperback books scattered about on the floor or stacked in piles are practical: wiring, plumbing, how to get ahead in business. Comic books are also popular. On the whole the sects look inward, within their own walls. They rarely speak of other sects, particularly in the presence of outsiders. One has the impression (mistakenly) that each hut or fortress is self-sufficient. Visitors must in fact pay to stay, even when they have come to help farmers.

The life in these huts and fortresses seems at first glance to be completely different from life in farmers' households. Farmers rarely lock their doors, and their compounds, though walled, are relatively open. But the inward-looking life of the militants has more to it than meets the eye. Despite the cramped quarters of the solidarity huts and fortresses, and despite the sense of beleaguerment inside the walls from police surveillance, one can find a great deal of personal space and privacy. One can also find, especially after a successful rally or confrontation, moments in which the feelings shared inside the fortresses are best described by Freud's term, in *Civilization and Its Discontents,* as "oceanic." Within the huts one finds, too, the representations of structure Barthes refers to in *Sade, Fourier, Loyola*—self-isolation, articulation, and ordering.

Boredom is a problem, and many of the things that must be done are mundane: dishes must be washed, meals cooked, leaflets written, cars repaired. But some activities provide novel experiences, such as learning about the families and lives of the farmers. Militants discover differences between farmers and workers, recognizing that no matter how radical a farmer may sound or how much involved he has been in earlier radical activities of the JCP or the JSP, he retains an essential conservatism in his sense of responsibility about his property and in his desire to protect the patrimony from the state. The militant discovers very quickly how deeply attached farmers are to their way of life. From militants farmers gain a sense of their relationship to a much wider world, but farmers also impose limits on the militants. Farmers may speak of revolution, or regard themselves as revolutionaries, but they do so in a way more metaphorical than real. Militants are not too clear about such matters, either. Most are hesitant about their commitments and have private differences with their sects' doctrines. They suffer over the meaning of those differences, some virtually every day. Ask a revolutionary in a fortress if he or she is "really " a revolutionary, and the answer, almost invariably, is, "Not quite."

Such characteristics are contrary to the conventional wisdom about "true believers," particularly radical left ones, which leaves us with the interesting question of how there can be so much public commitment when there remains so much private doubt. The question is not easy to answer. Most theorists assert that commitments are easily made because radical beliefs are integrative, self-reinforcing, and, in the end, simplistic. The present research suggests that this is not true. While there may be superficial resemblances be-

tween a militant's life and that of the zealot in a commune, these resemblances tend to disappear on closer inspection. Many militants
in fact drop out. There are many disappointments. Those who remain, however, are not allowed to think in terms of failure. Setbacks
are seen as temporary and to be confronted so that remedies can be
found in a correct praxis. Details of individuals' performances will be
scrutinized. At all levels of leadership self-criticism is practiced. The
program is a kind of continuous education. The implications of daily
activities are examined, and general questions are posed; then the
general questions are translated into practical guides for the immediate future.[4]

Compared to people "outside," militants have a different sense of
time. They see two kinds of accomplishment: on one hand, short-
term events, confrontations, battles; on the other hand, very long-
term transformation. The revolution will come, they say, even
though it may take a long time. What is missing is what might be
called an intermediate perspective, precisely the perspective of those
who are engaged in conventional activities. The present is not seen
on its own terms. Rather, the present is composed of "heroic" episodes—the "movement of July 22nd," the "March 28th takeover,"
the April march, the Fall of Fort Komaino, rallies, jailings, beatings,
individuals serving as surrogate victims of imperialism, capitalism,
and the state, witnesses providing solemn testimony at public gath-
erings. Time is discontinuous, jumping from one heroic episode to
another like a series of photographs taken months apart. In their
surrogate roles, however, the militants represent a realism more
stark than any photograph.

Witnesses, exemplars, surrogates for the revolutionary process—
what militants share is the belief that the forces they see in motion
can only end with a final Althusserian disjunctive moment when no
force will be left that is powerful enough to rescue those in power.
Vietnam, China, even the October Revolution can be recapitulated
in Japan, a function not only of the decay of capitalism (the class
struggle) but also of the steadfastness of the revolutionaries. There
can be no discouragement at temporary setbacks. The proper end
will arrive when it is time for it to arrive.

This, at any rate, is what many militants will say in a first interview. After a third or fourth, separated by intervals long enough to
allow a relationship to be established, a militant is likely to reveal
another side, a dissatisfaction with the rhetoric, nagging doubts
about personal backsliding, and a desire to maintain an indepen-

dence of mind and spirit that suggests both self-respect and a willingness to respect others.

THE PUZZLE is that one can believe so much and so little at the same time. One can accent the view that failures are good because they serve to deepen one's revolutionary understanding and test one's commitment. Even if one's revolutionary work produces no popular support or mass conversion, and even if one is rebuffed by the people when one reaches out to them, such setbacks can be used to reinforce conviction. One needs to be steadfast, particularly in Sanrizuka. But, alternatively, living close to the farmers can raise one's respect for precisely the way of life one is supposed to redeem; the more understanding one has for the qualities of individual farmers and their way of life, then, the harder it is to be a revolutionary.

Most militants agree that to be a revolutionary one must hold to one's beliefs even in the face of disconfirming evidence or unpopular views. As Hans Toch says of social movements:

> The premise here is still that beliefs have intrinsic merit, but this does not lead to the inference that they must have general appeal. On the contrary, the believer argues that it is precisely the validity of his beliefs which makes them unpopular. He thus becomes one of a select few who can benefit mankind by recognizing meritorious solutions to universal problems.
>
> The changes that follow the act of conversion are directed at the task of consolidating psychological gains. As soon as new beliefs are adopted a stocktaking follows, which records the advantages of the new beliefs over the old. Simultaneously, the reinterpretation of reality begins. Old facts are given new meanings. Premises sprout conclusions, and then proliferate into systems.[5]

In the fortresses each person is made to feel important. Each has a special role. To use Erikson's terms, where individuals are important and numbers are few, relationships of trust, autonomy, initiative, industry, intimacy, generativity, and integrity are all reinforced by participation. Yet each event will also impose mistrust, shame, guilt, inferiority, confusion, isolation, stagnation, and despair.[6] Mediating between these "negative" and "positive" sides of the dichotomy requires a tempering wisdom even among the most romantic revolutionaries.

More than with other people, what counts most with militants is not what they do from day to day or week to week but how they struggle with the inner meaning of their beliefs, those preoccupations that are intensified by living within the solidarity huts and fortresses. Meetings are frequent within the huts. Some of the huts are organized in an almost military fashion, with sect members acting as "soldiers." Virtually everyone develops a specialty. Some will work on getting out the sect newspaper to be distributed to members of the Hantai Dōmei; others will make posters and handouts describing political events and announcing rallies. Publicity work goes on more or less all the time.

Meetings are serious, and all sorts of problems are discussed at them. The topics of greatest concern tend to be shifts in government policies that will have repercussions for the movement, such as a change in tax laws or in the noise abatement ordinance. Of great concern, too, are agricultural matters—reports on yields from the land being farmed by the sect, or news of the effects of changes in irrigation. Other items include the posting of individuals elsewhere, reports of rallies or mobilization efforts, or perhaps a review of a member's act of misconduct or irresponsibility. Sometimes a meeting will be held on a specific subject (agriculture, the fuel pipeline being built to the airport from Tokyo), preceded by a film or by a lecture with diagrams. Drinking is allowed only after the meeting is over. Evening meetings with farmers and outside supporting groups are held frequently also. At such meetings people introduce themselves, give their age, describe their work and their relationship to the movement, and then sit down to tea or sake.

Despite the tension, there is rarely an open dispute between sect members. Most tend to be good-humored with each other, and quiet. A few will gather in the evening after a meeting to drink beer or whiskey or sake, and talk until very late at night. The senior officials more or less responsible for running things may or may not have an official title, but there is always someone acknowledged to be the leader. The most militant sects are in general the most hierarchical, but that holds true more for the headquarters offices than at Sanrizuka.

Some of the top sect leaders are skilled at demagoguery in a rather special way. The Japanese language can be spoken as a series of staccato bursts that sound like machine-gun fire. The sound drills home certain messages. Used in this way, language obliterates thought but generates an immediate mass response. The effect is particularly ferocious when done in a high-pitched female voice from a platform in front of a large audience. The body becomes stiff, immobile—an instrument, like a gun, from which sound crackles in a shower of sparks. The purpose is to electrify rather than communicate; the audience responds with guttural noises and grunts. Few of these performers live in the fortresses and huts in Sanrizuka, but every major sect seems to have one or two of them who speak occasionally. They are very effective in mobilization efforts and in projecting the image of complete dedication and militancy.

ONCE ONE GETS behind general labels like "sect" and "militant" or "New Left," one is struck by divergences and differences within each category. Even in the most militant sect, members continuously reinterpret their experiences. It is this, perhaps the greatest strength of the movement, that is also a great weakness, for individuals may at any moment reconsider their commitment and decide to drop out.

Each sect is what Neil Smelser calls a value oriented movement: "A value oriented movement is a collective attempt to restore, protect, modify or create values in the name of a generalized belief. Such a belief necessarily involves all the components of action; that is, it envisions a reconstitution of values, a redefinition of norms, a reorganization of the motivation of individuals, and a redefinition of situational facilities."[7] There is little fundamental estrangement from society or what is frequently and carelessly termed "alienation." Some people very much influenced by parents or older brothers are committed to standards of moral conduct that simply cannot be met in daily life. Many are anti-intellectual in the sense that they dislike abstractions and consider formal education a system of hierarchy, a hierarchy of words and of information. Some militants who seem to be the least articulate will suddenly open up. One young militant, very taciturn, whose father had been born in the United States and whose family came back to Japan just before World War II, became voluble when interest was shown in his archeological work. He had been locating Yayoi archeological sites not far from Sanrizuka and was extremely knowledgeable about them.

The older women—that is, in their thirties and forties—are, by any standard, quite remarkable. Two in particular might be mentioned, impressive not only for their commitment to the cause but also for their determination to transform the role of women in

Japan. One, a professional organizer for the Fourth International, was extremely efficient and highly intelligent. With a shrewd sense of what was going on politically, she had moved from a hard left JCP position to one favoring the Japan Socialist Party. She knew, although she was no theorist or intellectual, how to apply a "dialectical" wisdom to political situations with shrewdness and common sense.

The other, a woman in her mid-forties, came from a very old, distinguished, liberal family that had lost its property after the war. She was the daughter of a well-known "fauve" artist and art dealer. Highly educated, she married an engineer in 1960 and they built a house in Yokohama. Her transition to life in a solidarity hut came about gradually. As a responsible, educated Japanese woman, she began working as a volunteer to help out those in need in various neighborhoods. Perplexed and troubled by what she saw, she became concerned over the condition of the aged, the poor, and the helpless in some of Yokohama's poorest areas and sought reasons for the profound inequalities and injustices she found. She became an anti-war activist and moved close to the JSP. She divested herself of her material possessions. Then, as the contradictions mounted between the life she was living and the one toward which she was headed, she became an ardent feminist. But it was only when the responsibilities of being a wife and mother in a middle-class family conflicted with the work she had chosen for herself that she took the step of leaving the family, a decision of great and continuing anguish. Her husband, outraged by the injury done him, prevented her from seeing their two teenage daughters. Eventually she joined Chūkaku-ha. Her style of thinking is hesitant. She fears that the sect might be too hard on individual preferences. Her role is a nurturing and mediating one; in the fortress she is a healing spirit. The cadres are now her family. She asks nothing for herself, maintains a quiet humor and charm, and has a no-nonsense approach to doing good. She is very practical, very "Japanese," and very feminine, but these qualities disguise a very strong will. She believes Chūkaku-ha provides the framework for personal and social discipline.

Both of these women were very close to the Women's Corps of the original Hantai Dōmei, many of whom were more militant than the farmers themselves, and who still go about Japan, clad in "peasant" costume, making speeches. All are determined to change the subordinate position of women in the ordinary Japanese household. They doubt that even a revolutionary transformation will automatically free women and men simultaneously.

One would expect to find the most extreme militancy among the top leaders of the sects who have remained in the fortresses for the longest period of time. But almost the last thing one encounters is fanaticism. Some, on first encounter, tend to dogmatism, to think in slogans, replying to questions in stock ways that signify an appropriate commitment to Leninism or Trotskyism. But if one gains their confidence different qualities emerge. Two of the most important leaders of two of the most important sects can be used as examples. Both are committed to a way of life that is harsh and in many ways lonely, despite communal living. Both consider themselves to be revolutionaries. Both live with doubts and reevaluate what they are doing almost continuously. They are relatively compassionate and humane individuals, although they would probably be called "hardcore fanatics" in police reports.

One of them—we will call him Aki—is about thirty-four. He is a graduate in business from Tokyo University, which he entered in 1968, one of the most politically active periods. He himself was not involved in any of the political movements at the time, although he was of course concerned with many of the issues, most particularly the Vietnam war.

On leaving the university he first began looking for a job. It occurred to him that a job was a means to an end but that he did not know what the end was for him. Aki realized that until he understood something about the goals of life he would not be satisfied by a job. He discussed this with his friends and came to the conclusion that his best course would be an involvement with other people. His first plan was to go to Vietnam, mainly because that was the defining struggle of the time. If he could see it first-hand, he thought, it would help him define his relationship to other issues and people. He gave up the idea because it was too dangerous physically and also because he was not in the best of health at the time. He then decided to join the crew of a fishing boat and spend some time experiencing the life of a fisherman, although he had no intention of becoming one. A friend agreed to arrange this. The fishermen who interviewed him for the job—at best high school graduates—were very suspicious of his motives. They thought it very strange that someone who had graduated from Tokyo University would be interested in such a life. He did not get the job.

Aki became bored and dissatisfied with himself and decided then to look for a regular job. But a friend from the university who was involved in Sanrizuka and who was looking for someone to send out asked him to go. He was not particularly interested, but since he had nothing better to do he decided to go for a month. Farm work might provide a good opportunity for him to build himself up physically.

At the end of that month there were so many rumors of various police actions, among them the pulling down of the steel tower at Iwayama, that he decided to wait and see what would happen. Meanwhile, his body had been strengthened by working hard with the farmers. He began to think about parallels between Sanrizuka and Vietnam. Both were places where imperialism and capitalism collided with the force of popular resistance. This, he felt, was the real meaning of the class struggle. It was the beginning of his politicization.

After the confrontations of 1971 he began to question his own perspectives. When there were no big events, militants simply sat around and read a little or slept. It was boring and meaningless. Aki realized that life had to have a certain rhythm in order to have meaning; one needed discipline. This he regarded as the main lesson of farmers' lives. Accordingly, he and his fellow militants began to farm. They were not very good farmers, though, and in the battle between plants and weeds it was usually the weeds that won. Gradually they realized that farming was a full-time job.

In turn this posed a crisis. If one farms, that is all one does; there is no time for anything else. It dictates the terms of one's existence. How, then, immersed totally in the requirements of farming, can one retain the necessary consciousness of the larger struggle? By the third year of Aki's life in Sanrizuka, this was the prime question. It was resolved by a particular strategy—not simply to farm, but to locate farm sites at strategic points where the government intended to build a road or a facility related to the airport. In this way farming became the basis of a confrontation, forcing the police to take the site and raising the issues of appropriate land usage, the rights of cultivators, the aggressiveness of government. Farming was turned into class struggle.

Quite often these tactics were misunderstood by other sects. When Aki's group began introducing tractors and mechanized farming, they were criticized for becoming "bourgeois." A small issue that we might call the affair of the lunch boxes became a symbol of such criticism. When Aki's sect went out to the fields they began taking lunch boxes containing rice and vegetables. Since no one else used lunch boxes this was regarded as bourgeois. Such petty concerns loomed large, especially under the circumstances of isolation and boredom in the solidarity huts and fortresses.

It was through such activities as the farming that the militants gained the trust and respect of the farmers. After Aki's sect led the way, it became customary for all the sects to help the farmers and for outside supporters to come to the huts not only to fight but to farm as well. In turn, the farmers would not have been able to continue the political struggle without such assistance. Gradually they came to rely on the free labor provided by the sects.

Aki is the leader of a solidarity hut that represents a coalition of sects including the Fourth International. Supported by a number of intellectuals, journalists, writers, and others, it is the least ideologically militant of the groups on the site. Aki accepts—and indeed makes a principle of accepting—those with various points of view who would like to associate themselves with the movement.

By contrast, the person in charge of one of the most militant groups—we will call him Ishi—is almost completely different. The son of a shopkeeper, he was married before he became interested in politics. His wife and three children live with his wife's parents. He became involved in politics and in the Sanrizuka movement in 1968 while a student. When he first came to the site he stayed at To-mura's house and got to know him slightly.

Ishi believed that the workers' movement, on which revolutionary change would ultimately depend, was insufficiently radicalized because of the failure of the two dominant radical political parties in Japan to do effective work. Accordingly, he joined what seemed to him the most organized and radical Leninist sect, one which would have both an above-ground and a below-ground structure and which would not be afraid of using violence and guerrilla warfare if necessary, but only under circumstances that would mobilize popular support. (In this regard Ishi's views differ substantially from the Japanese Red Army or other terrorist groups.)

Ishi spent many years organizing workers in various parts of Japan. Unlike Aki, he has spent very little time in Sanrizuka itself. Sent to Sanrizuka by the central headquarters of his sect in January 1981, his senior and intellectual mentor having fallen ill, he spent much of his time writing articles and interpreting events both for Hantai Dōmei members and for the large membership of his sect not on the site. He did no farming and had no intention of becoming involved at that level. His direct connection with the farmers was through the original Hantai Dōmei itself and most particularly Kitahara, the secretary general, with whom he had a daily early morning meeting. He now remains identified with one of the two Hantai Dōmei organizations and is deeply committed to its success.

For him the political nature of the Sanrizuka struggle is essential. His sect has made its main field base there, so the future of the movement is perhaps of greater importance to his sect than to any other. He sees the inspiration of his sect as an extension of the Bolshevik revolution and the Leninist inheritance. For him, despite the variations in technique and development, the basic institutions of capitalism remain unaltered, and revolutionary struggle remains the only valid basis for transformation from finance capital to a workers' socialist society. There is, he thinks, a two-front war: against those who would represent fascist elements in the revolution and against those who represent the capitalist state. The German experience shows that it is necessary to deal with both simultaneously; otherwise a revolutionary condition may lead to a fascist outcome. For this reason, Ishi believes, one must support both violent and peaceful means.

Ishi considers his sect to be part of the worldwide revolutionary movement. It has offices in Tokyo, a network throughout Japan, and an international bureau with representatives in other parts of the world. The formation of a worldwide socialist system he regards as essential. Indeed, he believes that no socialist state can function properly as an independent entity: its productivity remains low. Only when a universalized socialist system has been achieved can socialism realize itself as an effective alternative to capitalism. He sees the two principal enemies of socialism as imperialism and Stalinism. It was Stalin who abandoned the principle of worldwide socialism and created the bureaucratic state capitalism of the Soviet Union.

As one might expect, Ishi considers himself a professional revolutionary, which, he admits with a grin, causes his children a certain degree of embarrassment in school when they are required to fill in their father's occupation on various forms. One might also expect him to be unshakable in his beliefs and doctrinally rigid, but this is not the case. He has doubts about the movement. He is sustained in part by his sense of responsibility to those whom he has recruited to the sect.

Aki and Ishi are opposite kinds of people. The one came to Sanrizuka with few political beliefs and immersed himself in farming; only gradually did the movement come to have political meaning for him. Ishi was involved in various struggles from his university days on, and has been arrested, beaten up, and involved in violence. He is part of what might be called a revolutionary bureaucracy. Both are highly intelligent. Both are responsible. And while they are discreet about matters affecting the movement, they are frank and articulate in expressing their views. Neither one thinks in slogans.

PERHAPS THE TWO most important groups at Sanrizuka today are Chūkaku-ha which has a network well established throughout Japan, and a coalition of sects that support the Farmer-Workers Solidarity Hut (*Rōnō Gasshuku-jo*) in Yokobori Village. These two represent very different tendencies. The most important single sect associated with the latter is probably the Fourth International, which has worldwide links to the Fourth International as an international Trotskyist movement. Chūkaku-ha also has great respect for the views of Trotsky and by no means ignores or repudiates his importance. It is a highly militant organization with a well-defined structure, which follows the Leninist principle of democratic centralism, perhaps more in principle than in practice. The Farmer-Workers Solidarity Hut, like the diverse group of intellectuals and leading trade unionists who support it, leans toward the Japan Socialist Party. It was through the Farmer-Workers group that links were established between the Sanrizuka movement and the Larzac farmers' movement in France. A number of Hantai Dōmei farmers visited France in the late summer of 1981, and in turn a Larzac contingent visited Sanrizuka in March 1982.

The importance of both groups derives in considerable part from the outside support they receive. Each has professional organizers who help rally and mobilize members and collect funds. Each confronts different circumstances. Because of its "war" with Kakumaru-ha, Chūkaku-ha operates under circumstances that require exceptional care and watchfulness. Kakumaru-ha members have followed individual Chūkaku-ha members to their homes and have often raided or burned the houses in a campaign of violence and harassment. The Farmer-Workers Solidarity Hut is a much looser group. It has a "sage," Maeda Toshihiko, who lives in a small house on the edge of a rice paddy. Other intellectuals are also associated with it, particularly those mobilized by the newspaper *Rōdō Jōhō* (*Labor Information*). Some famous left-wing journalists like Mutō Ichiyō are among the key supporters.[8]

The main emphasis of the Farmer-Workers group is that the airport issue is a clear case of government violation of the rights of farmers and an example of state oppression. The airport is intimately connected with imperialism and war; it is part of Japan's effort to penetrate Southeast Asia and part of the U.S. defense perimeter. Hence the airport issue is a lightning rod for citizen participation groups struggling against a variety of issues. In November 1976 a national supporting organization, the National Solidarity Group, was established to enlighten the public on the nature of the airport issue. The body has no formal membership, most of those involved in it are what might be called "New Left workers." The organization has regional chapters—the Tokyo metropolitan area, the Kansai area, and so on. The national leader, from the Kansai group was originally a telegraph worker; he became active in the union, then joined the JCP, and eventually became a full-time JCP organizer for ten years. He dropped out and remained aloof from the New Left groups for a time, and then worked in the Tomura election campaign in 1974. Although the National Solidarity Group began as a support structure for the anti-airport movement, today it is active in protesting other issues as well, including the New Osaka International Airport, nuclear power plants, and lake pollution. Sanrizuka liaison offices are maintained in a number of regions. Most prefectures have such headquarters.

One of the group's organizational purposes is to establish a citizens' coalition or solidarity movement; another is to attract those who have been offended by sect conflict. The Farmer-Workers Solidarity Hut claims to be non-sect, or to be above sectarian conflict, and the National Solidarity Group attracts those who would otherwise not have anything to do with sects and yet at the same time have become disenchanted with party politics. The membership, a mixture of those who were Zenkyōtō, Beheiren, and other groups not directly involved in New Left sects, contrasts sharply with the five hundred or so full-time professionals of Chūkaku-ha.

The basic policy of the National Solidarity Group is formulated by National Representatives Conference, which consists of delegates from the regional chapters. The Conference meets about once every three months, particularly after a major rally. A National Executive Committee, responsible for implementation of the policy, meets once a month. The main office is in Tokyo and is financially supported by certain sects, most particularly Fourth International. Relationships to sects vary according to region and branch. The

Kansai branch is the best organized and includes representatives from the Fourth International, the Bund, and the Revolutionary Communist League.

Support comes not only from intellectuals but also from workers, civil servants, teachers, and others. During rallies some of these supporters have been arrested and need financial and legal support to fight their cases. The Solidarity Group enlists the support of young lawyers, mobilizes defense groups, and raises money on their behalf. The control tower attack alone resulted in several hundred arrests, and the legal proceedings have been lengthy and costly.

The leadership of the National Solidarity Group regards the sects as lagging behind events, lacking in imagination, unable to transcend provincial and doctrinal prejudices, and less sophisticated than the general body of workers and intellectuals who support them. Within the sects they see corruption and a lack of genuine discussion.[9] As well, the "no-compromise" position of New Left sects has influenced farmers who in the end *must* compromise and find ways to contend with the impact of the airport. What is needed, the National Solidarity Group believes, is a broader and more sophisticated citizen's action movement.

Chūkaku-ha, in contrast, is a revolutionary action movement that has chosen Sanrizuka as its main battleground. It is less interested in educating farmers and militants than in using them in the wider struggle. Its permanent cadres, on which it relies heavily, pursue the struggle by recruiting support in trade unions and other outside bodies. Chūkaku-ha's success against Kakumaru-ha is, Chūkaku-ha members believe, a testimonial to its correct tactics, and its dominant position among the sects supporting the Hantai Dōmei is an example of its "correct position" relative to the state. Support for Chūkaku-ha by Dōrō Chiba, the Chiba branch of the locomotive union, is repeatedly used to show how the movement can revolutionize workers.

Chūkaku-ha hopes to come to power in a revival of the same kind of mass movement that characterized AMPO 1960, that is, through the mobilization of a broad spectrum of popular support. Rather than seeking a grand coalition of citizen protest, however, they want to intensify the class struggle. For them militarism and the growing pressure for war between the superpowers can only be stopped by popular resistance. They are encouraged by movements opposed to nuclear arms in Europe, especially the confrontations occurring at missile sites. In Japan this movement is centered in the Sanrizuka struggle, and Chūkaku-ha is leading the fight. Chūkaku-ha uses confrontational but not terrorist tactics. Time, they believe, is not on the side of the Japanese government or of governments generally, but on the side of revolutionary Marxism.

Chūkaku-ha is organized on a cell basis outside the Sanrizuka site. But it has a popular supporters' organization, the Tokyo Mobilization Committee, which is more or less equivalent to the National Solidarity Group. The leader of the Tokyo Mobilization Committee considers his task as primarily devoted to transforming the Sanrizuka movement into a large coalition of anti-war and anti-nuclear groups in collaboration with the sects. The Committee (formally known by a much longer name: "Solidarity with the Sanrizuka Movement with the Support of the Chiba Locomotive Union") was organized in 1977.

The National Solidarity Group and the Tokyo Mobilization Committee perhaps define the opposite ends of the New Left political spectrum. It would be inaccurate to conclude, however, that one is "liberal" and the other "radical." It was the Fourth International, a sect involved in the National Solidarity Group, that was mainly responsible for the control tower takeover on March 26, 1978—perhaps the single most dramatic act of the drama of confrontations. Moreover, individuals close to this coalition may consider themselves to be extremely radical, either as intellectuals or in activist roles.

BRIEF CHARACTERIZATIONS of two remarkable Sanrizuka "outsiders"—people on the fringes of the sects—may help to give a clear picture of sect life. One is a mentor of the "nonsect sect," the Farmer-Workers Solidarity Hut. The other is a well-known elderly woman who is a supporter of Chūkaku-ha. Maeda Toshihiko, the mentor of the Farmer-Workers group, was born in 1909 in Fukuoka Prefecture. He joined the Japan Communist Party in 1931, was arrested in Kyoto in 1932 and not freed until 1938, and became an anti-war militant. After the war, disappointed with the policy of the JCP, he left the party. He served as the mayor of the town of Miyako in Fukuoka Prefecture from 1948 to 1953. A personal newsletter that he distributed was so well received that it came to have a circulation of several thousand, and he wrote a book based on the newsletter articles. He became friendly with Tsurumi Shunsuke and Oda Makoto and joined Beheiren in 1965.

Maeda's ideological views are quite idiosyncratic. There is something of the flavor of an old-fashioned anarchist about them. He deals with themes of power, freedom, production, and the division of labor, in terms popular enough to appeal to the experience of ordinary people. His slogan is, "People should be free in mind and equal in spirit." His house, on the edge of a rice paddy, was built for him by volunteer labor. To the members of the Farmer-Workers Solidarity Hut he is like a father, the head of the family. Under a deliberately simple exterior, a manipulated innocence, there is considerable artfulness and shrewdness, and he has a good sense of humor. To raise money, for example, he took to making illegal sake, inviting government tax officials to come see how it was made. His argument was that rice, being a private property, could be used in any form by the people, and the government had no right to regulate the use of private property. He wrote a book on how everyone could make sake; it sold very well. The tax officials did not quite know how to deal with him.

Kawata Yasuyo, the supporter of Chūkaku-ha, has also written a book—hers is on torture and the violation of human rights in South Korea. A woman of causes, she is one of the founding members of the Japanese branch of Amnesty International. She is from a powerful shipping family; her father was the publisher of an English-language magazine. In 1938 she was an Olympic swimmer. When she discovered that her husband was trying to make money by investing in Okinawa, she divorced him. She was the editor of a monthly women's magazine, *Fujin Kōron*. Among her friends and associates are Maruki Iri and his wife, Toshi, who together painted the famous Hiroshima murals, a series of panels depicting the nuclear holocaust.[10] Kawata knows virtually all the important Dietmen and government officials, radicals on the run from the police, and highly placed politicians in the LDP. She goes out to Sanrizuka quite often and is part of the Chūkaku-ha network to the outside world.

There are many others with links to the movement. Some are old, like Maeda and Kawata. Others are of a middle generation, like the organizers of the supporting networks. Some are very young. The movement also exerts a pull on a number of outstanding journalists, among them Takagi Masayuki of *Asahi Shimbun* and Mutō Ichiyō of *Rōdō Jōhō*.

Not everyone who was involved in events and confrontations was a member of a sect or one of its wider supporting groups. Many who saw television broadcasts of what was going on, or had friends or relatives involved, went individually to Sanrizuka to help out in what they considered to be a good cause. Some were caught up in the events in ways they did not anticipate, with tragic consequences. The case of one twenty-nine-year-old woman—let us call her Hashi —is perhaps illustrative.

She was born in Sapporo, where her father worked as a minor official for the Ministry of International Trade and Industry. When she was in the sixth grade he was transferred to Tokyo. The family got into debt and the mother had to work. Many of their possessions were pawned. She went to live with her grandfather, who died when she was in high school. She was never much interested in student activities. In her high school the student movement was extremely active, but she did not take part. Her parents, without much of an education themselves, stressed its importance to her. She worked all the time. She delivered newspapers, worked as an elevator girl, and worked in a research institute while attending pharmaceutical college in Tokyo. Her life was hard, but she was determined to get her degree.

Hashi first heard about the Sanrizuka movement in 1971, when she saw on television the storming of the farmers' broadcasting tower by the police during the first expropriation. Particularly impressed by the farm women who had chained themselves to the tower and had fought police bulldozers and other equipment, she wondered if these women might have evolved a new way of living. She was surprised by how powerful they seemed to be.

After the event, she more or less forgot about the movement. People she knew talked about it with contempt, dismissing it as an example of the egotism of farmers. When she graduated from college she went to work for a health-care center run by the Tokyo municipal government, even though the pay was low and she had been offered a better job in the private sector. She found the job boring and a disappointment after all the years of hard work. But she came to have friends among those working for the center. Some of them had had experiences in the student movement, some as former Chūkaku-ha members. They began to tell her about Sanrizuka. When Tomura stood as a candidate for Dietman in the national elections, her friends helped in his campaign. She voted for him, convincing her parents to do the same.

She joined the Tokyo municipal government employees' labor union, which had about three thousand members. It was an exciting time, because the Tokyo municipal government was trying to decentralize its union and make the ward organizations into more autonomous union bodies, a hotly disputed issue. Hashi also became interested in the problems of the *burakumin* and asked her union officers if she could take a leave to help out in a campaign for them. The officers were horrified by the idea, which surprised Hashi because they, and most union members, were affiliated with the JCP. The JCP had decided, however, that the *burakumin* issue was not an important one. The union JCP leaders began to regard her as a troublemaker especially when she tried very earnestly to convince them that innocent people were being victimized and that it should not be a matter of ideology but fairness. Her supervisors called for her isolation, and for a while no one would talk to her. Nevertheless she stood as a candidate for a union post and won. After that most of her activities centered around union matters. Since her branch of the union consisted largely of women workers, she concentrated her efforts on women's activities.

She heard about Ōki Yone and of events in Sanrizuka. It all seemed remote until a militant was killed during the Iwayama steel tower confrontation. That upset Hashi; such things were, she thought, an embarrassment to Japan—but still she did not get involved. Although she and her friends thought something very important was happening in Sanrizuka, they were too busy with union affairs.

The heroism of the militants and farmers was widely publicized, especially the case of the two militants in the tower sprayed for forty-eight hours by police water cannons in freezing weather, and in 1977 her union local took a stand in support of the Sanrizuka movement. But because the union was dominated by the JCP (which had been expelled from the site), actual support was lukewarm, and those who went to Sanrizuka had to do so on an individual basis. Hashi joined an ad hoc youth group that proclaimed its solidarity with Sanrizuka, participating in the control tower takeover. She and some other women were asked to provide medical care and set up a post at a point far from the airport. She had little idea of what was actually going on and no connection with the Fourth International, the main group involved in the takeover.

Arrested by the police on March 27, 1978, charges were preferred on April 16. She had to wait over a year for her case to come up.[11] In October 1980 she was sentenced to two years in prison and then released on appeal. After her release, her union expelled her, she was dismissed from her job, and she lost four years of pension rights. The police kept her under surveillance. Her parents, ashamed, became estranged from each other and separated.[12]

Without sect affiliation she has had no outside assistance and no money for legal fees. She lives alone, supporting herself as best she can. The JCP has ignored her financial situation; only her mother and the women from the health-care center for whom she worked as a union official have contributed money. With her record, it is practically impossible for her to get a decent job today; she is considered a "national enemy." Many of the 216 people arrested in the takeover incident have been caught in similar circumstances.

7

The Christ of the Crossroads

TOMURA WAS the real leader of the Hantai Dōmei. Even today, when the Hantai Dōmei has split into two, each group claims him as its ancestor. He remains the patrimonial figure for everyone, farmers and militants. His portrait adorns the walls of most of the fortresses. He continues to be revered even by those who profoundly disagree with his politics and his tactics. Less a prophet than a redeemer, he was always a lonely figure. But once the movement started he came to occupy a unique place in its pantheon. Some likened him to the Buddha at the center of a Tantric circle, defining a sacred terrain, a heaven and a hell, and surrounded by angels, disciples, and devils. Tomura, as a devout and fundamentalist Christian, saw himself as doing Christ's work, perhaps even as a reincarnation of Christ himself. Defending the sacred soil polluted by the Airport Authority and government policy, it was to redeem the land and the people from Satan, the secular authorities, that he took his sword in his hand.

From the start of the Sanrizuka Hantai Dōmei, Tomura saw more clearly than others the broader issues involved and the difficulties that the Hantai Dōmei confronted. He was the one to bring in the students. Despite his old-fashioned ways, he liked students and enjoyed exchanging views with them, perhaps because he didn't have children of his own. As he himself became more militant, he came to share the students' outlook more and more. Yet his outrage always retained its deeply conservative core. In this he remained close to the attitudes of the farmers.

It was in part his Christianity that helped him become an effective leader of the Hantai Dōmei. He phrased both events and principles of the airport struggle in Christian terms and biblical parables, something he had been doing all his life. Like his father before him, he was concerned about finding and sustaining the social relationships that would enable him to lead a life of integrity. The continuing search for true principles kept Tomura more open to ideas than most people. He was responsive to new solutions just as he was open to new forms of art, and he found it easier to look to young people for ideas than to his contemporaries. There is, indeed, a sense in which he never quite grew up. Yet he was capable of profound stubbornness and rigidities, whenever his sense of appropriateness was offended.

Tomura's grandfather was born in Yachimata—one of the places, along with Tomisato, later considered as a possible site for the airport. He served in the Imperial Army in 1877 during the Seinan War and took part in the battle at Kagoshima. Traveling back from Kyushu by boat he heard a foreign missionary preach in Yokohama, and he was so impressed that he converted to Methodism. He began working as a guard at the imperial meadow at Sanrizuka; later he became an iron smith turning out agricultural tools for the experimental farming at the imperial estate. He was a second son, an emperor's man, and a very serious Christian. On the family compound near his house he built a small chapel that stood until 1982.

Tomura's father was also a strict Methodist. A very shrewd businessman, he opened a shop behind his father's house where he produced and sold high-quality patented machinery. It was so successful that orders came from all over Japan, including Hokkaido and Okinawa, and he employed twenty workers. On Sundays, Christian ministers came to preach in the chapel.

Tomura Issaku was born on May 29, 1909. A first son, he was given the name of Isaac after Abraham's son, and as a symbol of sacrifice. He believed that the story of Abraham and Isaac teaches the lesson of man's absolute obedience to his absolute God. Tomura later explicitly recognized the obligations of his name, and felt that since his father and grandfather had chosen that name for him he had to be willing to sacrifice his life for God. The Tomura children were very strictly brought up. At dinner each evening all the children were required to report on the day's happenings before grace was said. Tomura's father was politically independent but not without political ambitions. After World War I he ran for assemblyman of the Tōyama Village Assembly. The campaign staff asked him for money for bribes, which made Tomura's father very angry. When he did not give money his campaign staff left him or were fired. He ran the campaign by himself and lost the election. Afterwards he went to the Narita police station with the names of other candidates and the members of their campaign staff who had been involved in bribery. Several of them were arrested. Tomura's father and family were bitterly disliked for this by the neighbors for many years.

In 1925 Tomura entered Narita High School. Founded in 1887 for the sons of wealthy families or those very interested in education, it was originally under the control of the Narita Temple. It emphasized the teaching of English and Chinese script read in a Japanese way. Upgraded to a formal high school in 1898, it was the second oldest in Chiba. The school was extremely difficult to get into; only one of every five or six candidates passed the entrance examinations. Tomura failed twice before getting in. He was an indifferent student, graduating sixtieth in a class of sixty-two.[1]

At that time some very gifted people were teachers in high schools. At Narita High School there were two people who later became very well know. Nakano Yoshio, a graduate of Tokyo Imperial University, was to become a professor and a leading radical intellectual, and Nakayama Gishū, a graduate of Waseda University, would become an award-winning novelist. A nonconformist, Nakayama was popular among students. They came to his home on Sundays. He taught English to Tomura and introduced him to the work of Victor Hugo and as well to that of Marx—the "real" God, according to Nakayama. Tomura liked literature, but he was better at painting and playing the piano. He did not care much for studying. He, too, was a nonconformist. Other students wore their hair short; his was long. He hated the military training that was a required part of the school curriculum.[2] To the great irritation of the school authorities he kept the collar of his school uniform open. Once when the seniors, who didn't like him, told him to report to the school auditorium for discipline, he brought along a gun that he had found in his house. A teacher discovered the gun and warned Tomura's father about his son's behavior. On another occasion the students were told by the military training officer to visit the emperor in front of the imperial palace; Tomura was the only student who refused to participate. His excuse was that he did not like soldiers.

After finishing high school he worked in his father's shop. He continued with his literary pursuits, however, and he and some friends from high school started a magazine, *Makiba* ("meadow"), asking a local writer to be one of its sponsors. An essay by Tomura that appeared in the magazine in 1930 laments the corruption in the national election and advocates keeping one's goals high and not compromising with life's realities. Tomura's father was also a writer and published a book called *Life Is Like an Art*. Both father and son were preoccupied with the differences between principle and reality and tried to live their lives without compromising the first for the second. Not surprisingly, Tomura at this time was strongly influenced by Thoreau. The father, very much a businessman, was head of the firefighters' brigade, the chairman of an association to promote tourism, and a local boss. Tomura, however, was not a very diligent worker in his father's shop. He preferred to go to the imperial meadow to paint.

Hoping that marriage would have a sobering effect on him, Tomura's father asked a minister he knew to introduce his son to Hoshino Sumie, of a Christian family in Hokkaido. Tomura was twenty-five and Sumie twenty-three when they were married. After the wedding Tomura promptly went away to paint, leaving Sumie behind. He seemed to take no notice of her. Marriage, far from making Tomura settle down, seemed only to encourage his painting. A few years later Sumie got sick and went back to Hokkaido to her parents. To her surprise, Tomura followed her there, perhaps to get out from under parental control. They lived for five years in Hokkaido. Tomura worked for his brother-in-law's coal shop and painted portraits that he sold, while his wife sewed kimonos for a living. It was in Sapporo, the main city in Hokkaido, that Tomura won his first prize for painting. When the war broke out, Tomura was drafted but was then rejected for military service. He and Sumie went home to Sanrizuka. Although not a pacifist, he remained strongly anti-war and anti-militarist through the period.

Anti-militarism may well be the key to Tomura's own involvement in the anti-airport struggle. He was the only one from Sanrizuka to get involved in the Tomisato confrontations (beginning in November 1965), because he became convinced that the airport was designed primarily for military purposes. When the site was shifted to Sanrizuka, in July 1966, Tomura believed that the strategy adopted by the government was dictated by the urgency of the Vietnam war. Everything else followed from that first rash decision, Tomura thought—the government's failure to notify the people or to inform the prefectural authorities of the facts. When the decision was finally made, it seemed to come from nowhere. So affronted was he by the lack of due process that it represented for him a clear case of government "violence" against the 325 families in the airport site, not to speak of those in the larger Shibayama area outside. The only information received by inhabitants of Tōyama and Sanrizuka, the areas most directly affected, was a five-minute summary of the government's decision.

Anger aside, Tomura could not and did not do very much in the beginning. He was an abrupt man. He left the Tōyama Secondary School before the end of the Hantai Dōmei inaugural meeting at which his presidency was announced. Unity was the main problem Tomura saw. Sanrizuka, unlike Tomisato, was not at all unified, and it lacked both leadership and strength. In Tomisato there had been JCP involvement, which had given the movement strength, and in Shibayama there was strong JSP involvement; Sanrizuka, on the other hand, had a pro-government, pro-LDP past. Although former LDP supporters like Ishibashi joined the JSP, Ishibashi, from a loyal Meiji family in Tenjinmine, was hardly a radical. The JSP was not sufficiently radical for Tomura, who joined for a year and then left it when his involvement with militant students deepened.

The government's tactics were so successful in the beginning that within a month of the first meetings 80 percent of the original support for the Hantai Dōmei had eroded. Negotiations were at first left in the hands of prefectural authorities, who circulated questionnaires asking people where they would like suitable alternative lands. When some farmers repeatedly ignored these, the prefectural government notified them that those not answering would not receive land. People were frightened; deprived of solid information, they did not know what to do. Tomura could rage and thunder from his presidential pulpit, but he could offer little practical advice. As farmers began to negotiate in great numbers the outlook for the resistance dimmed. The turning point came on October 10, 1967, the land survey confrontation, when farmers fought against approximately two thousand riot police. JCP members ran away from that battle.

By this time Tomura and several others had learned about the anti-military demonstrations of the Zengakuren students, starting with AMPO 1960, and was very impressed. Its president had visited

him, and Zengakuren had already participated in a rally. To per
suade Zengakuren to come to Sanrizuka in a more organized way,
Tomura and several others went to Tokyo station to await the return of the Zengakuren leaders from a demonstration in Kyushu.
They agreed to come, but for a time were heavily involved in other
demonstrations. The building of the solidarity hut on Ishibashi's
compound marks the real beginning of sect involvement and also the
beginning of Tomura's influence. Now, for the first time, he could
pursue his principles with others instead of in isolation. The cause
seemed to him much the same as that of the early Christians. He
gathered up his disciples, the militants, and so became, in effect, the
Christ of the crossroads.

For Tomura, as for his father and grandfather, life was a continuous struggle. To harmonize one's internal and external lives one
had to do one's appropriate duty. When it involved withdrawal and
isolation, Tomura accepted this. When it required active participation, as in Tomisato, he became involved. He believed that one con-
structs one's life; one does not simply accept things as they are.

Tomura's secretary in the movement was a young militant very
close to the United Red Army (Rengō Sekigun), the part of the radical movement most involved in terrorism and most of whose members went to North Korea or Beirut. Through him Tomura became
increasingly intrigued not only by the PLO but also by the Popular
Front for the Liberation of Palestine. He was an anti-militarist, but
gradually came to accept the need for violence to stop militarism.
This too he saw in Christian terms. In his view Christ was a man
of God who represented absolute principle, not peace at any price.
As the events during the heroic period became more confrontational, and the struggle over the first phase more desperate, both the
militants and the farmers accepted his changing views about
violence.

IT WAS ON February 26, 1968, Tomura's "day of self-discov-
ery," that Tomura turned toward violence. On that day, the Hantai
Dōmei members saw the riot police go into action against the militant students. It began with a rally sponsored jointly by Zengakuren
and the Hantai Dōmei on what was then the Narita Municipal Athletic Field, a rally that aimed to "smash the Sanrizuka Airport by
force and to stop the expansion of the Sunagawa military base."
(The term used for "smash," *funsai,* is a word particularly associated
with slogans from AMPO 1960—"AMPO *Funsai,*" "U.S. Imperial-

ism *Funsai."*) The rally attracted about seventeen hundred participants and three thousand riot police. Zengakuren had announced its intention to break into the Airport Authority office behind the Narita City Hall and smash it.

First Tomura spoke, saying that thirty-two years ago some young military officers had started the February 26th Incident and that it was always the young people who changed society. This could be interpreted as a proto-fascist reference (the incident was associated with *Nōhon-Shugi*), which made the militants rather uneasy.[3] But Tomura was quite unconcerned with such distinctions. Led by Hantai Dōmei members, the militant students then proceeded to march to the City Hall. As they approached the entrance, they broke their placards and made them into sticks. The militants' way was barred by riot police, who were not, however, equipped for a real confrontation; they had only ten shields among them. When students began throwing stones, some 420 police were injured.

Late in the afternoon the police began their counterattack. When one of the students fell Tomura tried to rescue him. Police surrounded Tomura and hit him several times on the head. They had been planning to arrest him but were frightened by the amount of blood. Tomura was fifty-seven at the time.

In his book *Standing in the Field,* Tomura describes his feelings at that moment: "I thought I was losing my will to fight. What was I more concerned about, protecting myself and not capable of being more aggressive? Probably I was frightened by the blood. But I was even more frightened to find that I was caring about myself. When I saw that the blood was coming from my head, I thought it was really serious. The thought of dying frightened me and made me control myself." He had been beaten in the face, arms, and back as well as the head. Taken to the Narita Red Cross Hospital in Kitahara's car, he needed seven stitches in his head. Mrs. Tomura said that she had never seen him look so bewildered or frightened.

For Tomura the event was decisive. It drew him closer to the militants, and it made the Hantai Dōmei more willing to accept militants as their partners in the struggle. On the other side, however, there was also some soul-searching among the police. They had been severely criticized by the public for their violent behavior at a rally protesting an American nuclear submarine in Sasebo the month before. Despite Tomura's beating, they felt they had exercised control in the February 26 incident.

For Tomura there was to be no compromise. When Governor

Tomonō of Chiba Prefecture visited Tomura early in March at the hospital, bringing an orchid plant, Tomura took off his bandages and said, "Look at what the government does to us. After what has happened to me, I must change the way I look at the world." Nevertheless, he accepted the orchid plant (which still grows in the compound of his house).

When another rally was held at the Municipal Athletic Field on March 10, sponsored jointly by the Hantai Dōmei and the National Anti-War Youth Committee, Tomura left his hospital bed to join the protesters. He addressed some forty-five hundred participants, many of whom were carrying wooden sticks. "The state power which allowed police sticks to beat me is inside the barricade today," he said. "I hate this power." In the confrontations that followed, police used tear gas and water guns. Late in the afternoon, as the participants were leaving the scene, they were suddenly attacked by police who claimed they were trying to arrest those who had engaged in illegal acts. Over one thousand were wounded and some two hundred militants were arrested.

In the February 26 encounter, because so many police were wounded, public sympathy was with them. At that time the prefectural police had had little experience in dealing with confrontations. (The big event that they had policed were major horse races.) They were re-equipped and given additional support after the February 26 rally; by the time of the next confrontations, on March 10 and March 31, the police were better prepared and much more violent than before. For each side, then, February 26 was the turning point. It was the event that precipitated what can be called the legitimization of violence.

TOMURA ENUNCIATED the need for moral violence by making explicit references to biblical parallels. Those who were not with him were against him, he made clear. He collided with other groups, like the JCP, who had "betrayed" the Hantai Dōmei; he had the JCP expelled. He fought others who might have become the intellectuals of the movement. While he believed in grace and could accept different points of view, this was true only up to a point.

His interpretations and parallels did not stop with the Bible itself. Recalling previous radical Christian movements, he cited especially the instances that had involved bloodshed. The government would kill people, he believed, in order to complete the airport. He saw the struggle in terms of Christians against Romans. When the Hantai

Dōmei built tunnels and underground bunkers he likened them to catacombs. He and the others were prepared to die in them. Later he would compare Prime Minister Sato to Nero. His two main heroes during this period were probably Thomas Munzer and Tanaka Shōzō. He drew a parallel between the German farmers' wars of the sixteenth century and Sanrizuka, and like Munzer he was prepared to die on the battlefield. The parallel with Tanaka Shōzō was even more direct. Tanaka Shōzō was a Christian and a member of the Diet representing the Ashio area, where farmers' lands were slowly being destroyed by the pollution of surrounding streams and water as a result of mine wastes. As in Sanrizuka, farmers, workers, and militant students were mobilized against a state that ignored its citizens. Tanaka led two protest marches on the capital and risked his life petitioning the emperor on behalf of those from his constituency who were most affected.[4] For Tomura, the imperial policy at the time of the Ashio mine struggle—a policy that the Meiji government called *Fukoku Kyohei:* Rich Country, Strong Army—was only an earlier version of Prime Minister Sato's industrialization scheme.

The movement of popular protest at Ashio, led especially by radical Christians and militant socialist students, was so powerful that the government was forced to do something about the pollution it caused. It decided to confine the polluted water to a large pond, buying up the land for this purpose around Taninaka hamlet, an area they picked in part because the anti-pollution movement was particularly strong there. To construct the pond about four hundred households had to be relocated, but some sixteen families refused to move. The government took over and dismantled their houses. Tanaka came to live in a small shack with some of the farmers. He spent all his money on their behalf, leaving his wife and friends behind. He lived simply and died on a pallet, his only possession a Bible.[5]

The example of Tanaka Shōzō at Ashio impressed Tomura in several different ways. He saw the Hantai Dōmei farmers as the "sons of Shōzō." Tanaka had moved during his life to the left, steadily becoming more radical, more militant, and more pure. But he was also very worldly, a Dietman and politician; he knew how important it was to participate in legal and institutional politics. So Tomura followed his example. On the one hand he moved to the left. On the other he ran for political office in hopes of defending the Hantai Dōmei better. He stood several times as a candidate for the Narita City Assembly, winning each time. He ran for the National Diet House of Councillors in 1974; that contest he lost. A special ad hoc organization had been formed during his campaign, an organization composed of trade union intellectuals, journalists, supporters from sects, and a variety of other people; it was an AMPO-style affair. Out of the 600,000 votes that were needed to win the election, he obtained 234,000, a surprisingly large number for a person totally uninvolved in national constituency politics, and with no practical political experience or organization. Moreover, the election helped to build a massive support structure that was crucial in the later mobilization of outsiders and assisted in the confrontations and rallies that followed.

In the Narita City elections his way of campaigning was much like his father's. He had decided to run in part because the Narita City Assembly, which was originally opposed to the airport and had passed a resolution condemning it, was suddenly persuaded to reverse itself by pressure from above. This convinced him that the Hantai Dōmei needed to have its own representative there. Three Hantai Dōmei members were already on the Shibayama Town Council. Although Tomura himself was inexperienced, within the Hantai Dōmei there were some very shrewd old local political figures. Ishibashi, for example, had been on the campaign staff of Mayor Fujikura of Narita City. Ogawa Gen had also been involved in election campaigns. In Shibayama were several farmers who had worked for the election of JSP Dietman Jitsukawa. Tomura did not initially want to run for Narita City assemblyman but finally agreed to accept the nomination. One of the Hantai Dōmei vice-presidents, Tsuji Masao, became his campaign chief. Like his father, Tomura refused to allow his campaign staff to drink sake at his headquarters (they had to go secretly to nearby restaurants). Despite his severe style, Tomura won 804 votes and was elected.

Representation on the Narita City Assembly did not do Tomura much good; indeed, he came to distrust elective institutions. He also came to dislike the main radical political parties, which he saw as being a part of the system as much as any other parties. But his greatest contempt was reserved for governmental and prefectural authorities. In the early days of the movement he had been willing to meet with prefectural and other governmental officials—even with police officials. Most Hantai Dōmei members, in contrast, wanted nothing to do with the officials. Tomura argued, "It is not good to build a wall around us. We should discuss with the people from the Ministry of Transportation and the Prefecture." Eventually, however, he would avoid any contact with officialdom. Ishibashi had originally represented the hard line of the Hantai Dōmei and protested Tomura's meeting with the governor; subsequently their positions would be reversed.

For Tomura there were several simple rules of the Hantai Dōmei that had to be followed: opposition to the airport; a willingness to collaborate with unions, groups, and individuals who shared the same objective; and a commitment to continue to fight until the construction project was abolished. Despite the looseness of the guidelines, however, he also believed he had a superior, almost revelatory knowledge of who could be trusted and who could not. As his own militancy increased and as many farmers dropped out of the struggle, he came to phrase the farmers' struggle in dramatic terms. Since farmers would not be able to live away from the soil, the airport construction, Tomura believed, was a sentence of death for farmers. Land had mystical properties; it was the first thing that God had created. (In Genesis God created heaven and earth.) Tomura came to see the buying and selling of land as against God's will and the Airport Authority's efforts to buy land as the act of Satan. Farmers on the land are the blessed of the earth, thought Tomura; in turn farmers should take care of their land, and protect it. Selling it to the government he saw as a betrayal of that trust.

Along with Tomura's growing hostility to government and the institutions of government, then, went a hardening of his political views. But there remain paradoxes. He was hard on "betrayers," yet on a personal level he was capable of great understanding and acceptance of individuals and households who had dropped out. Despite his radicalness he remained far more sympathetic to rich farmers than poor ones; the rich ones he considered to be the better farmers. Indeed, he had little respect for households settled in the postwar period and placed his confidence instead in the wealthier farmers in old villages like Komaino and Tokkō. Yet it was precisely those older villages that sold out en masse. In Komaino a local boss, Nakano Masayuki (currently a Narita City Assemblyman), not only got people to drop out but mobilized about 70 households to join the pro-government Narita Airport Countermeasure Hamlet Council, which already had about 130 household members from among the postwar settlers of Furugome, Kinone, and Tōhō. Indeed, as early as 1967 farmers from old villages began dropping out. So much for Tomura's "vision."

THE MORE Tomura moved to the left, the more his difficulties with the Japan Communist Party mounted. The decision of the JCP to act as a legal party was, as we have already commented, one of the factors that led to the formation of the New Left in Japan. Although the JCP had been very active in Tomisato and was among the first outsiders to support the Sanrizuka-Shibayama Hantai Dōmei, Tomura was critical of it because it intervened too much in Hantai Dōmei politics and was too critical of the Hantai Dōmei allies. The JSP, which was more reliable, was insufficiently militant. While the JSP Youth League was a very radical part of the anti-JCP Zengakuren, the JSP, despite Hantai Dōmei support from Dietmen, was not very active on the movement's behalf. For different reasons, then, both the JCP and the JSP became suspect.

A major turning point in the movement occurred when the militants came to the site on a permanent basis and the JCP was expelled. Tomura had received a letter from Miyaoka Masao, the deputy commander of the Action Corps of the Sunagawa Military Base Hantai Dōmei, introducing and praising Akiyama Katsuyuki, the president of Zengakuren, and suggesting that Akiyama could help in the Sanrizuka struggle. Tomura moved fast. He already knew of the role of anti-JCP students in three Sunagawa struggles that had occurred in spring 1967. He asked Akiyama to come and explain his views. In reply Akiyama linked the airport to AMPO 1960 and to the Sunagawa movement. He said that Zengakuren held an anti-war position and that the state was merciless. Tomura brought Akiyama to a meeting of the Hantai Dōmei Executive Committee at Chiyoda Civic Center on September 1, 1967, and asked him to give a speech explaining these views. Akiyama did so, over the objections of JCP representatives. To Tomura the JCP's objections violated the general principles enunciated by the Hantai Dōmei, and he charged the JCP with being exclusivist.

Other events contributed to the expulsion of the JCP. On October 8, 1967, in a protest demonstration against the prime minister's visit to Southeast Asia, a Kyoto University student, Yamazaki Hiroaki, died. This seemed to Tomura a demonstration of what Akiyama meant about state power. He began to argue in favor of mass support from Zengakuren. To prevent this, the JCP distributed stickers and handbills attacking the students and built several solidarity huts in a campaign that began attracting the support of local farmers. The circulation of the party paper, *Akahata (Red Flag)*, increased.

On the evening of November 12, after the second Haneda struggle to keep Prime Minister Sato from going to the United States, about 150 Zengakuren students came to Sanrizuka. They were exhausted. Some 330 of them who had been involved in the confrontations at

Haneda had been arrested. Tomura welcomed them at the Chiyoda Farmers' Cooperative. Hantai Dōmei members took them home, gave them hot baths, and served them food and sake. JCP organizers tried to convince the farmers not to welcome the students but they were surrounded by Hantai Dōmei members. In the ensuing scuffle the *Akahata* photographer's film was taken from him. Thereafter JCP members were kept from attending the regular Friday meetings of the Hantai Dōmei.

During a later confrontation JCP members departed from a battle at a crucial moment, leaving the Youth Corps in a very vulnerable position. It was this event that precipitated the final break in Hantai Dōmei–JCP relations. Up to that time, despite Tomura's hostility to the JCP and despite rumors being spread by the JCP about the activities of certain Hantai Dōmei members (which hinted at collaboration and secret negotiations), many farmers on the Hantai Dōmei Executive Committee, including Ogawa Meiji, felt a loyalty to the JCP and did not want to expel it. On December 15, 1967, however, it was decided that the JCP was trying to destroy the organization and it was expelled. Immediately thereafter the sects belonging to Zengakuren came in force. Chūkaku-ha came first, to Tenjinmine, followed by Kaihō to Ōshimizu, and the Socialist Student League to Tōhō.

IN ALL THIS Tomura was the key person. Not only was he very drawn to these students, he began to think of them as his sons and daughters. They, in turn, were fascinated by him, his words, his commitments, his physical bravery. They needed an older person to look up to. On the face of it Tomura scarcely looked the part. A large, rather stocky man, quite formal and severe, often wearing a suit and tie to rallies, he was much a man of the community, but he remained an outsider to the end. He kept his door open to students. There was an air of freedom about him that was attractive to them. Yet he was preoccupied with himself, even to the exclusion of his wife. Although he enjoyed social events and an occasional glass of whiskey, he was serious always.

Some people have seen Tomura as a village intellectual thrust onto a stage by accident and forced to play a part he could not have anticipated. But that is too simple a formulation. He was always aware of large forces both in his society and in the wider world around him. On a public platform, with a bullhorn in his hand, he was effective in whipping up emotions and connecting local issues with national ones, the farmers' struggle with the nature of the state. But often the farmers could not understand him. As he became more militant he referred more frequently to biblical myth and historical antecedents, which he brought down to the present time and place, in the earth and soil of Sanrizuka. Sanrizuka became his crossroads for the confrontation between good and evil, people and state. His world consisted of two sets of opposites that did not always mesh successfully. One pair was "smallworldness" versus "largeworldness"; the other was "goodworldness" versus "badworldness." The problem was to prevent badworldness in one's life, community, and society. Between these almost Manichean poles, life was a continuous struggle, struggle in one's personal life and in one's community, against those in either the small world or the large who would prevent the good and elevate the evil.

Smallworldness consisted of Sanrizuka and the fields, meadows, and streams around it, and the farmers who bought his farm machinery. (He never gave discounts, but he did extend credit.) In its smallworldness his was a completely inward provincial life. The Hantai Dōmei became a congregation, a religious "hamlet." When he was elected president of the Hantai Dōmei he heard someone say that he was a *Yaso* (the derogatory word for Christian). Immediately he replied that he had joined the Tomisato movement because he was a *Yaso* and that the government was taking away the farmers' land, "opened with sweat and tears" against God's will. There was no more talk about *Yaso*s. As he became more radicalized, his projections of the kingdom of heaven and Hantai Dōmei evangelizing became more political, and he drew closer to the militants without losing his sense of tradition, place, and smallworldness.

Tomura was not an easy man to deal with; he had many of the attributes of a village bigot. If he believed he or the movement had been betrayed (as in the case of the leader of the Women's Corps), he could be cruel in his retaliation. He believed in the democracy of the insider but had a deep suspicion of the outside, whether it was a political party or the government. The exception was, of course, all "people's movements," from the PFLP to the Viet-Cong, for all were part of that same struggle for liberation that was first defined by Christ himself. That view was linked to his largeworldness concept, the revolutionary struggle converting the bad into the good. The epitome of largeworld-evilness was the state, and the militarism that went with it.

As the president of the Hantai Dōmei, Tomura played on the larger scale rather than the small: he remained aloof from small conflicts and even from tactics and strategy and day-to-day events. He had little patience for meetings, often leaving discussions to go off and paint. He always carried a sketchbook with him. His art gave him an escape, provided a way out to a more idealized pictorial world, uniquely personal, where others could not follow. Even during the 1971 expropriation confrontations with riot police and right on up to 1978, he would sit calmly in a fortress during a quiet moment and paint or sketch the surrounding scenery as if nothing were going on. At home he could pick up a piece of paper or cardboard and become so involved in fashioning an object that he would forget a guest completely. Mostly he did sculpture even though he rarely found a buyer for his pieces.

He never really had an art teacher; he had taught himself by looking at art books. In the Narita City library he read everything remotely connected to art and started to experiment with kinetic sculpture and mobiles in the late 1940s. He began to use iron for sculptures, using techniques introduced from the United States but not widely known in Japan. Iron, something that had been part of his everyday life, he regarded as a particularly intimate material. Despite his efforts he was not highly respected within the community of artists. Although he participated in exhibits every year after 1956, only once did he win a grand prize.

Tomura's life did not neatly fit into a bounded universe. At one end of the compound in which he lived were the shop and house of his grandfather and father. On the other end of the long narrow plot in which he lived there stood the old chapel built by his grandfather. The small, lovely wood-and-plaster church presently used by the tiny congregation was designed and built at Tomura's request by Yoshimura Junzō, a very distinguished Japanese architect. The church's small scale was appropriate to the smallness of the congregation. In the study of Tomura's house, next to the helmet he used in confrontations, was a small library with the writings of Pascal, Calvin, Tanaka Shōzō, Jung, and Karl Barth. He might not have understood them, but he had certainly read or tried to read them.

Despite such evidence of largeworldness in his study, Tomura was capable of smallmindedness in his dealings with others. One example of his intolerance centers around the church on his compound. In June 1966, just prior to the announcement of the Cabinet decision on the airport, Tomura asked the Reverend Kawashima Masayuki, the

pastor of the Sanrizuka Church, to oppose the airport. Since Tomura had organized the Christians in Tomisato into the Tomisato
Airport Christians Hantai Dōmei and had fought with them, he now
expected the Christians of his own congregation to follow suit. To
Tomura's surprise, the Reverend Mr. Kawashima refused, saying
that a church is a place where people with diverse views should
gather. Neither as an individual nor as a minister would he take a
stand on the airport issue. Tomura, deeply angered, stopped attending services, and from then on he gave no more contributions to the
church. He placed a sign in front of the church that said: "At this
time farmers are shedding blood under the power of the state. But
the blind minister and congregation who do not see this reality are
like the ones who put Jesus on the cross. They are agents of the establishment. They should realize what is happening around the
church."

Kawashima was the fourth minister of the little church, a building
of the United Church of Christ. Although the church was an independent organization it was very dependent on the Tomura patrimony. The facilities included a small bathroom, toilets, and a tiny
kitchen underneath a ladder that led to a room in the belfry where
the minister lived, a room the size of six *tatami* mats. The construction cost had been 780,000 yen, of which the Tomura family had
loaned 300,000 yen. Withdrawal of Tomura support represented a
serious crisis for the tiny congregation. Kawashima, who was thirty-
five and newly married, was very upset and did not know what to do.

The matter turned out to be more complex than a personal dispute. Tomura made his own position clear in a book called *My Cross,
Sanrizuka*. Sanrizuka was the cross he had to bear. He wrote: "I
tried to talk with the ministers in Chiba Prefecture about the airport
issue, but they regarded me as disloyal to the church and looked
upon me as a pagan. The ministers considered the airport issue political and said that the church should be independent from any political activities. By being neutral, they stood with the establishment. In
order to make my beliefs consistent with my conduct, I must stand
on the farmers' side, the side of the oppressed. I wonder which is
more Christian."

The lack of support from his own congregation had come after
many frustrating attempts by Tomura to get a hearing from local
Christians. He had spoken about the airport issue at the Sakura
Church without getting any response. He wrote to all the ministers
in Chiba, but some returned his letters unopened. For Tomura the

issue was clear enough. The responsibility of Christians was to try to do God's will. The land was the creation of God and should be protected. The state power, supported by the riot police, used force to violate the land. The state in Sanrizuka, he said, "is an apparatus of organized violence. I see un-Christianlike evil control in the state power. If you don't see the controlling power of Satan, where do you find Satan?" To fight the airport, then, seemed to Tomura a way to spread the gospel.

Poor Kawashima. He believed that God's will was somehow different from such precise determinations. In his congregation, moreover, some members were pro-airport. Kawashima thought that the airport issue should not be decisive in determining who was or was not a good Christian, but Tomura saw his stand on the issue as the essence of Christ's teachings. Christianity was both nonconformist and engaged in a continuous struggle. Without this original fighting spirit, Christianity was like "salt without taste." "Christ," Tomura said, "approved of violence and even used it at times." For Christians to stay away from the conflict was the ultimate hypocrisy.

When the Reverend Mr. Kawashima came to visit Tomura in the Narita City hospital after his beating, Tomura would not be mollified. In the spring of 1969 he raised the rent from 4,000 to 10,000 yen. He put signs on the kindergarten saying, "Let's Oppose the Airport." He refused to let the toilet (a non-flush kind) be cleaned out by the regular "honey cart" man. Tomura and his wife were expelled from the congregation, along with Tomura's brother and two other members of the family. The fight still goes on. Mrs. Tomura, although devout, will not attend the Sanrizuka church. But Tomura's son-in-law and adopted daughter, who live in Tomura's house, are members of the congregation, and young Tomura looks after the new church building.

The debate raised wider questions about the Sanrizuka movement. While Tomura accused the church of not helping the struggle, Kawashima argued that it was not the role of the church to throw stones and fight with sickles. Christianity stood for the recovery of humaneness and the improvement of society by freeing people from sin, Kawashima said; Tomura replied that the farmers were weak and had no recourse but to fight with sickles. Kawashima agreed that for the government to use riot police to force farmers out was undesirable, but he argued that if everyone acted on Tomura's principles and took the law into his own hands, society would fall apart. In the larger non-Christian community in Sanrizuka much the same debate was taking place. Many of those who had the same view as the Reverend Mr. Kawashima were actually opposed to or not at all enthusiastic about the airport.

For Tomura, the loss of the church was the loss of his personal instrument of social life and reform, part of the smallworld-largeworld combination that was so important to him.[6] This was in fact not the first confrontation Tomura had with a minister of his church: the first one left after a dispute with Tomura. Today the minister in charge lives in Tokyo. He comes to tend to the congregation every third Sunday in the month. A sophisticated and thoughtful man, he remains sympathetic to the Hantai Dōmei.

DEPRIVED of his church, Tomura moved more directly to Zengakuren and the sects and became the head of his own congregation, his own band of revolutionaries. He acted as a Christian even though he did not expect others to become Christians. It was not necessary, he thought, for in the militants he saw equivalents to those bands of militant Christians who throughout history had represented good against evil, small worlds against large, and the people against the state.

In this role he became increasingly monopolistic and jealous of his own position as the key symbol, interpreter, and intellectual of the movement. He had little use for intellectuals outside, not even supporters. What they wrote on behalf of the movement was fine, but they were not allowed to get too close. He got along well with Maeda, the wise man who lived at the edge of a rice paddy and wrote books with a distinctly anarchic tinge that helped popularize the movement. Maeda had no following among farmers, however; his immediate influence was limited to certain sects.

One man, Yamaguchi Bushū, who came to Sanrizuka to give his support when the tunnels and underground bunkers were being constructed, did challenge the moral and intellectual authority of Tomura. Naturally enough, the two men clashed. Yamaguchi was a tall, thin man, about fifty when he began coming to Sanrizuka. He would stay at the solidarity hut at Tenjinmine. He had been the leader of the farmers' movement in Ibaragi Prefecture and was called *Sensei,* "teacher." He had organized twenty-five thousand farmers in Ibaragi and founded the Jōtō Farmers Union, which was successful in virtually paralyzing the economy of Ibaragi in a land liberation movement that focused on the government's sweet potato pricing and agricultural loan fund policies. In 1947 and 1949, running as a Japan

Communist Party candidate, he had been elected Dietman. Later he separated himself from the JCP and dissolved the Jōtō Farmers Union. He became more interested in citizen protest movements and action groups in the Hokota area.

Originally Tomura regarded Yamaguchi as a predecessor and leader in the struggle. But early on, Yamaguchi made known his reservations about Tomura's leadership. Speaking at a rally by invitation, he criticized the Hantai Dōmei for not being able to gain the widespread support of citizens in the area. This was very different from the usual rally speeches, where everyone praised the Hantai Dōmei and promised solidarity with it. Tomura was not used to criticism—certainly not in public—and he took it personally. He considered Yamaguchi too much of an economic determinist and his idea of mass involvement out of touch with the situation. For Tomura, the Sanrizuka struggle was unique precisely because it did not depend on the economic motivation of farmers or conventional political parties, the vehicles for mass mobilization. Tomura distrusted public support. Yamaguchi considered it essential.

In almost no time after Yamaguchi came to Sanrizuka on a long-term basis, he clashed with Tomura on the issue of tactics. Tomura was not much of a tactician. He fought the battles of principle and justice and articulated them very well, but he had a tendency to confuse symbols with reality and to place his faith in the former as if by doing so it would become the latter. There is some merit in this approach, of course, but it works only occasionally, and even then for only a short period of time.

Tomura's belief in the efficacy of the underground tunnels and bunkers provides a good example of his way of doing things. With farmers and militants inside the tunnels, ready to sacrifice their lives, Tomura believed the government would not go ahead with the expropriation. Yamaguchi disagreed. At a Hantai Dōmei Executive Committee meeting at the Chiyoda Farmers' Cooperative, held just after Ogawa Meiji's funeral, he offered a different strategy that he called "counter-siege." Yamaguchi pointed out that no matter how well defended a tunnel or bunker was, it could be easily isolated and conquered by the police if there were not enough farmers or militants to provide sufficient support. What was necessary was a mass mobilization of the public which could then be used to besiege the riot police and isolate them. If those in the tunnel could hold out for long enough to let the mobilized public go into action against the police, the opposition would hold. Tomura did not believe it would be possible to get spectators to take action against the police. But Yamaguchi insisted that with modern mass media techniques such as publicity vehicles with loudspeakers, such mass support would materialize. Yamaguchi provided a set of strategies that he thought would be appropriate, and many of the people at the meeting listened to him, in part because they respected his record. Tomura walked out.

Tomura, however, did not try to stop Yamaguchi or convince the Hantai Dōmei of an alternative strategy. Yamaguchi promised that his way would represent the first step in a civil war that would so threaten the Cabinet that the airport would be brought to an end. Some people thought this strategy was correct and that Tomura's "fight to the end" strategy in the tunnels was too much like what they were told during the war. Yamaguchi's strategy was adopted. The twenty-four-meter broadcasting tower was rebuilt in a more strategic location. Mobilization handbills were printed and distributed. Postcards were sent to neighboring towns in thousands. Cars with loudspeakers drove through the streets.

Yamaguchi's strategy was only partly successful. Meanwhile, rumors circulated that he had engaged in certain economic activities near Sanrizuka that would enable him to profit personally from the farmers' struggle. In the end Tomura triumphed: Yamaguchi left Sanrizuka.

AROUND HIS COMPOUND Tomura's large, rusting, powerful forms still stand. Not visible are a pair of large steel gloves made of movable parts with large sharply pointed spikes sticking out on all sides. These he designed to be worn to fight the police. They have a medieval quality, like a fragment from a chamber of horrors.

In Tomura there was romanticism that converted to anger, and passion that converted to violence. He was indeed God's angry man who saw his violence in symbols, and he acted on those symbols as if they were embodiments of principle. He made trips to the United States, to the U.S.S.R. and Eastern Europe, to Southeast Asia, to China. In 1978 he went to Lebanon and in Beirut participated in an international exhibition of paintings. Increasingly he began to believe that weapons would be necessary if the struggle was to succeed. The more he doubted that one could rely on public support, the more he believed that all revolutionary and underground movements in the name of justice and in opposition to the state, if sufficiently radical and militant, could form a universal alliance. In this he was perhaps following his original logic. The conclusion was inevitable given the nature of the struggle. He would have, if he had lived, "internationalized" the struggle, perhaps even by an alliance with the PLO, yet it is not clear that in this he knew what he was doing. More than anything else, he remained a first son trying to be faithful to the ideals of his father's book *Life Is Like an Art* and to his notion of revolutionary Christianity. He died before his logic could be put into effect either by the militants or by the Hantai Dōmei itself. Indeed, perhaps only three people really knew how far his anger had taken him: Mrs. Tomura, who understood it, Matsui, his private secretary, who encouraged it, and Kitahara, the secretary general, who still plays with the idea from time to time.

III

Political Dynamics

The garden that is looked at becomes the garden looking back at us, the garden of contemplation turns into a garden on the march, and the reversal from one role to another in either direction is immediate.

Yukio Mishima, *Imperial Gardens of Japan*

8

The Hantai Dōmei

TOMURA, the moral architect of the original Hantai Dōmei, gave the movement its voice. So pervasive was his influence that the leadership and organization remained largely unchanged for over a decade. Memories of Tomura survive in the two Hantai Dōmei organizations today.

During the period when Tomura was president there were four vice-presidents, all of them farmers representing their villages. Ogawa Meiji from Kinone was the most important of the vice-presidents. After he died in 1971, his grave was obliterated to make way for the airport runway. Another was Seri Makoto from Shibayama; he betrayed the movement. A third, Tsuji Masao from Ōshimizu, was an elementary school teacher with a small piece of land on the airport site. He left the movement in 1969 because he opposed the use of the Boys' Corps in confrontations. Ishibashi Masaji, the fourth vice-president, became acting president after the death of Tomura in 1979, a post he held until he was forced to resign in January 1982.

From the time of Tomura's death until 1983 when the Hantai Dōmei split into two organizations, the most important office was that of secretary general, occupied by Kitahara. It was an office that had been created specifically for Kitahara by Tomura. In that position Kitahara played a key role in linking the Hantai Dōmei with the sects and in representing it outside Sanrizuka, but he had little autonomous decision-making power. The farmers did not entirely trust him, which may account for the tensions between him and other key Hantai Dōmei leaders such as Ishibashi and Shima. In earlier days even Tomura never completely trusted Kitahara, despite their collaboration.

The original Hantai Dōmei was structured along two lines: territorial (that is, each hamlet had its own organization) and functional (the Old People's, Women's, Youth, Boys', and Action Corps). Together these groups made up the Hantai Dōmei. Two bodies governed the organization. The first of these, the Hantai Dōmei Committee of Representatives (*Jikkō-Yakuin-Kai*), was made up of representatives from twenty-seven villages and was headed by the president of the Hantai Dōmei. Tomura, of course, first held that post and was succeeded by Ishibashi. The second governing body was the Executive Board (*Kambu-Kai*) of ten members; it included representatives from the Committee of Representatives and from each of the corps groups, and it was presided over by the secretary general, Kitahara. As secretary general Kitahara was also the main link between the Hantai Dōmei and a body representing the seventeen sects involved at Sanrizuka, the Supporting Organizations Liaison Council (*Shien-Renraku-Kyōgi-Kai*).

Issues were raised in several ways. An individual farmer could present a concern to a senior official of the Hantai Dōmei—the acting president or a member of the Executive Committee, for example. Important matters were usually sent to the hamlet Hantai Dōmei for its consideration and recommendations before being decided upon by the Hantai Dōmei as a whole. An issue could also be brought forward by an individual at the hamlet level and then sent to the Committee of Representatives for deliberation. Often the farmers most concerned with a particular issue would hold informal meetings before bringing up the matter formally. Sometimes, too, when two hamlets had an especially close relationship, like Heta and Kinone, representatives of those hamlets might discuss matters in a very informal way before taking any action. Representatives from all the villages within a school district also tended to get together to discuss an issue. Thus the procedure varied, depending on the nature of the issue itself—how complex it was, how many discussions were needed to resolve it, who was involved—and on the existing links between hamlets and between people.[1]

There was no single model for the Hantai Dōmei. Among the

Organization of the Hantai Domei

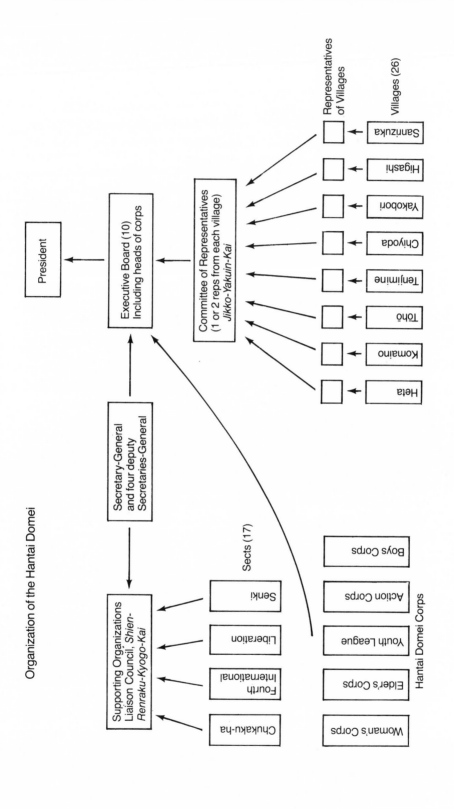

President

Executive Board (10)
Including heads of corps

Committee of Representatives
(1 or 2 reps from each village)
Jikko-Yakuin-Kai

Representatives
of Villages

Villages (26)

Sanrizuka

Higashi

Yakobori

Chiyoda

Tenjimine

Tōhō

Komaino

Heta

Secretary-General
and four deputy
Secretaries-General

Supporting Organizations
Liaison Council, *Shien-
Renraku-Kyogo-Kai*

Sects (17)

Senki

Liberation

Fourth
International

Chukaku-ha

Hantai Domei Corps

Boys Corps

Action Corps

Youth League

Elder's Corps

Woman's Corps

sources for its organizational structure was the earlier alliance between farmers and militant sects in the long and successful struggle over the Sunagawa military base expansion. Another model, one that was especially important in shaping women's role within the Hantai Dōmei, was the Kita-Fuji movement. Kita-Fuji representatives came to Sanrizuka to teach their tactics. Perhaps most of all it was the Yachimata-Tomisato Hantai Dōmei that served as the organizational basis for the Sanrizuka-Shibayama Hantai Dōmei. When the airport site was shifted from Tomisato to Sanrizuka, about thirty or forty members of the Yachimata-Tomisato Hantai Dōmei visited the hamlets and villages around Sanrizuka. Among the visitors were its president, Umesawa Kiyoshi; its secretary general, Hosono Michio; its Youth Corps commander, Yoshida Sōichiro; and its Women's Corps commander, Ebara Masako. Their positions and titles were copied in forming the Sanrizuka-Shibayama Hantai Dōmei. The dual principle of hamlet and corps organization was in itself a traditional, familiar arrangement.

When it first became known that the government intended to shift the site of the airport from Tomisato to Sanrizuka, an attempt was made to find a president for the new Hantai Dōmei that was being formed. The organizers' first choice was Kanzaki Takeo, president of the Narita City Farmers' Cooperative. He said he was too busy. Others who were asked to become president on the same day—June 25, 1966—were Nogami Hideharu, a former Narita City assemblyman, and Kanzaki Kenzo, a member of the City Agricultural Committee. Both declined, saying they had no confidence in the movement. All three were local "bosses," people with local political power; they had been chosen because it is virtually impossible, particularly in an agricultural community, to have a successful organization without the leadership of a recognized boss. The organizers were worried that the Hantai Dōmei, which was to have its inaugural celebration only three days later, would be stillborn if the leadership role could not be taken by one of the bosses.

Deciding to ask Tomura, then, represented a sharp departure from local precedent. Tomura was neither a local boss nor a farmer. He wasn't even particularly sociable toward local people, and he was a Christian. But he was the only person in Sanrizuka who had participated in the Tomisato movement. Prior to actually asking Tomura, the Hantai Dōmei organizers met at Sanrizuka Park. Among those who didn't think Tomura would make a suitable president, Ishibashi Masaji was the most outspoken. He didn't get along with intellectuals, he said, and he went home. But Ogawa Meiji argued that it didn't much matter who was president as long as the farmers on the site continued to fight. Despite grumbling, Ogawa Meiji's views prevailed. Once Tomura was agreed upon, Ishii Kōji (a JCP member), Ogawa Meiji, and a carpenter named Takahashi visited Tomura at his compound. He was working on a piece of sculpture when they asked him to become president. At first he refused, saying that the leader should be someone who lived in the airport site. He pledged his support nonetheless. Asked to reconsider, Tomura finally agreed. He asked his wife to make him a sash. He wrote on it, "The truth shall make you free," and wore it at the inaugural rally on June 28 at the Tōyama Junior High School auditorium. More than twelve hundred farmers came. Tomura gave the inaugural speech, and representatives of the Yachimata-Tomisato Hantai Dōmei and the JSP politicians also spoke.

Two days later the Shibayama Hantai Dōmei met at the Shibayama Junior High School to choose Seri Makoto as president. The two organizations merged on July 10 to become the Sanrizuka-Shibayama Hantai Dōmei, with Tomura as president and Seri the vice-president. The office of the Farmers' Cooperative became the first headquarters. (Eventually the headquarters moved to Tomura's study, where meetings were held amid books on Christianity, paintings, calligraphy, and mementos.) Later the Old People's Corps was formed under the leadership of Sugasawa Kazutoshi of Hishida village. Wearing a "red guard" badge, he made a speech to the farmers in which he said that sovereignty resided in the people, that the people did not have to become victims of national policy, and that agriculture and the environment were being destroyed. Old people must stand up and fight.

The original group of farmers was willing to negotiate with government authorities. Some of the farmers, like Ogawa Meiji, were former ward bosses; many were members of the LDP. Others had been taught by the JCP and the JSP. They were practical men, eager to deal with the government. The transition to a hard line came gradually, along with the escalation of violence. The Zengakuren chairman first visited Sanrizuka on September 1, 1967; on December 15 the JCP was expelled. The New Left sects entered in force early in 1968, occupying the first Zengakuren solidarity hut (taken over by Chūkaku-ha) on Ishibashi's compound. To the police, the presence of the sects was a change in the rules of the game. The major turning point came on February 26, 1968, when Tomura was badly beaten up by riot police and taken to the hospital. At that rally 249 people were arrested and 1,380 injured, ushering in a phase of violence. On September 16, 1971, three riot police were killed during the second expropriation struggle; 3,200 people fought against 5,-300 riot police. As some people saw it, violence was an illustration of the power of the Hantai Dōmei itself, a power that reached its peak in the control tower event of March 26, 1978, when 280 organizations sent 23,000 participants. After the airport opened on May 20 of that year and the government promised to be more conciliatory, violence declined. Although Tomura died on November 2, 1979, the atmosphere remained violent. A large number of riot police still stand guard around the airport.

To the sects the violence represented class struggle; but it is a bit more difficult to interpret the importance of violence to the farmers. Most of them oppose it in principle. Tomura had his own views, of course; his attitude toward violence was closer to those of the militants than of the farmers. For everyone, violence symbolized resistance to marginalization. The old woman Ōki Yone, the only person in the first-stage airport site who to the end refused the government's offer to negotiate, provides a vivid example of that kind of resistance. It was Ōki Yone who made Tomura understand better the strength and character of the farmers' commitment and gave substance to what otherwise would have remained a set of abstract principles. Her story, retold many times, has come to represent the indomitable spirit of the Hantai Dōmei.

Ōki Yone was born into a farm family in Yachimata. The family was too poor to keep her; at the age of seven she was indentured for life. She never went to school and could neither read nor write. When she was fifteen she ran away from her owner and then made a living as a servant and a waitress in Yokohama, Tokyo, Narita City, and elsewhere. She lived with a man for a time, but they drifted apart. After the war she met Ōki Minoru, and together they built a hut in Tokkō. Because of land reforms they were able to buy a small plot of land, which they began to cultivate as a pioneer family. In addition they cultivated a small rice paddy owned by the Fujisaki family. Then Ōki Minoru died, and she was left alone.

At the time of the first land expropriations most of the farmers from the main villages affected were strongly supportive of the Hantai Dōmei, but as time passed they began to negotiate with the government. Individual households and whole villages dropped out, even Iwayama village (which in 1972 became the site of the steel tower constructed as the symbol of opposition). Finally Ōki Yone was the only one left on the site. Kasé, who stayed with her in her tiny house for a while, asked her what she did when she was sick. She said she would crawl to the well to drink water and crawl back to her futon and sleep.

The government offered her compensation in accordance with the procedures they had worked out with the other farmers. But unlike the others she refused it, saying that she would not take money from a thief or burglar. She faithfully attended rallies and took part in the physical confrontations. She never failed in her duty. It is this sense of obligation (*giri*) that was perhaps the most essential quality of the Hantai Dōmei itself.

When the government tried to negotiate with her for her house, she went to Hantai Dōmei members in Tōhō and Tenjinmine to ask them to establish a policy and give her some guidance. The Hantai Dōmei, however, did not know quite what to do. It had no money to give the farmers being threatened; it could only exhort them to hold firm. So Ōki Yone decided to visit Tomura himself. First she collected locusts in the field and cooked them as a special delicacy, and she bought a bottle of sake with some money that supporters had given her. She brought the locusts and sake with her. Tomura, delighted by this gesture, was impressed by her grace and power.

As the airport construction came closer to her house, it became more difficult for her to survive. The rice paddy was filled with sand. The well dried up. She was harassed by riot police shouting epithets at her. She shouted back at them, asking if they were not human beings and had not come from a mother's womb. If they tried to take her house while she was having a meal, she said, she would throw pots and pans and dishes and hot *miso* soup at them. If they came while she was in the field she would fight with her plow and sickle. (It was from Ōki Yone that Tomura got the idea of using farm equipment as the symbolic weaponry of the Hantai Dōmei.) She startled the police by saying that if they wanted to remove her from her house they would have to put their police sticks up her vagina, and then she flipped up her kimono. The police fled.

Nevertheless, on September 21, 1971, Ōki Yone's house was dismantled. She fought back, was beaten, and had to be carried off on a police shield. The land was "swept" by the surveyors. For the farmers this was a moment of grave crisis, but for Tomura, standing in the field with some others who had pitched a tent, the scene was the Bible come to life, the parable of John the Baptist telling the people in the field about God.

By the time of her death, Ōki Yone, perhaps more than anyone

except Tomura, had become the symbol of the movement. In Tomura's eyes, she was the last who was first—the last in her poverty
and social status, the first in her will, incorruptibility, strength. To
the farmers she represented the qualities of the pioneers, the spirit
of the tough oldtimers who had to do everything by themselves and
became good farmers the hard way, in contrast to those from the old
villages, particularly ex-landlords, who in the end collaborated with
the government. To all those who had sold their lands and left, Ōki
Yone was a reproach.

The militants, too, valued her spontaneous radicalism. Childless,
she adopted as a son an ex-student, Koizumi Hidemasa, who had
come to Sanrizuka to work for the movement and eventually became
a farmer and a leading member of the One-Pack Movement. With
this adoption she demonstrated her sense of responsibility for the
continuity of the movement and for the integration of militants and
farmers. Finally, and perhaps most important, as a woman she symbolized the liberation of women, especially the farm women who had
been taught to be subservient to men, always decorous in their conduct. Neither the subservience of women's role nor the decorum of
age had any place in Ōki Yone's scheme of things. Yet she had an
essential delicacy and grace and sense of appropriateness that en-
deared her to all.

If Ōki Yone was the heroine of the movement, another woman
represented "original sin," a Judas figure, at least for Tomura. In her
story one sees the kind of tragedy faced by individual households.
Her name was Ōtake Hana and she was deputy commander of the
Women's Corps. She, too, was born into a peasant family. She married Ōtake Kinzō (later one of those who persuaded Tomura to
become president of the Hantai Dōmei) and went with him to Manchuria. After the war they returned to Japan and settled in Furugome.

They were so poor that they could not afford to bring up their
children; the children were sent to relatives. Their firstborn son
eventually came to live with them. He did not like farming and got a
job in a woodworking factory. A successful worker, he saved some
money and bought a wagon, then a small truck. The family began to
prosper. He decided to begin his own woodworking factory and obtained a loan of 700,000 yen. The factory was completed just as the
airport issue arose.

Ōtake Hana threw herself into the work of the Hantai Dōmei. Tomura was deeply impressed by her commitment; he regarded her as
one of those closest to him. Then the unexpected happened. After

the airport project was approved the government prohibited the installation of high-voltage wires. Ōtake Hana's son was unable to open his factory, which was dependent on electrical power, and he could not repay the loan. Then a second disaster occurred. Years before, the Ōtake family had been induced to switch from growing potatoes and peanuts to planting mulberry trees when the government had inaugurated the Sanrizuka Area Structural Improvement Project, part of its comprehensive agricultural policy. But the program was abandoned when the airport project was conceived. Farm support disappeared. Mulberry cannot easily be replaced by another crop.

The family was left in a very vulnerable position. When Ōtake Kinzō then got ulcers and had to be operated on, no one was left to earn a living by farming. Ōtake Hana could not remain in Sanrizuka; she had to drop out and leave. The farmers understood her predicament very well, but Tomura did not. He never forgave her.

There are several other people whose beliefs and actions give a better idea of the ideology of the movement than any description of it. We have already mentioned Ogawa Meiji, one of the Hantai Dōmei organizers, who originated the idea of the underground tunnels. His last will and testament have become part of the Hantai Dōmei legend. Also part of that legend is the story of Sugasawa Kazutoshi, the first commander of the Old People's Corps, who came up with the tactic of throwing feces and urine bombs at the police and who wanted the elders to commit mass suicide on the imperial estate when the cherry trees were to be cut down. And there is Ishibashi, an ex-LDP man and a former emperor's man, who saw the struggle as a fight against the state. Each of these individuals defined the movement in a different way and endowed it with a different meaning.

One of the most important leaders of the Hantai Dōmei was Uchida Kanichi, a dairy farmer. As commander of the Action Corps he was an active, courageous Hantai Dōmei member. A man of great stature, Uchida was one of the founders of the Maruasa Cooperative, which became a great source of support for the Hantai Dōmei. There were many reasons for Uchida's importance to the Hantai Dōmei. For one thing, he came from Shibayama, a very traditional farming area but also the place where the first farmers' unions in Japan were organized. As people from the area describe it, Shibayama has a history of peasant rebellion and landlord-tenant conflict, especially in Yachimata and Tomisato. A Farmers' Union was established there in 1924 under JCP auspices (it gradually moved toward the JSP, which is Marxist rather than social-democratic). It was in Shibayama that landlords, who had relatively small holdings, confronted deteriorating agricultural circumstances and to save themselves severely repressed their tenants. In 1928 there were forty peasant uprisings there, and in 1929 eighty. Uchida represents such "memories." He is the village headman for Iwayama, where his grandfather owned land, even though he actually lives in Asakura village.

Uchida is also a firm JSP man; he joined the party in 1950. Before that he belonged to the Farmers' Union Youth Group, as did his brother and a cousin. It was this union, which has many more members than the Hantai Dōmei, that collected about five thousand signatures in opposition to the airport and presented them to Governor Tomonō of Chiba. It mobilized a motorcade of one hundred cars that invaded the airport site. Uchida has been a candidate for the JSP Executive Committee as a representative of the farmers. He was the member of the Hantai Dōmei Executive Committee who was most responsible for a smooth working relationship between the sects and the farmers, both in hamlet Hantai Dōmei organizations and in more general Hantai Dōmei politics—a very delicate assignment, to say the least.

During the period in which he was commander of the Action Corps, Uchida's strength was partly organizational and partly personal. He was one of the first to fight back in the early days and one of the first arrested by the police. In an organization based on "inward-looking" familialism, he was an anomaly: from the start he looked outward. Long before the One-Pack Movement, Uchida was concerned about the future of farming. After the war he had looked for ways to improve farm income in the area. The land had deteriorated while the men were away; the women had carried on the farming, but the quality of the produce—peanuts, rice, some vegetables—had declined. So the cooperative was organized around the principle of scientific farming. It shifted its products to potatoes, watermelons, and carrots and other vegetables. About twenty or thirty households became involved.

Another important person, although he had no official role in the original Hantai Dōmei, was Shimamura Ryōsuke, a successful chicken farmer who was originally a worker. A Tōhō village pioneer in the second-stage site of the airport, Shimamura is one of those who phrased the Sanrizuka conflict in a wider context well understood by the other farmers. "How can one have democracy when a government can come to a village and destroy the house and life of

an individual citizen without recourse, as in the case of Ōki Yone?"
he asked. "How can one believe in parliamentary democracy if it ignores the wishes of the people and provides no means for their views
to be heard?" Before the Sanrizuka affair Shimamura had little interest in politics; today he believes the fight must go on because "the
government does not listen to its people." He sees the airport as simply the occasion for ventilating these larger grievances that should
be of interest to every Japanese citizen. "A parliamentary government is above all a government of laws. But has the government a
right to ask people to obey those laws if it does not itself remain
faithful to the spirit of the law? Should one simply accept its decisions on the basis of authority? Our past experience suggests not."
His views, widely respected, are shared by many farmers of the
Hantai Dōmei.

Not all of the Hantai Dōmei concerns had to do with farming or
with the tradition of peasant rebellion. The movement became
deeply involved in contemporary politics in Japan. Farmers quickly
came to believe that the airport was an instrument of militarism and
imperialism. They saw the underground trenches as a symbol of
Vietnam and the police and their equipment as surrogates for an
alien state power. As early as September 4, 1967, when *Zenshin,* the
Chūkaku-ha newspaper, defined the purpose of the new airport as
serving the troops going to fight in the Vietnam war, the theme
found popular support among the farmers, who as ex-soldiers vowed
they would never again let themselves be fooled by governments. In
one of his earliest speeches Tomura spoke of the problem of air
space and pointed out that the air lane "Blue 14" was a route for
U.S. military bases in the Yakota area. Blue 14, by continuing across
Tokyo Bay to Ōshima Island, constricted commercial passenger
flights from Haneda, which were not allowed to cross Blue 14 but
had to skirt it by flying around to Kisarazu in Chiba, then down the
Bōsō Penninsula to Ōshima, and then on to Osaka, Kyushu, and
points beyond. In turn Tomura linked this problem to the Status of
Forces Agreement, an implementation of the Japan-U.S. Security
Treaty which gave the U.S. military force and Japan's Self-Defense
Force exclusive rights not only to Blue 14 but also to other air lanes
that crisscrossed Japanese air space. So the Hantai Dōmei believed
that cramped air space, the chartering of commercial passenger
flights for transporting troops through Haneda to Vietnam, and the
priority treatment received by U.S. military personnel (which interfered with normal traffic at Haneda) were the reasons for the government's decision to build the airport at Sanrizuka.[2]

As such issues became more important and the Hantai Dōmei drew closer to the militant sects, the organizational links between the Hantai Dōmei and the sects became more enmeshed. Through the sects' Supporting Organizations Liaison Council and the Hantai Dōmei's Executive Board the two groups maintained their official connection. But what began as a marriage of convenience for both groups became a labor in the vineyards on the sects' part to raise the farmers' "consciousness" and provide a broader understanding of the political nature of the confrontation.

The closeness began to create problems for the Hantai Dōmei. One problem was to prevent sect division from weakening the movement. Another problem was for the Hantai Dōmei to keep control of its own movement—a lesson learned at the time the JCP was expelled. The Hantai Dōmei had to insist that the sects keep to their own organization, although it allowed them to make representations to the Hantai Dōmei and to receive representations from their own outside supporters. Most of all, the Hantai Dōmei did not want sects involved in the farmers' decision-making bodies. Most of the hamlet and village organizations adhered strictly to rules against the participation of outsiders, even just as observers, in the farmers' own meetings.

A close look at the diagram suggests obvious points of tension. As Hantai Dōmei membership declined, it was more difficult for the Hantai Dōmei to keep control. The balance of power slowly shifted away from the Hantai Dōmei Committee of Representatives and Executive Board and toward the Supporting Organizations Liaison Committee. The Hantai Dōmei secretary general became less responsive to the first two and more to the last. In turn, the Liaison Committee was more and more dominated by Chūkaku-ha. As Chūkaku-ha became more powerful (to the concern, particularly, of the Youth Corps, and the farmers more favorable to the JSP), it began to act as a watchdog: it carried out patrols and surveillance of farmers, watching for evidence of possible secret negotiations between the farmers and the government. Farmers resented that. Chūkaku-ha's actions, some people believe, produced a public conformity and a rigidity of policy within the Hantai Dōmei while inducing duplicity under the surface.

If there were tensions between the Hantai Dōmei and the sects, there were also divisions between the farmers living inside the second-stage construction area and those outside it. The two groups have had different problems, and over time the government has de-

Sect Organization in Relation to the Hantai Domei

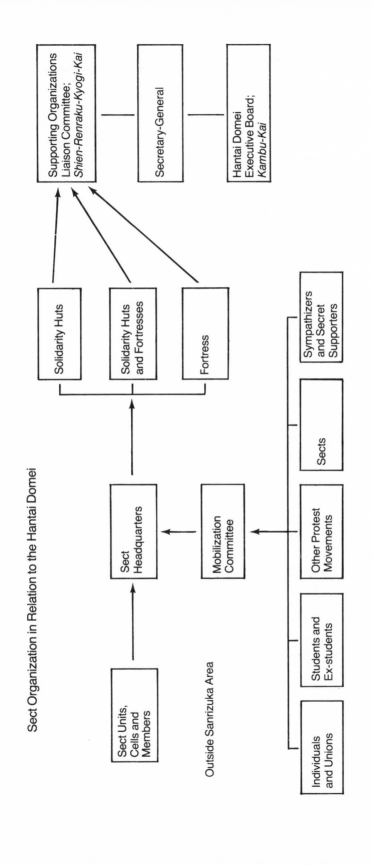

veloped a strategy of keeping the two groups apart and conducting secret negotiations with individuals from each group. The problems faced by the farmers outside the airport site are, as we have mentioned, largely ecological; irrigation is a chief concern. The government has made very generous offers to provide appropriate facilities to alleviate the problem. New land has been made available to farmers inside the site, along with the necessary preliminary support required to bring the land up to high-yield standards. Increasingly, it has seemed that holdouts have been acting petulantly and in defiance of the more general public interest—matters that farmers have always taken very seriously. The questions of how to deal with these internal matters and how to control the sects fell most heavily on the shoulders of the Executive Board members responsible for Hantai Dōmei policy. These included Atsuta Hajime, the Action Corps commander; Hasegawa Take, the Women's Corps commander; Akiba Tetsu, in charge of the "rescue corps" that helps those in prison; Sugasawa Shōhei, deputy secretary general of the Hantai Dōmei; and Ogawa Gen, representing the farmers of the second-phase construction site.

Hantai Dōmei organization counted most when a crisis occurred. In between the short intervals of crisis, the organization was sustained mostly by its hamlet institutions and by the loyalty derived from farmers' commitments to one another, commitments cemented by heroic exploits. In effect, the organization created its own past and cast its members as heroes and heroines.

DESPITE CONFLICTS, then, the Hantai Dōmei was able to survive quite well for a number of years, even without many leaders. Perhaps, too, it survived because of the common concern of its members on three important questions: private property, "equality," and the future of farming. All three were bound up with the question of succession—that is, with transferring property from one generation to the next. Most farmers, whatever their political persuasion, considered themselves defenders of their private patrimony. In the older hamlets they defended what was inherited and what was left of a social structure in which most were landlords; their visible claims to power and prestige are residuals of that earlier privilege. These farmers, radical only in their anger and hostility to the LDP and the government, remain for the most part deeply conservative. Also fiercely defending their patrimony were the pioneers like Shimamura and Ogawa Meiji. They were defending what they themselves had created.

Equality, the second issue all Hantai Dōmei farmers were concerned about, does not mean dividing land equally among members of the Hantai Dōmei, something that most farmers would regard as unnatural, but refers rather to the problem of equalizing the burdens placed on farmers as a result of their obligations to the Hantai Dōmei itself. The issue was of special concern at the time of the first land survey. The farmers had decided on a strategy of fighting for ninety days, but the government initiated the survey during the summer, the busiest time for farmers. To prevent economic disaster, the Hantai Dōmei mobilized all its members in certain hamlets and had them plant just peanuts, enabling them to use time-saving group farming methods so that there were always some farmers available for action. This strategy provided the Action Corps with a mobilizable core ready for confrontation.

Sometimes the collective strategy failed, however. During the rice harvest, those who finished early were asked to help others still working. But rice and vegetable farmers work on different schedules. Moreover, the farmers who needed help the most were, of course, the wealthier ones with the largest land holdings. Those who could finish work early were mainly the poorest farmers, who ordinarily supplemented their incomes by work outside. If the poor were to help the rich, the poor would have to give up their outside income. A different system of "support farming" had to be devised.

To keep farm income up during the main period of confrontations, farming was carried out illegally on "vacant" airport land—land that had already been vacated, and land being cultivated by farmers who had sold out but had not yet evacuated their farms. (In fact, Hantai Dōmei members began stealing peanuts from some of these farmers on the grounds that they had betrayed the movement.) Ogawa Meiji, for example, began growing wheat on government land, and farmers mobilized against a government bulldozer that had been brought in to stop him. Eventually Hantai Dōmei farmers were able to continue to farm Airport Authority land. (Indeed, farming such land is still a major source of revenue for some farmers.)

Some of these improvisations worked reasonably well, but it became more and more imperative for the Hantai Dōmei as an organization to come up with some agreed-upon policies about land and the future of farming. In their "Yokobori Declaration" the Hantai Dōmei established the principles that all land belonged to farmers; that no land in the entire airport area belonged to the government; that no distinctions on the basis of previous land ownership would be recognized; and that land vacated by farmers who had sold out to the government would be occupied by the Hantai Dōmei and cultivated, the income going into a common "struggle fund." It was left to each hamlet to implement this policy, come up with its own production plan, and allocate the labor force in an appropriate way. As a result of continuous experimentation, a satisfactory arrangement was worked out in which Heta hamlet members went to Kinone to help the Ogawa brothers (kinship counting for a good deal) and Shiramasu farmers went to Tenjinmine. The Youth Corps farmed in common on the the so-called People's Farm out of which came the One-Pack Movement.

Such experiments made people think more imaginatively. For the first time the future of farming was being seriously examined by the farmers themselves. Could farming on small holdings, the largest not much more than five *chō*, continue in the absence of direct government subsidy? Would farmers within the Hantai Dōmei use the struggle to expand their own holdings and increase their claims to government compensation? Would secret deals be made with the government by farmers who wanted to rent vacant airport land? Vice-President Seri, for example, ordinarily harvested enough rice— about eighteen bales—for his own family's subsistence. Cultivating airport land (under Hantai Dōmei policy) he was able to produce a surplus of seventy bales, which he sold through the Farmers' Cooperative for his own private benefit (against Hantai Dōmei policy). Should this be allowed? Even members of sects followed suit. As their skills improved, they too desired to profit from the situation. In thinking about the future of farming, the Hantai Dōmei tried to come up with a general plan in which a more systematic relationship between production, investment and fertilizer control would help farmers. Part of the profit would be used to finance Hantai Dōmei activities, the organizers hoped; another portion would be kept by individual farmers.

No group has been more interested in the question of the future of farming than the Youth Corps. It sought to deal with the question in a practical context; it tried, for instance, to secure the advantages of proximity to the Tokyo market. Most Youth Corps members remain deeply committed to farming. Their fathers may have taught them to farm, but they believe it necessary to find their own perspectives and techniques.

First sons, and a few first daughters, made up the largest part of the Youth Corps membership. Few farmers have enough land for subdivision, so most second and third sons and daughters leave the farm and go to Tokyo and other cities. As their parents age, first sons do more and more of the work. But parents are afraid of giving up their farms because of possible successor conflicts and because they do not want to be entirely dependent on the good will of their children for care in their declining years. It is an awkward situation for young people, who are anxious to change the structure of rural life but do not want to look as if they are waiting for their parents to die. They are caught between filial devotion and powerlessness.

A few Hantai Dōmei farmers, aware of the situation, have "retired" early. But this too has had its problems. In trying to pass along their land to the children who seem to have the best prospects for making a go of farming, some farmers might be depriving their first sons of their traditional right of inheritance. Few guides exist for resolving these questions. "Rural philosophers," even radical ones like Yamaguchi Bushū, who involved himself in the Hantai Dōmei for a time, can offer no answers to such practical problems.

During the period of confrontations, the Youth Corps, along with the Old People's Corps, was the most militant in the Hantai Dōmei, more daring than the generation in between. (In fact, the cautiousness of the Action Corps was often mocked: members of the Women's Corps would jeer at their husbands and goad them to action.) The Youth Corps was small, perhaps seventy active individuals, and had its own publications. The publishers and editors of the publications are all under indictment for past confrontational activities; many are still fighting expensive court cases. Many of the Youth Corps members lacked the experience with party membership that their parents had, and lacked also their parents' fluency in ideological language. Anxious not to be brought into the internal disputes of the sects, they were angry that the Hantai Dōmei involved itself in the war between Chūkaku-ha and Kakumaru-ha.

One descendant of the Youth Corps is the small group of people who formed the One-Pack Movement. One-Pack is a utopian group; it is trying to resolve large issues in a practical immediate context, hoping that its principles can then spread throughout Japan. One-Pack members are all in couples. One couple is Shima Kansei and his wife. Shima played an important role in the Hantai Dōmei. Another is Koizumi Hidemasa (the adopted son of Ōki Yone), who is in his early thirties and lives with his wife and three children in a hut in Tōhō. Ishii Tsuneji is a third member; his father, Ishii Takeshi, was an important member of the Hantai Dōmei Executive Board and traveled all over Japan to gather its support for the organization.

Ogawa Naokatsu, a member of the Action Corps, inherited land on his father's death and became the head of the household; he has a wife and two children. Ishii Shinji, responsible for his mother as well as for his wife and two children, was a member of the Hantai Dōmei Executive Board. A sixth "couple" is neither married nor living together, but by other One-Pack members it is regarded as a working couple: it is made up of two people who provide the same amount of labor and receive the same amount of money. Both are older women—Someya Katsu was Ōki Yone's closest friend, and Tanaka Tomi is the widow of a devoted member of the movement who died in 1980. Except for Shima, all the men married ex-student activist women.

The members of One-Pack share the work and the land, and together have invested in equipment such as trucks, large tractors, and sheds. They sell the vegetables of the season, all grown according to principles of organic farming. These are packed in a single carton and periodically distributed to subscribers, mainly in Tokyo. They also distribute recipes and suggestions for how to use the vegetables that they grow, many of which are unfamiliar in Japan.

There have been other groups of experimental farmers as well. A four-family "Vegetable League" sold its produce to a local cooperative pickle factory. A larger group of about twelve households, the Sanrizuka Organic Farming Group, was the first to engage in a program of improving agriculture; some of its members overlapped with One-Pack.

Perhaps the most perplexing problem for all these groups and for the Hantai Dōmei is the future of the role of women. In the original Hantai Dōmei, women were among the most militant. It was not only Ōki Yone who set an example. The women who visited from the Kita-Fuji movement taught the Sanrizuka women their techniques of violent protest, such as chaining themselves to bulldozers or trees, and standing well in front of the men in confrontations with the police so that they took the first blows. In some families, including quite traditional ones, such actions had the effect of changing basic family relationships, particularly those between husbands and wives.

Confrontations interrupted the rhythm of life. Rules changed; eating times became quite different; mothers-in-law had to expect altered behavior from their daughters-in-law. Some women went all over Japan making speeches. For the women of the Sanrizuka area, who had rarely been allowed away from the farm and whose opinions no one had paid attention to, the changes the movement brought were dramatic indeed.

One key activist woman had lived a totally harsh and bleak existence for eighteen years. Not until the Hantai Dōmei started and she became a participant in the movement did her husband accept the idea of her going out, meeting with friends. Then even her mother-in-law accepted her new role, which on one occasion involved preparing meals for a hundred people. In effect, the movement released her from bondage.

The behavior of the police was a turning point for some women. Scandalized at first by what the police said and did to them, the women then came to understand that the police were only following orders, orders that must have come from the government. Such a betrayal by the government made the women reexamine their own position. With civic obligations broken and family life restructured at the same time, women needed to rethink their total situation. Explicit movements in favor of women's liberation they found entirely unattractive. The women felt that change must take place within the family; the struggle must involve the family as a unit. In their view, change from within required reading, discussing, and participating in the Women's Corps.

The Women's Corps was organized almost by chance as women got together to discuss how best to adapt to the movement. Each family was represented in the Women's Corps by one woman, usually the housewife—the most "oppressed" person in the house. Hamlet meetings were held once a week and larger meetings once a month. Topics included everything from funerals to taxes.

The Women's Corps had a commander and two deputies. Like other Hantai Dōmei bodies, the group depended on the talent, interest, and availability of individual members. One woman would be asked to organize a meeting, and someone else to make arrangements to look after the old people and the children while the meeting was going on. It was an informal structure, but it seemed to work. The women had an important effect on the decision-making within the Hantai Dōmei, which they regarded as an indication of how the status of women had changed in the area.[3] But the Women's Corps rarely discussed matters it regarded as appropriate to other Hantai Dōmei organizations. For example, the One-Pack Movement was regarded as part of the Youth Corps. Women's Corps members did not help the ex-student wives of One-Pack members, not even those who were having great problems in adjusting to family life in Sanrizuka.

If it was a difficult transition for them to make, they nevertheless had to make it on their own.

Many of the Sanrizuka women have become part of other movements and other struggles and now define their political sympathies as explicitly leftist. Hasegawa Take, the Women's Corps commander after Ōtake Hana left Sanrizuka, is a woman in her late sixties. She was a schoolteacher for many years, beginning in the days when a teacher was a model citizen and a representative of the imperial system, and after the war, when the Americans came, she became interested in democracy. She joined the teachers' union. She regards being "left" as something quite different from being a Marxist or a communist, which she does not believe in at all. Most of each month she spends away from the area, organizing. She visited the People's Republic of China for two months in 1970–71 but opposes the present Chinese regime.

Most of the women were, until the confrontations, LDP supporters. Afterward they did not become particularly anti-state (they were barely aware of the existence of the state), but they turned away from the LDP government and toward the JCP and the JSP. These two parties were attractive not because of their ideologies but simply because they were alternatives to the LDP. Many of the women have been arrested. Some have deep scars on their faces, permanent mementos of encounters with the heavy shields of the riot police.

THE ROLE of young people and women, the changes in generations and family relationships, the shifting of power between the Hantai Dōmei and the sects, and the pressures generated by the change in government tactics from confrontation to negotiation—all put heavy burdens on Hantai Dōmei members and exacerbated tensions within the leadership. Some of the tensions came to a head in January 1982 with the resignations of Ishibashi and Action Corps commander Uchida, setting in motion a chain of problems that led to a division of the Hantai Dōmei into two separate and hostile bodies in 1983.

The immediate issue was Ishibashi's alleged violation of Hantai Dōmei rules forbidding direct negotiations with government authorities. There were, of course, early precedents for such negotiations. Tomura had met with Governor Tomonō of Chiba Prefecture three times prior to the rally on February 26, 1968, at which he was wounded. Indeed, Tomonō had given Tomura a secret "hot-line" telephone number. After Tomura was beaten, however, the Hantai Dōmei decided that direct negotiations were useless. No official negotiations followed. (In 1979, however, Shima engaged in some preliminary discussions that were leaked to the press, and he thereafter was considered suspect. But he retained his duties in the Youth Corps and as a deputy secretary general and a member of the Executive Board.)

The events leading to Ishibashi's resignation were fairly simple. In August 1981 Ishibashi, the acting president of the Hantai Dōmei, went on a vacation. At the invitation of an LDP Dietman, Mizuno Kiyoshi, he visited the lovely Katsura Detached Palace in Kyoto, something that is more difficult for a Japanese to arrange than for a foreigner. At the end of the month Ishibashi had a meeting at the house of an Airport Authority official, Maeda Nobuo, with Nishimura Akira, who had been skilled in negotiation between the government, farmers, and fishermen and who also worked for the Airport Authority. This occurred after private meetings between airport officials and several key Hantai Dōmei members, among them Uchida and Iwasawa. The next month the same Dietman took Ishibashi to a *sumo* game and they had dinner and drinks, charged to the Airport Authority.

On October 23 five Hantai Dōmei members (Ishibashi, Uchida, Iwasawa, Umezawa, and Iida) met with high-ranking government officials, among them Hattori Tsuneji, director general of the Transportation Ministry; Matsui Kazuji, chief of the Aviation Bureau; Katō Kōichi, a former deputy secretary of the Cabinet and presently a Dietman; Maeda Nobuo of the Airport Authority; and Nishimura Akira. From the government's point of view, the meeting was an important breakthrough. The government had just made the decision to implement the Fourth Airport Consolidation Five-Year Plan and the Cabinet had approved an appropriation of 320 billion yen.

In December, Hattori of the Transportation Ministry visited Tenjinmine in an attempt to convince other farmers to join with Ishibashi in negotiations. His visit was discovered by the Chūkaku-ha cadres at the headquarters on Ishibashi's compound, who alerted other Hantai Dōmei leaders to Ishibashi's violation of the rule about negotiating. Ishibashi then requested that Chūkaku-ha leave the headquarters site. An emergency Executive Board meeting was called on January 22. The agenda included the forced resignation of Ishibashi as acting president of the Hantai Dōmei, and the removal of the headquarters and Chūkaku-ha from Ishibashi's compound. In reponse to the question of why he had negotiated, Ishibashi said that he had been having exploratory contacts with the government in order to protect the Hantai Dōmei. Asked by eleven Chūkaku-ha members to engage in self-criticism, Ishibashi not only ignored the request and demanded that the sects cease patrolling the Tenjin-mine area and that the staff of the headquarters on his compound be changed, but he also called for the return to Tokyo of a special Chūkaku-ha troop sent in when the crisis arose. These requests, under the signatures of Kitahara and Ishii Shinji, were sent to Chūkaku-ha for a reply.

An expanded Executive Board met on January 29 at the home of Atsuta, the deputy commander of the Action Corps. It rejected Ishi-bashi's requests about patrolling and moving the headquarters. The committee wanted to know more about what had actually happened and whether or not Chūkaku-ha's accusations had been correct, and they asked for letters of self-criticism from Ishibashi and Uchida. The letters were not written until after the deadline for them had passed. Representatives from the Tenjinmine Hantai Dōmei did not want to accept Ishibashi's letter. The Executive Board, however, ac-cepted it and his resignation from office as well. Ishibashi remained a member of the Hantai Dōmei, as did Uchida, who was replaced by Atsuta as commander of the Action Corps.

The loss of two such stalwarts was a tragedy for the Hantai Dōmei. In their defense, Ishibashi and Uchida claimed that the Hantai Dōmei had become too rigid in its policy, duplicitous because of excessive conformity, and no longer an open organization. Ishiba-shi in particular argued that his exchange of views with government officials was aimed at getting the government to understand the plight of farmers, not to discuss conditions of compromise. In his let-ter of self-criticism he apologized for the lateness of his reply, a delay caused by the illness of Commander Aikawa of the Old People's Corps, and he apologized for his secret contacts with the govern-ment. He said that the structure of the Hantai Dōmei was in need of reorganization, something he had not managed to do anything about. He had discovered, he said, that five families in Toyomi were considering leaving. This had precipitated his decision to tell the government how hard the situation was for farmers, especially those whose lands were subject to the Land Acquisition Act.

In an interview with *Asahi Shimbun* on February 11, Ishibashi said he had wanted to tell the government that Hantai Dōmei mem-bers were like victims facing the death penalty for sixteen years. It was time to reconsider basic Hantai Dōmei policy, he said; many people, including those who sounded the most militant, were engaging in secret negotiations. Finally, he charged that the Hantai Dōmei had lost the initiative and that Chūkaku-ha was now playing a leading role instead of a subordinate one, and he ended the interview by saying that it was necessary for the Hantai Dōmei to find some visible and public means of communication with the government.

The Youth Corps, in commenting on the situation, reminded its members of the negotiations attempted by Shima three years earlier. It argued that the time for negotiations would come later. It sympathized with those in the second-stage site but criticized the Hantai Dōmei for making protestations of victory while ignoring growing fears and uncertainty, circumstances under which farmers think negotiation the best opton. While commenting negatively on Ishibashi's personal weaknesses, the group also pointed out that the Hantai Dōmei had not backed him up, and that by depending too much on Chūkaku-ha, Ishibashi had become isolated. Stung by Yough Corps criticism, Chūkaku-ha replied that negotiations had to be stopped completely. It criticized the Youth Corps for calling Chūkaku-ha "deviators."

As for Ishibashi, he was unhappy, confused, and sick, and even had to go to the hospital for a while. Uchida, also unhappy, was pleased that at least the problems were out in the open now that the surveillance being done by the sects had been exposed. Ishibashi said he felt better after drinking a lot of sake. A year later the Hantai Dōmei split into two bitterly hostile and separate bodies.

9

The View from the Top

So FAR we have looked at the Sanrizuka struggle from the bottom, from the perspective of the Hantai Dōmei and the New Left sects. In their eyes the enemy is the state—and within the state, the government; within the government, the bureaucracy; within the bureaucracy, the Airport Authority. Being against the state extends to the LDP, the JSP, the JCP, and parties in general, for these are institutional mechanisms that make the system work and give it legitimacy but also render null and void the efforts the farmers have made on their own behalf, because the parties serve both their own interests and the interests of their more powerful clienteles. For different reasons, both the farmers and the sects have gone well past indifference to a deep hatred of the state itself.

The term "state" presents a problem: one can hate the state, but it is, after all, an abstraction. In this case violence has translated the abstraction into something real. To farmers and militants the state shows itself in the form of riot policemen, sticks, shields, and bulldozers. But if one asks farmers whether they really hate the state, they become evasive. It is really the sham of parliamentary government they hate, they say. If one probes further, they say they are troubled by the sham rather than parliamentary government. The sham, in turn, the government's failure to listen, to pay attention to the obligations it has incurred. Being against the state has its immediate aspect, then, but it has a certain tentativeness, too.

If we consider the state as an ensemble of organized political institutions and try to see it from the perspective of those most intimately involved in them—the president and vice-presidents of the Airport Authority, past and present, officials of the Ministry of Transportation, members of the Aviation Council, designers of the airport, Dietmen, prefectural authorities in Chiba, city and town councillors—we get an entirely different picture. It is a picture of plans and programs, expertise and performance, and, behind them, the individuals and factional leaders whose personal and political conflicts constituted a dynamic quite separate from the struggle of the farmers and militants, and subject to interpretations completely different from theirs.

The difference in the two views of the state is not really caused by what one might expect—that is, by the government's remoteness from ordinary life in Sanrizuka or Shibayama. Certainly remoteness is not the problem today. Hattori of the Transportation Ministry can recite, with an astonishing familiarity and ease, the names and family situations of all the farmers involved. He cannot do this for the sects—but then, he doesn't want to.

The government thinks it has been responsive. After all, it moved the site from Tomisato as a result of public protest there. The Tomisato area was heavily LDP-affiliated, and the government recognized that it could not cope with protest from so many people. Sanrizuka, thinly populated and with public land available, seemed a good alternative. Another piece of evidence of the government's willingness to compromise was that in 1966, when the site was shifted, the size of the proposed airport was cut down by half. Originally, after the Ikeda government had approved an Airport Long-Term Consolidation Plan in March 1962 with an initial exploratory grant of 1.8 million yen and sent a study team abroad to examine other international airports, a master plan was drawn up that proposed a five-runway airport of 2,500 hectares. This was accepted by the government in August. The first phase of the construction was to be done by 1970 and the entire airport by 1973, at a total construction cost of 200 billion yen. There were to be two 4,000-meter runways, two 2,500-meter runways, and one 3,000-meter runway. The proposal called for a site compatible with prevailing conditions of aviation control, an hour's drive or less from downtown Tokyo. Negotiations began quickly under the direction of the prime minister's office, in particular the Metropolitan Consolidation Committee headed first by Kōno Ichirō and then by Kawashima Shōjirō; thus they had special access to an extremely profitable project. Chiba was selected as the most appropriate prefecture. Kawashima, an important LDP boss, came from Chiba. He was very pleased with the plan because of the benefits it would bring the prefecture.

There were several reasons why the government scaled down the original plan. Some were economic, particularly uncertainties about the cost. Others were political. The sheer size of the original undertaking in a land-poor country aroused widespread opposition, even within the Cabinet itself.

Shimamura, one of the intellectuals of the Hantai Dōmei with a gift for putting matters well, again and again made the point that a parliamentary government could not work unless it listened to the people (and he meant people like himself). From the government's perspective, the LDP and other political parties and interest groups—indeed, the entire network of representative institutions— had plainly conveyed the citizens' needs to the government. Shifting the site and reducing the scale had seemed to be the appropriate change in public policy, the appropriate expression of the government's accountability. The government differed from Shimamura not so much in principle as in degree. Both sides understood the relationship between listening and obligation, between information and action. The government knew very well that to listen is to be obligated, but it established the limits in such a manner as to exclude Shimamura and his colleagues. The result was disaster—with coercion and violence following.[1]

Worse, the government refused to "hear" after the farmers had made every effort to petition and bring to its attention their circumstances. Many farmers saw the airport affair as a breach in obligation. Their underlying complaint was not that the airport was wrong; that came later. It was the treatment they received, compounded by coercion, which seemed to them to break the social contract. They were not speaking metaphorically when they said they were defending their lives and their existence.

But there is of course a limit to how much any government, democratic or not, can respond to all the demands made upon it. For one thing, too much responsiveness simply increases the load, encouraging the government to pay attention to more and more localized interests. If a government is to maintain a larger perspective and make an effective policy for the longer run, too much fine tuning may be a mistake. In fact, any policy is bound to give offense to some, and to benefit some more than others. The problem is to find the right balance.

At the same time, the more complex a society becomes, the more the government needs to intervene in order to mediate the consequences of complexity. What is required, then, is greater intelligence and rationality rather than less, and a sphere of competence and network of jurisdictions that, if not above politics, at least allow issues to be considered on their more general merits. As the government takes on the responsibility for doing more of these things, the greater is its need for coordination and control.

These are delicate problems in all democracies. How much obligation and to whom, what kinds of accountability, the scope of effective decision-making, the nature of information available, are all matters of continuous concern. No political system ever decides finally where the boundaries are. Where they are drawn at one time can cause enough problems to require that they be changed at another. The cost of error may be high. In the worst cases the need for coordination and control takes such precedence that governments become authoritarian, turning to coercive methods to accomplish results. In other cases, the bureaucracy retains more power than is customary in parliamentary democracies. Then a challenge to its authority becomes a challenge to the legitimacy of the state. That is what happened in the Sanrizuka case. The movement took matters into its own hands and ignored political parties and other institutions in favor of extra-institutional citizen protest.

There has been a fundamental question implicit in our discussion so far. If the discrepancy between the view from above and the view from below is too great, and if the institutional mechanisms for one reason or another fail to convert the information from the bottom into obligation at the top in some appropriate mediating policy, is there then a place for extra-institutional action in democracies? In one sense the answer must be no, for the very basis of democracy is the adaptation of institutions so that such kinds of activity are not necessary. But if it is assumed that there must be a limit to the defined limits of government obligation, the answer must be yes. Without limits to the government's obligation a decision would have to please so many that it would become nugatory, and compromise would not differ much from corruption.

Hence one can expect the boundaries of conventional and legal politics to be challenged. In this the Sanrizuka movement has had much in common with environmental, ecological, and peace movements. Indeed, studies of nonviolent movements have shown that over time, as government fails to respond to their demands, the members tend to become more violence-prone. They generalize the specific objects of their campaigns to an attack on the legitimacy of government. Once dissent changes from a tactic to a principle, escalation of principle and piety follow, and violence is likely to become more acceptable.

These circumstances may not in fact shake the power of democracy or of a particular political system, but they may appear to do so. The Sanrizuka movement created a great deal of concern both within the government and outside it. Moreover, although the pattern of extra-institutional dissent is old in Japan and has led to periodic violence, causing at least one prime minister to resign, over the years the conflict has become part of an authentic radical tradition. The consequences of the Sanrizuka struggle can be measured in both human and material costs. The first phase of the airport construction was not completed until 1978, and the second phase has not yet properly begun. For an airport of sixteen hundred hectares and one runway the direct investment costs were 160 billion yen and indirect investment costs of 800 billion yen. The human costs include four policemen and two militants dead, thousands injured, and innumerable lives deeply affected by court cases, legal proceedings, and other disruptions.

Perhaps one reason why there has been so much difficulty is that coordination, control, political information, and the use of intelligence (in the largest sense of that term) are so much a function of the Japanese bureaucracy that no one much questions the bureaucracy's power. The overall benefits of that power are regarded as one of the secrets of Japan's successful economic transition. Everyone wants to applaud institutions that work so well, and the individuals responsible. The LDP is returned to power in election after election.

How DOES the government hear, and to whom does it listen? A brief outline of the institutional mechanisms of Japan as a democratic state will make it possible for us to address those questions.

Japan has a parliamentary government with two houses—the lower House of Representatives, and the upper House of Councillors. It is modeled along cabinet government principles of parliamentary supremacy. There is an elaborate network of standing committees. Most of the initiative for bills and legislation comes from the government. The Cabinet has a legislative bureau which, in collaboration with relevant ministries, is responsible for drafting basic legislative proposals. Proposals go through a complex series of steps in which they are discussed and modified by Cabinet and Liberal Democratic Party bodies before being presented to the two houses of the Diet. A bill goes from a ministry conference to an administrative vice-minister's and a political vice-minister's conference by way of the Cabinet secretary's office and then through the Cabinet itself for presentation to the Diet. At the same time it will proceed through LDP Diet committees—first the Policy Affairs Research Committee (PARC),[2] then a PARC Deliberation Commission, then the LDP Executive Council,[3] and finally the Diet Policy Committee—prior to entering the Diet itself. This ensures a smooth working arrangement between the Cabinet and the LDP. Once the bill has been passed, it is sent to the Cabinet for promulgation.

There is also a battery of advisory councils to the various ministries, as well as bureaus within the ministries. Consisting of from twenty-five to fifty members—bureaucrats, scholars, private-sector representatives, and so on—each council's job is to review important policy issues and give recommendations at the request of the minister. Council members are appointed by the minister for a renewable period of two years. In the Transportation Ministry, the one which we are most concerned with since the airport falls within its general jurisdiction, there are ten such advisory councils. In turn, these councils have counterparts in the LDP standing committees of the Diet and the PARC. Ad hoc committees of the LDP may also be established, such as the New International Airport Construction Promotion Headquarters. Similarly, ad hoc committees may be set up at the Cabinet level. One important one was the Cabinet Ministers' Discussion Group. When an influential minister, Kōno, died, the discussion group became a council.

The Aviation Council is perhaps the most single influential body in a senior consultative relationship to the Cabinet. At the end of World War II Japan had about 150 airports. For six years Japan was prohibited from owning and operating aircraft or airports. By 1953 the number of airports had dwindled to 90, of which 52 were under U.S. military control. Haneda was officially returned to Japanese control on July 1, 1952, becoming the Tokyo International Airport, but not until 1957 did Japan take over full control. In that year the number of people making international trips by air between America, Japan, and Europe exceeded those who traveled by sea.

Political Dynamics

Just a year after the handing back of Haneda in 1952 the first Japanese flag carrier was permitted to fly, and the first Aviation Council was set up in an advisory capacity to the Minister of Transportation. The council's first concerns were with the reestablishment of a Japanese aviation industry and commercial airlines. The government accepted its three-year proposals for development of the airlines. Later the emphasis shifted to development of airline facilities, including in particular the airports in "category one": Tokyo International, Osaka International, and the New Tokyo International at Narita. The council has had five chairmen since its founding. At present the chairman is Dokō Toshio, the former chairman of Keidanren, the most powerful group representing business and technology in Japan. Members include the president of Japan's two leading airline companies, Japan Airlines and All-Nippon Airways, as well as representatives of shipping, research, trading, and aviation businesses, senior banking and communications officers, and several university professors, including the professor of aviation engineering at Tokyo University, Nakaguchi Hiroshi, and Nakamura Mitsugu, professor of economics at Tokyo University. Also on the council are editorial writers from *Asahi Shimbun, Yomiuri Shimbun,* and *Mainichi Shimbun.*

Several members of the Aviation Council sit on the Transportation Policy Council, which has thirty-three members and is concerned with Japan's overall policy on transportation. This council, established in 1970 and now headed by a well-known economist, is a completely separate entity from the Transportation Council, which was established in 1949 and includes representatives from bodies such as the Atomic Energy Council. The Transportation Council's members, mostly ex-bureaucrats and technicians, work full-time in their positions on the council.[4]

The Japanese system is highly consultative within specific ensembles of jurisdictions. A great deal of discussion takes place among the various Cabinet and Diet bodies, and these groups heavily influence both the drafting of legislation and its implementation. By the same token, the power of the ministries and of the bureaucrats within them is much enhanced because of the complex process of decision-making. Once a decision is arrived at, it stops being "political" and becomes "technical." The transition from political to technical effectively removes a piece of legislation from the direct questioning and meddling of parliament. Hence, despite the fact that the Sanrizuka movement was political in the most direct sense, "politics" appeared to be, from higher up, simply a factor complicating technical matters, particularly coordination and construction.

There was, of course, a more elaborate hidden agenda. Building and constructing the Sanrizuka airport was not, especially for the officials in the Transportation Ministry, simply a technical problem. Rather, it represented Japan's coming of age as an industrial power and as a newly independent political entity. A completely new facility attuned to the jet (and the supersonic) age was meant to be a symbol of national pride and independence. In both the wider symbolic sense and in the narrower technical aspects, it was a perfect project for a ministry. But this did not mean that there was smooth sailing even on the government side. The airport also symbolized, as we have seen, a major change in domestic priorities, one of which was to push small farmers off the land by deliberate design after having brought many of them there by equally deliberate design. The effects of that policy switch were already visible in Chiba Prefecture, much of which had become an industrial slum. If democratic decision-making involved elaborate consultative procedures, these were all at the top; the prefecture level was the cut-off point. In the Sanrizuka case the lack of consultations from below was clear enough. The farmers were not the only ones who had been ignored. Neither the governor of Chiba Prefecture not the mayor of Narita City was provided with proper advance information. The public meeting at which the Cabinet decision was presented lasted for about five minutes. Farmers and their families were told that they would have to get out, and that they would be appropriately compensated.

Even so, the government's decision was not especially badly received. About half the population of the area was initially in favor of the airport. More followed when the government offered to provide proprietorship of concessions and shops in the airport to some of those who sold their land. From the standpoint of Imai Yoshifumi, the extremely intelligent and capable chairman of the Airport Authority during the most difficult days of confrontation, the policy he followed was eminently correct.

For the government the airport was also an experiment in Japanese planning. Since the Meiji period, economic improvement has had very high priority. Japan was the first country to engage in indicative planning. After all, the only resources Japan has in abundance are an extraordinarily well cultivated intelligence, a high level of education, and the shrewd use of both to mobilize the abilities of its population. Otherwise, lacking in raw materials, overpopulated, with only about fifteen percent of its land arable, Japan would appear to have grim prospects indeed. To survive requires continuous and careful scrutiny of the relative efficiencies of capital and investment in each productive sector. The costs of errors in innovation are extremely high. It is not a multiple-chance society.

Responsibilities for planning are concentrated mainly in the bureaucracy. The best brains in the country find their way into the ranks of the senior civil service; the best in the service find their way into the most important ministries; and within the ministries, despite a system of regular promotion and age grades, it is the best who rise to the top—and not only to the top of the civil service. Many spill out of the ministries and into the Diet.

The entire system can be defined in terms of jurisdictions, competence, scope, excellence, and performance. Even the people most hostile to it have to admit that the bureaucracy has been extremely successful when defined in these terms. It is able to recruit remarkable and intelligent people. Excellence, power, and prestige go together. The meritocratic hierarchy is based on open competition, both for the educational system and for the higher civil service. The best high school students go to the University of Tokyo Law Department. Carefully screened from a pool of the best applicants, the best of these become candidates for the senior civil service. This is, of course, an exaggeration. Not all the "best" people go to the University of Tokyo; some choose not to. Nor do all the "best" graduates choose careers in the civil service. But in general the pattern compares with the system of the *grandes ecoles* and elite recruitment in the French civil service. Both systems rely on bureaucratic elites determined by competitive recruitment and each has exceptional political autonomy. Compared to France, however, Japan has a bureaucratic elite that is much less politically accountable. Different, too, is the method of decision-making. In the Japanese case, the desire to maximize political intelligence requires that the bureaucracy have a relatively high degree of autonomy. Bureaucratic jurisdictions are relatively sealed off from political pressures. Yet officials maintain closer and more personal links with parliamentary commissions, committees, and political bodies than is common in most Western societies.

Political parties, especially under the long reign of the Liberal Democrats, are less inclined to exploit their legislative powers of review and questioning than in the West. Except for a few important leaders of powerful factions, party members have a smaller share in making important decisions than civil servants. The LDP is made up of a broad coalition of factions. The faction with the greatest number of supporters inside and outside the Diet is the most powerful. Supporters are attracted largely on the basis of how much money the faction can obtain and how successful its leader is in gaining and exploiting revenues. Scandal is endemic; the most famous is the Tanaka case. (The scandal did not prevent the Tanaka faction from remaining the most important in the party, however.) Thus the political marketplace is, in good measure, an arena for raising revenue from the special interests most able and willing to pay. This crude political marketplace is balanced by a relatively uncorrupt and sophisticated bureaucracy with a degree of discretionary power unknown in Western democracies. The Cabinet mediates between the two by means of its complex system of advisory councils.

Those at the top of the bureaucracy constitute a functional elite. All are recruited through a highly competitive examination. Within each ministry the career course is precisely defined. A sub-section chief will spend six years in his post, a section chief seven, and a department chief up to ten years before becoming, if selected, a deputy bureau chief.

University connections link up diverse jurisdictions and networks of power. School cliques (*gakubatsu*) are much more important in Japan than old-boy networks in the United States. Most bureaucrats were graduated from the University of Tokyo Law Department (a few from Kyoto University).[5] In the Diet, too, University of Tokyo graduates predominate among those drafting bills. One can say, then, that Japanese party politics is dominated by factions and decision-making is dominated by bureaucrats; in turn, both are dominated by cliques (*batsu*) and cliques by *gakubatsu*.

The most successful bureaucrats go on to higher appointments after they retire. Some take lucrative positions in industry; some move into other branches of government. A high proportion of Cabinet officials are former civil servants. Almost a third of Diet members are former bureaucrats. Informal networks link organs of government as well as bureaucratic jurisdictions. Former high-ranking officials of the Ministry of Transportation are now in such posts as president of the Airport Authority, director of tourism, and senior executive for Japan Airlines.

Within the bureaucracy regular discussion is virtually mandatory. Before a decision is made everyone is consulted; all views are aired.

This means that no one person is a decision-maker; decisions are truly collective. It means, too, that everyone is bound by them. Such a system creates problems of coordination between jurisdictions, but it is assumed that the consultation will enable the most rational course to emerge and prevail. The jurisdiction is itself a limit, a sphere of discretion; decisions can be made without too much popular pressure. The person at the top is responsible mainly for seeing to it that the decision is carried out. Once made, a decision is very difficult to reverse. Review is unnecessary unless exceptional circumstances arise, since the decision would come out the same way a second time.

In general the principles of bureaucracy in Japan are closer to the French, the Prussian, and the English traditions than to the American. The implicit premise is that a concentration of intelligence is necessary for effective government, and that a concentration of power is needed for this process to work. In contrast, in the American system a great deal of emphasis is placed on the "service" part of the civil service. But comparisons are not very useful here. For the most part the Japanese bureaucracy remains distinctively Japanese, despite the fact that its modern version, codified in the Meiji Constitution, was modeled after the principles of Western constitutional monarchy. Traditionally the bureaucracy always had a privileged position and shared to some extent the emperor's supreme power; civil servants stood, to a degree, "above politics." This principle remains embedded in the modern conception. In spirit and meaning, however, the principle is quite different from the ideal of the disinterested civil service that is common to Western practice and dear to the Weberian scholar.[6]

The power of the bureaucracy, then, has remained very well entrenched for some time. The public considers the bureaucracy to be serious and upright. If fault can be found, the criticism might be that the bureaucracy is somewhat lacking in versatility. Given its structure of recruitment and insulation this last point should not come as a great surprise.[7] Certainly it would not surprise the Sanrizuka farmers, who would put it rather less politely.

Along with a great deal of power at the top of the structure there is an absence of power at the bottom, at the local—that is, prefectural—level. The problem is one of substance rather than form. Organization charts will show an elaborate network of local institutions, including school districts, cooperatives, city assemblies, wards, and so on. But the local government system is one in which a derivative governmental largesse or spoils is distributed by local committees manipulated by bosses representing the factions and parties to which they belong. Such a system greatly reduces the independence of villagers. They have learned that councillors, mayors, and minor local government officials need to be handled gently and with respect.

Closely connected is Japan's lack of an effective system of due process. Compared to the West, Japan is a society without lawyers. On the one hand this encourages honorableness in negotiating. But the dearth of lawyers makes it difficult for individuals to protect their rights, especially against the government. That is what particularly upsets Ogawa Kakichi—he is fed up with the way mediation occurs through family, business, or political connections. Such mediation, especially in hamlets, provides exceptional opportunities for political bosses to serve as go-betweens. It leads to manipulation and corruption, among other things. Yet one must take care not to offend the bosses. Indeed, recourse to the law is almost the surest way to offend, and most offensive of all is a suit against the government. Moreover, the individual rarely can win. Legal recourse is, then, truly a court of last appeal (save conflict itself).

The process of mediation through influence and manipulation can be seen in the case of Ishibashi. Once he had decided to accept offers to negotiate with the government, there were informal visits, drinks charged to the Airport Authority, arranged trips. A network of social relationships began to evolve that would have surely turned into a network of obligations and compromises. Ishibashi, who understands politics very well, saw this as the only way back for the farmers. For other Hantai Dōmei leaders, however, this was the way down for the Hantai Dōmei. These practices are as old as politics in Japan, and if one acts too differently one is likely to give offense, as did Tomura's father when he took a case against corrupt politicians to the local authorities. Where due process is lacking, the alternative is a politics of principle, which can quickly become the politics of no compromise. And the politics of no compromise requires one to turn one's back on the legitimacy of the state itself.

How WAS the original decision to build the airport made? By looking at the methods of consultation and mediation that were used and at how the political party system, the interested clienteles, and the bureaucracy worked together, we can begin to understand the different perspectives of the groups involved and the different kinds of information the groups represent. The parties, which represent a broad spectrum of the public, or populist information, had their greatest say at the beginning. From then on, the interested clienteles (business, military, and the like), who constitute interest information, and the bureaucracy, who represent more technical information, had the lion's share of the decision-making. Once the Cabinet decision had been made, from the standpoint of the Ministry of Transportation, which had the primary responsibility for building and running the airport, the matter became a technical rather than a political problem, one that primarily involved coordination between ministries and other governmental bodies.

To some extent, of course, each group within the government *must* select the clientele to which it will be responsive. The more responsibilities a government has, the more necessary it becomes to establish limits. The limits can never be fixed, though; they are always shifting, depending on the issue itself, public opinion, the groups and factions involved. In any particular instance the government might draw the limits too narrowly. Indeed, as virtually everyone in the government now agrees, that is what happened in Sanrizuka. The government was saddled with a predicament of its own making and from which, once a certain point had been reached, it could not extricate itself.

What began as legitimate redress of citizens, then, became (at least for those farmers in the Hantai Dōmei) legitimate violence against the state. The Sanrizuka case opens the question of what the government and the public should do when the limits of obligation are blurred and public listening restricted. Such a question is only asked after the event, after some unanticipated difficulties have revealed failures in current procedures. Misunderstanding is virtually assured. What at one point may appear to be an exaggerated demand may turn out to be a well-founded concern. Hidden agendas become visible, and visible ones may be obscured by the flow of events. At the earliest stages in the Sanrizuka case, when internal politics between party and bureaucracy played a crucial part, most farmers were oblivious to what was going on. The farmers were interested in the airport not as a symbol of Japan's industrial coming of age but rather a symbol of imperialism and militarism, a view the bureaucrats regarded as rhetorical and irrelevant. Both sides were in a sense correct. On the matter of militarism, farmers are more than ever convinced that they were right, as remilitarization proceeds. At the time, though, the government saw the airport as a matter of internal conflict between politicians and bureaucrats, whose preoccupation with each other was exacerbated by the initial consultative procedures employed by each group. The consultative process served to screen out "irrelevant" information from farmers as so much noise.

Despite the Vietnam war, the government considered military use for the airport as a remote contingency at best. The equation of economic, political, and military power was ignored. Except for some opposition from JSP politicians who indeed did see their connection, the bias of politics from the top was on where the airport should be built, not least because a project of this magnitude was bound to involve both spoils and corruption. "Humane" considerations too prevailed when the site was changed from Tomisato. Only after it was located at Sanrizuka did it become more than a technical problem. Few questions were asked; none dealt with large issues of purpose. Even after violence escalated, the airport matter was regarded as so politically residual that the government's most important relations with farmers remained within the jurisdiction of the Airport Authority and the governor of the prefecture. The question is, why?

Several answers are plausible. One is that local government in Japan consists mostly of mediating networks at the end of a pipeline of government jurisdictions and financial disbursements, the residual part of a spoils system. It lacks local resources and official power, and it has particularly narrow limits to effective participation. A second answer is that the LDP, because of its long reign, is shorter on popular representation (and populist information) than on interest representation, particularly those interests connected to business, commerce, and industry. A third is that political intelligence and the sense of a public interest is so concentrated in the bureaucracy that political problems are immediately converted into problems of technical information, which fall within the appropriate jurisdiction of the bureaucracy. The third reason may of course be due in part to the first two, or the first two may be a function of the third. After all, the bureaucracy has had a privileged place as a functional elite for a very long time.

One of the reasons why the airport was considered a technical problem rather than a political one was, simply, that it was indeed a technical problem, and of mammoth proportions. Politics was involved at every stage, of course, but as long as the bureaucracy was seen as the appropriate jurisdiction for decision-making, the more hidden agendas—who would benefit, how various interests could be

Political Dynamics

placated, how the powerful factions and their leaders could be satisfied—were obscured. There was as well great antagonism between politicians and ex-bureaucrats in the Cabinet. Politicians tended to be of more plebeian origins and were hostile to the ex-bureaucrats, who were highly educated. The latter were concerned about the quality of the soil, distance from Tokyo, availability of land, and other technical matters. Politicians were more sensitive to the involvements of officials from the Metropolitan Consolidation Committee in the Cabinet, the Prefecture, and diverse ministries, committees within the LDP favoring promotion of the airport, the advisory committees, and so on. In a sense the bureaucrats won. All these matters were considered to be part of a coordination problem, admittedly delicate because it involved all sorts of relationships between groups and persons, but a coordination problem nevertheless. Only at times did the hidden agenda emerge, and when it did it was crude and brutal.

The dual nature of the prefectural government also has an impact on the way in which a technical problem unfolds politically. The prefecture is, on the one hand, an instrument of national government ministries. Three-fourths of its revenue comes from the central government. On the other hand, the prefecture constitutes the order of local government jurisdictions. In this latter role it is much closer to the people of the area, and its officials are more responsive to their needs, than is national government. Indeed, at one point several governors had leftist orientations. Not a few governors have shown considerable opposition to government policy, particularly comprehensive planning schemes which negatively affected their prefectures. The position of governors is difficult and their powers ambiguous. In the case of the airport, there was tension from the start about how best to respond to opposition. The prefectural authorities were pulled in opposite directions by the public sentiments in the prefecture and the responsibilities imposed by central government.

Such tension was exacerbated, too, because those in the central bureaucracy were what might be called "impact oriented": they wished to make a positive impact on their careers by their job performance. That is, they were less concerned with what they were asked to do than with how to do it effectively and so to help their careers and reputations. The prefectural authorities were more concerned with social consequences. Caught in the middle between the need to mediate and the need to administer, they saw the need for proceeding cautiously, while central bureaucratic authorities were anxious to get the job done.

THREE DIFFERENT PHASES can be distinguished in the decision-making process—political, administrative, and implementative. The first dealt with the airport itself within the larger context of the change in government policy decided in 1960. The second occurred after the decision was made to construct the airport and the Ministry of Transportation was given the major responsibility. The final phase involved cooperation between the Airport Authority, a government corporation within the Transportation Ministry, and the prefecture government.

The first period began in 1962, when the Ikeda government decided on a second, inland airport for the greater metropolitan Tokyo area, and lasted until 1966, when the Cabinet shifted the site to Sanrizuka. During the period between the formation of the original study group and the final site selection, a variety of agencies, committees, and other structures were involved, linking the LDP, the Diet, the bureaucracy, and the Cabinet. The politics of transportation was at its height. Special urgency was added to the negotiations by several major airplane disasters (All-Nippon Airways, Canadian Pacific, and BOAC). The Transportation Committee of the LDP established a special subcommittee, the New Airport Construction Promotion Headquarters, to try and facilitate construction. Pressure from Japan Airlines and other major foreign companies increased; pilots were complaining of the small size of Haneda. It was a time when air networks were dramatically expanding, both domestically and internationally. Supersonic transport was considered to be extremely likely, and Japan Airlines requested major subsidies to make it competitive with other flag carriers and to enable Tokyo to become one of the world's main centers of commercial and international travel. International prestige, Japan's future as a world industrial power, and Tokyo as a major world center were all considerations in the decision, seen from the top.

The transition from the political phase to the administrative one was by no means smooth. Many Cabinet ministers, but not all, were former civil servants. During this first phase there had been a long battle between one of the more "political" Cabinet ministers and the ministers more likely to see the problem in bureaucratic or technical terms. Of the people most directly involved, four were of particular significance. One was Kawashima Shōjirō, vice-chairman of the

Political Dynamics

LDP, who came from Chiba; another was Ayabe Kentarō, minister of transportation; Governor Tomonō of Chiba was the third; and finally there was the minister of construction, Kōno Ichirō. Kōno, an old-time political boss, had contempt for bureaucracy generally and thus was particularly involved in this issue.

Kōno was the first son of a large landowner from a hamlet called, appropriately enough, Narita, in Kanagawa Prefecture, where his father had served as village headman and chairman of the Kanagawa prefectural assembly. Although the father was wealthy and an influential political boss, his mother tried to convince him to follow more respectable pursuits. Kōno tried to get into the Engineering Department of Waseda University, but after failing twice he went into political science instead. After graduation he took an examination to become a reporter on *Asahi Shimbun,* but he failed there too because he could not pass the English examination. However, helped by an influential journalist from his home town, he was made a reporter in the economic section, covering the Ministry of Agriculture and Forestry, and then moved up to the political section covering the Cabinet and the political parties. He resigned in 1931 to become a secretary to the agricultural minister in the Inugai Cabinet and was elected a Dietman in 1932, winning eleven consecutive elections. His main interest continued to be agriculture and he particularly resented bureaucrats and military officials. After the war he remained in politics and was extremely important in Liberal and Progressive party affairs. Then he suffered a period of political reverses and disappeared from the political scene for a while to become the head of a fishing company. When the Liberal Party formed a political coalition with the new Democratic Party, Kōno became agricultural minister. He was an important mediator during the formation of the Liberal Democratic Party in 1955, and continued to hold his ministry under successive prime ministers. An aggressive figure and a skilled manipulator of LDP factions, he had many friends and many enemies. He was an excellent negotiator; he had been responsible, for example, for successful dealings with the Soviet Union on a fisheries agreement and, more important, Japanese-Russian normalization, meeting with Khrushchev on several occasions. The Yoshida school of the LDP opposed the negotiation and Kōno became known as pro-Soviet and anti-U.S.

At any rate, in 1962 he accepted the post of minister of construction in the Ikeda Cabinet. He was by then an extremely popular figure, and very influential in the areas of agricultural policy and road construction. Some accused him of being high-handed or authoritarian. There was no doubt that he interfered in whatever issues interested him.

The factional conflicts within the LDP as well as the differences in point of view about the airport centered for a time on Kōno. For one thing the factional leaders like Kōno play a crucial role in securing the position of political vice-minister for a key member of the House of Councillors or the House of Representatives. Dietmen particularly want the vice-minister position in the Finance Ministry, because of its role in budgeting, and in MITI (the Ministry of International Trade and Industry), the Ministry of Agriculture, and the Ministry of Construction, because of the role all three play in relation to the private sector. Being in such a position helps a Dietman get reelected because as vice-minister he can promote the interests of his prefecture and his constituency.

Very quickly the four-man committee—Kawashima, Ayabe, Tomonō, and Kōno—appointed by Prime Minister Ikeda to facilitate site selection and construction became the venue for three different struggles. One was between the officials of the Transportation Ministry on one side and Kōno and Kawashima Shōjirō on the other. Kōno and Kawashima, both political faction leaders, strongly disliked the bureaucrats. A second conflict was between Ayabe Kentaro and Kōno, in part because the former was minister of transportation but also because he represented those political figures who had come from the ranks of the bureaucrats, the so-called Yoshida school leaders. The Ikeda Cabinet was a delicate balance between the two, the factional politicians and the ex–civil servants. These conflicts were exacerbated by a third problem, differences of opinion about what kind of site was needed and where it should be located. Ayabe saw the issue as a technical one involving available air space, security, the capital already invested in Haneda, and so on. His staff prepared a report suggesting, among other possibilities, Tomisato and Kasumigaura. Anxious to move ahead, Ayabe began negotiating with the Finance Ministry for a budget to establish the Airport Authority, unfortunately neglecting to inform the other members of the four-man committee. Kōno in particular was furious when he found out. He thought it would be impossible to relocate the fifteen hundred households on the Tomisato site. The Aviation Council also recommended the Tomisato site, but Kōno remained adamant.

The three conflicts were not without wider political repercussions. Each time a new site was mentioned, there were some who were dismayed and some who were delighted. Kōno favored a proposal called the Kisarazu reclamation plan, part of the Tokyo Bay Reclamation Neopolis Plan proposed by an industrialists' conference. The chairman of the conference, Matsunaga Yasuzaemon, was one of the two most powerful political bosses behind the scenes. The proposal involved the reclamation of about two thousand hectares in front of the Japan Self-Defense Force base at Kisarazu, a plan opposed by Ayabe for a number of reasons, among them that there would be aviation control problems and that Haneda Airport would be adversely affected. Haneda was so inadequate, Kōno replied, that it should be turned into a vegetable market. In turn, Ayabe favored a land reclamation scheme at Urayasu, not far from Haneda, but this too ran into trouble with aviation control and with noise pollution as well.

The stalemate allowed rumors to fly thick and fast, so much so that Governor Tomonō of Chiba pleaded that a site be selected quickly because people in the prefecture were becoming too upset. Then suddenly, in July 1965, Minister Kōno died. By November Tomisato had been chosen as the site. Since Prime Minister Sato had promised Tomonō that he would obtain the governor's approval for a site six months before any final decision was made, Tomonō felt betrayed. Other influential people, including the secretary general of the LDP, also were unhappy with the way the decision had been made. It was as if, after Kōno's death, the committee members felt that the political side could be ignored in favor of the administrative. Some of the politicians favored a different site, Kasumigaura, where the problem of noise pollution would have been minimized.

One change in the decision-making process that at first seemed to be an improvement—the replacement of Ayabe by a new minister of transportation, Nakamura Torata, in June 1965—actually made things worse. Nakamura assumed that if he simply went ahead with the airport, the conflicting political positions held by influential politicians and bosses could be mediated. So concerned was he with the political problem at the top that he ignored the political problems at the bottom. He paid virtually no attention to local residents or to the mayors and other local officials most involved.

This concern at the top with the top is understandable in light of the way politics and administration intersect in Japan. But it obscured another side of political life that had been rapidly changing. The growing complexity of Japanese social and political institutions had shifted a good deal of responsibility onto the prefecture. It was not only the governors who were strong-minded and sometimes radical; mayors, too, were frequently members of the JSP or the JCP. Partly because they were outside the main lines of patronage and factional support offered by the LDP, they had to establish stronger local bastions. One result was a growing independence at the local level and the need for closer consultation with village bosses, a change that was never fully understood by the Transportation Ministry. When airport matters were placed jointly in the hands of the Airport Authority and Governor Tomonō, relations between the two remained uneasy. In Chiba, local revenues resulting from industrial development, much of it on reclaimed land, enabled the governor to take a more independent line.

On November 18, the Cabinet chose Tomisato for the new airport site. The town councils of Tomisato and Yachimata were opposed to the decision. On December 21 Shisui Town Council came out against the decision and on December 24 so did Shibayama Town Council. The Japan Socialist Party also came out in opposition. On February 7, 1966, about fifteen hundred anti-airport people, with the support of members of labor unions, marched to the Prefectural Government Hall and broke in. Kawashima, then vice–prime minister, asked the chief Cabinet secretary, Hashimoto, not to proceed with the Tomisato plan. It was around this time that the three aircraft disasters occurred and the matter became more urgent.

When the decision was made to move the site to Sanrizuka, the size of the proposed airport was halved. Sanrizuka, in contrast to Tomisato, had a small population and had the additional advantage of being in an area where the imperial estate and government land could be made available.[8] The prime minister met with the emperor, ostensibly for another reason but basically to inform him that the government wanted the imperial estate. This upset the Imperial Household Agency a great deal since they had not been consulted in advance. Finally, on July 4, 1966, the Cabinet officially decided on Sanrizuka.

Before the month was out, the Airport Authority was set up and a branch office was established in Narita City almost immediately. Ayabe now became head of the New Airport Construction Promotion Headquarters in the LDP. Another transportation minister, Ōhashi Takeo, replaced Ayabe's successor; Ōhashi outlined the basic plan to be followed, which scheduled completion of the first phase by the end of fiscal year 1970 and the final phase by the end of fiscal year 1973. In September 1967 the scheme was roundly criticized by the Aviation Policy Research Group, a body consisting of aviation experts, on the grounds that the new plan did not provide for enough runways, that it did not give sufficient access to downtown Tokyo, and that it would quickly become obsolete and in a few years would require a third airport to be built, a view shared by the new prime minister, Tanaka. The final plan for the airport site included 243 hectares owned by the national government, 152 hectares of other publicly owned land, and 670 hectares of private property owned by 357 households, for a total of 1,065 hectares.

Even before the Sanrizuka decision was announced by the Cabinet in 1966, rumors had leaked. On June 28 the Sanrizuka Hantai Dōmei was organized, and a few days later the Shibayama Hantai Dōmei was formed. On August 15 about one thousand people—farmers, members of labor organizations, and JSP and JCP National Diet and Prefectural Assembly members—held a peace rally; three hundred sat in the prefectural government building. On October 10, 1967, the Airport Authority went to the site and hammered three posts into the ground as a signal that the outer-rim survey would begin. Zengakuren chairman Akiyama Katsuyuki came to Sanrizuka and visited the Komaino hut. On November 17 the first ten hectares were bought from ten owners.

The political phase was largely a matter of politics in the classic sense—that is, a matter of disputes among politicians and a tug of war between ex-bureaucrats and more ordinary politicians. Disputes centered on personal hostilities, as in the conflict between Kōno and Ayabe, and on the bureaucrats' challenging of the old-time political fiefdoms. Omitted were what might be called the real politics, the underlying structural problems of the changes being wrought in Japanese society as well as the impact of external relations on internal Japanese politics.

The government never saw external issues—particularly those associated with U.S.-Japan treaty revision, the AMPO riots of 1960, and the elaboration of radical sects—as having any rightful place in the airport protest. All along, the government has made a sharp distinction between farmers' interests, which they acknowledge, and militants, whom they regard as exerting a negative influence on the farmers who would like to negotiate. The strategy of the government has been to separate farmers from militants and then to negotiate with farmers as a group and as individuals. For negotiation to become possible, however, principles must deflate and self-interest must become primary. The government's strategy has been to wait for the deflation of principles. Most officials now agree that it was confrontation that made the alliance effective precisely by enabling principles to be articulated.

Was there another acceptable strategy at the time? Given the political fighting and the delay of the decision for half a decade, during which period the larger political issues of Vietnam and militarism became identified with the airport, some would say no. Once the decision had been made and the Airport Authority took charge, the main preoccupation was with the coordination of activities among different ministries and agencies.

From the Airport Authority's perspective, the Finance Ministry was extremely difficult to deal with. Its uncooperativeness resulted in delays in financing and in obtaining subsidiary grants. The problem was compounded when several ministries were involved in the same matter. Building roads into the Sanrizuka area, for example, had to be done in cooperation with the Ministry of Construction, and all arrangements involving facilities and equipment had to be coordinated with the police. (Militants often blocked the roads.) The Ministry of Finance, then, had to be consulted by two other ministries (Construction and Transportation) and the financing worked out. The police, including those under the auspices of Chiba Prefecture, were largely autonomous. It was they who decided how many men would be required and settled on a strategy of confrontation. Since each ministry is itself an autonomous body, each with jurisdictions that had to be consulted, it was extremely difficult to adapt quickly to changing needs.

The public perception of the inflexibility of the bureaucracy takes on new meaning in this context. It is not that the bureaucratic mind is inflexible; rather, the consultative pattern within jurisdictions and the collective decision-making process make interagency or ministerial cooperation difficult. Many important matters then have to go to the Cabinet, but this, in turn, reveals an inability to work things out at a lower level. Ministers who cannot show progress are obviously inadequate. In the Sanrizuka case there was on the one hand a tendency to push things to the top for decision-making where coordination was required, but because of the political consequences of this there was on the other hand an equal and opposite tendency to push things down again to lower levels.

Such contradictory tendencies made decisive action difficult and also made it more difficult for agreement to be reached in the first place. For example, those at the lowest levels, the prefectural government and the Airport Authority, were given great responsibility for land acquisition and airport construction. But the Airport Authority had the pressures of the Minister of Transportation on it, the latter seeking results within the framework of a rapidly receding timetable, mounting costs, and increasing scrutiny from the Ministry of Finance. Meanwhile, Governor Tomonō, concerned with the people in the area, realized the need to exhaust all possible efforts to negotiate before proceeding with confrontations. Yet he had little room to actually negotiate, especially after Tomura was hit on the head and had the revelation that the government was determined to go ahead. Tomonō could only hope that he could persuade people to give up. Perhaps his most important contribution was to refuse to allow the provisions of the Land Acquisition Act to be applied. The Act would have allowed the government to take land by force without compensating the farmers. The various confrontations over land were in fact not over the expropriation of lands that farmers had refused to give up but rather over land being defended by the Hantai Dōmei which had already been sold to the government.

From the perspective of the Airport Authority, the main problem was not farmers but sects. In the year before the sects moved in, the government's policy was extremely successful; with the arrival of Zengakuren the situation changed completely. Indeed, both Tomura and the government knew that it was the sects which had saved the Hantai Dōmei. From the government's point of view the sects had no business there. They were revolutionaries and the farmers were not, no matter how radical the latter seemed to have become. Farmers, bound by village ties and obligations, were fighting for their lands. Sects were using the space, the physical terrain, to play war games, to act out a revolutionary fantasy. Moreover, the police were powerless to stop them: there is no law to prevent militants from taking the train or the bus to Sanrizuka. Indeed, there is no law to keep them from going to the airport. The police could only try to protect surveyors or government officials or construction workers who had to get on with their jobs. From a police standpoint, the security questions were like those in any large-scale confrontation. Prefectural police bore the main responsibility for peace and good order in the area surrounding the airport; Airport Authority police had jurisdiction over airport security itself and the adjacent area.

The Airport Authority regarded Tomura as the true leader of the movement. He was considered to be basically a pacifist who had moved toward the New Left sects as support dwindled for the Hantai Dōmei. The Airport Authority officials treated him with respect, as a Christian and a man of principle. (For Kitahara, however, they had contempt: their view was that he owned a tiny and not very successful kimono shop and he, unlike Tomura, was a totally insignificant person with no reason to be involved other than an opportunistic one.) But once Tomura came to see the airport as the state, which made it impossible for the Airport Authority to negotiate with the Hantai Dōmei as a body, he refused to consider the merits of the airport plan, the inadequacy of Haneda, and the difficulties of landfill in Tokyo Bay. He was, in official eyes, too preoccupied with the military aspects when in fact other aspects were far more important.

In looking back on what had happened, the man who was head of the Airport Authority for eight of the most strenuous years of confrontation, a former Aviation Bureau chief, put the main burden for the confrontations on the sects. Left alone, the Airport Authority could have handled the situation very well: it had successfully negotiated with almost all the farmers. He doubted that it would have been useful to engage in more local consultations. Consultations at the beginning would have changed very little, for the farmers had their own interests and there was no way to negotiate over the existence of the airport. Only the terms of relocation and compensation were negotiable, for which the means were always available.

Once the Airport Authority had been put in charge, the preoccupation was with such details as rapid transit, roads, construction of an industrial area, flight paths, construction of the pipeline for fuel, provision for rural needs, and so on. The Airport Authority was a new body. Its leadership consisted of people taken from other departments. Organized under three main heads—construction, operations, and general affairs—the Authority could not easily coordinate its activities. The senior cadres of the Airport Authority had all had considerable and diverse experience, but the situation was one that their previous experience and careers had not fully prepared them for. Moreover, the problem of coordination with other ministries, was, as already indicated, complex. Finally, in 1977, after the Airport Authority had failed to work out plans for the promotion of agriculture in the Sanrizuka area—a problem that required cooperation between the Ministry of Transportation and the Ministry of Agriculture—the Cabinet was asked to solve the matter. The Cabinet instructed the Airport Authority to have the airport open by the end of the next fiscal year and provided the necessary authority to the Ministry of Transportation to enable them to negotiate over irrigation, land resettlement, and other matters appropriate to the preservation of agriculture in the area.

Political Dynamics

Even during the political phase, local people did not have an effective working relationship with the government through their intermediaries, the political parties, and through parliamentary involvement, although some JSP and JCP Dietmen did try to be responsive. All the major parties were basically in favor of the airport. Local institutions had no way of making their own predispositions felt, other than township and city assembly resolutions against the airport. With arm-twisting by LDP politicians higher up and by prefectural authorities, these were in any case reversed.

When the technical phase began, after Minister Kōno's death, the politics of confrontation occurred within a year. The JCP was expelled, and the JSP lost influence in the area. The Cabinet took little official notice of the problem, although various prime ministers considered completion more or less urgent. Eventually, with some tacit support from above, a younger Dietman, Katō Kōichi, was able to act as a go-between. The son of an old LDP politician, Katō had been close to Prime Minister Ōhira (who was not particularly interested in the airport affair). The Dietman was of that generation deeply affected by the student movement and had, during his student days, been close to the Bund. On two separate occasions he was instrumental in initiating secret discussions between the Airport Authority and individuals from the Hantai Dōmei. The first time these involved Shima of the Youth Corps. Leaked to the press by an LDP Dietman, they aroused a furor within the Hantai Dōmei. The second time was the meetings between Ministry of Transportation and Airport Authority officials and Ishibashi, Uchida, and others, ending with Chūkaku-ha exposure and the resignation of Ishibashi and Uchida from their Hantai Dōmei offices, as we have seen.

WHAT HAS the government learned from what has happened at Sanrizuka? For one thing, it has learned that a public must be prepared, different sectors of the public consulted, and the mobilization of support orchestrated before a large-scale public venture of this kind is undertaken. The lesson is visible in the way in which the government has been negotiating over the New Osaka International Airport. But for the most part, the government regards the Sanrizuka struggle as unique, a consequence of a particular time and of some unfortunate episodes, not requiring any drastic change in current practice or procedures. The government is not about to alter the structure of political participation, especially at local levels. Whether local government will become more important is less a matter of principle than a function of the pressures it confronts and the responsibilities it assumes. If there is an institutional gap, a kind of political vacuum at the bottom, those at the top do not perceive it. Quite the contrary: factional politics, local bosses, political parties, the network of branch offices of the parties, prefectural authorities responsive to lower echelons, all seem to them to be perfectly adequate to handle legitimate politics. Only if the sects are involved, or the citizen protest movements that are closely linked with sects, and only if these are granted legitimacy, does a problem arise. But groups favoring revolution, or groups that stand in opposition to the broad majority of voters, put themselves outside the range of institutional politics. If they resort to strategies ranging from violence to public mobilization, that is done on their own initiative and does not require a structural response within the political system.

By and large, then, one must say no, the government has not learned anything specific from this struggle, and it does not see what should or could be learned. There were special circumstances. The time was unusual. And airports are, after all, attractive targets for all those groups opposed to most of the things governments do. But this does not mean that the government has learned nothing. Rather, it now recognizes that the political process includes more than parties, factions, the bureaucracy, and interest groups. Local authorities and citizen protest groups are—or must be—included as well.

If one asks whether or not the airport itself is satisfactory, the answer is also a qualified no. The airport is too small, and will be even after the second stage is completed. Construction of the Shinkansen, the bullet train to Tokyo, is in abeyance. The pipeline for bringing in fuel is being built, but very slowly. It is not the solution it was hoped to be.

Local government may in fact be more flexible, more ready to try different tactics and to learn from what has happened, than the national government. A case known as the "1.1 billion yen scandal," involving the construction of a pipeline, is an interesting example of local government's willingness to try a new approach. In 1971 the vice-president of the Airport Authority, who had been a mayor and the chairman of the National Town Mayors Association, hoped to conclude agreements with the mayors of towns that would be affected by the construction of a pipeline, roads, and storage facilities. Involving Chiba and Ibaragi Prefectures, the agreements would have infringed on plans for a national pipeline then under construction. The "scandal" occurred when Mayor Araki of Chiba City said that before he would give his approval to the pipeline construction the

Airport Authority would have to establish a committee of experts to discuss feasibility, safety, and other matters over which there had been public concern and protest. He also wanted the Authority to authorize compensation of 1.1 billion yen to Chiba City for environmental purposes, building community centers, and so on. Without this fund, the city would refuse to allow the Airport Authority to use the 11 kilometers of roads in the city necessary to build the pipeline.

Here, then, is an example of local authorities responding to public reactions to environmental problems, in effect blackmailing the Airport Authority. It suggests that local authority is not as helpless as it might appear. Indeed, Mayor Araki won. The Airport Authority agreed to his terms, which included more than the compensation scheme. The Ministry of Transportation was upset by the agreement; the Ministry of Finance was outraged. Relations between Chiba Prefecture and Ibaragi were strained. When a new political vice-minister of the Ministry of Transportation took office he had to make amends. Concerned about the disputes and recognizing that the government would be dependent on the cooperation of city authorities for a variety of national projects requiring civic support, he apologized for the government's mistakes and traveled around the country trying to persuade people that the problem of national and local disputes was based on a misunderstanding rather than a lack of sincerity on the government's part.

The questions raised by the Sanrizuka struggle are not easily answered. How can the institutional gap found in Japan, a gap that has its counterpart in all modern democratic societies, be filled? When dissent arises, particularly if it is localized or if the issues are more important than the number of voters involved, the normal channels of representation—local government, the political parties, the Diet—are inadequate. But how can governments respond to citizen protest outside the normal channels? Is violence endemic in order to force governments to respond? To what extent should there be institutional mechanisms for converting protest into information and information into obligation? And, most generally, what are the limits of government obligation in a democratic state?

Perhaps most of all there is the question of whether or not governments need to recognize that citizen protest has always been a factor in democratic politics, and violence too. It is a variable and fluctuating phenomenon. Deploring the need for it only makes it more effective. Issues of popular protest, then, will continue to be troublesome, and there are probably no institutional answers to them.

10

Reflections on Protest

THE SANRIZUKA MOVEMENT is only one of many recent expressions of citizen protest. Typically, such movements seek to gain their ends by means of extra-institutional pressure on the state. A radical coalition that started by opposing certain governmental policies, the Sanrizuka movement ended up bitterly hostile to the state itself.

The issues were certainly real enough: political economy, rural change in Chiba, pollution, the declining circumstances of agriculture in Sanrizuka and Shibayama, the marginalization of farmers. In examining the range of concerns that the movement came to represent we have tried to follow what Bourdieu calls a "theory of practice," showing how daily activities convert to a strategy of struggle in the full "sensuousness," as Marx put it, of living actors touched with a sense of the sublime.[1]

The starting point, a mistake made in the way the government decided on the airport site, was compounded rather than resolved by the events that followed. But beyond a certain point it is questionable whether or not the error could have been rectified even if the government had drastically changed its position. For what this movement demonstrates, in common with many others, is how difficult it is, once deeply felt principles have been invoked, to reconcile them through bargaining. Those who represent the principles refuse to be compromised by negotiation. Those who would compromise are bound by prior obligations and commitments. Under such circumstances, it is more and more difficult for governments to make "right" decisions and to assure those concerned that recognizable justice will be done or that some satisfactory rationality will be achieved.

Although this is a growing problem in all democracies, no one is quite sure how seriously to take it. After all, democracy is precisely a product of the overcoming of such difficulties. Each successful democratic system is a living example of how extra-institutional protest can be transformed into institutional reform. Protest, even in its extra-institutional form, is a commonplace of democratic politics, but when it occurs, both in Japan and elsewhere, it is regarded as a particular affront.

It is impossible, then, to separate extra-institutional protest from democracy itself and particularly those forms of political accountability which dilute authority by means of multi-purpose instruments of popular participation. By making accountability a function of direct opposition, the two become inseparable, a relationship converting democracy from a form of government in which political participation is passive, a form of complicity in power, into something dynamic, an expression of mutual responsiveness. Democracy, when it is properly functioning, does not simply accept the principle of opposition: it actually depends on the legitimate exercise of opposition. A more informed political decision-making process is the result—a process of political learning. If institutional opposition makes democracy creditable, it is extra-institutional opposition which defines the limits of that creditability.

In Japan institutional opposition is both present and constitutionally provided for along with appropriate channels and instruments for its expression. However, there are serious constraints at work which are relatively absent in most other democracies. We have described some of these; the lack of effective local government and the powerlessness of opposition parties in the face of the LDP's long dominance are two factors that help to explain why extra-institutional protest in Japan has been so bitter and violent for such a long time. But there is a more important factor. Even today, and especially in the ranks of the civil service, there is a distrust of opposition of all kinds, even institutional. Mediation, yes; opposition, no.

Nor are such views limited to the bureaucracy. Many senior officials of the LDP share them as well, so much so that despite its competitive factionalism, the LDP has suffered from a kind of hardening of the arteries. The situation is made much worse by the fact that the opposition parties' exclusion from national power attenuates and debilitates them. Where party opposition is so ineffective, offended public opinion is more likely to resort to direct political means.

But the problem of extra-institutional protest is not limited to Japan. Moreover, such protest can be found in countries with effective opposition parties. Nor is Japan alone in experiencing hostility to opposition from senior ranking bureaucrats or even high party officials. This suggests that we need to inquire further into the causes of extra-institutional politics, which in turn forces us to confront what might be called the limits of institutional politics in the modern state. The larger problem, common to all democratic states, is how to maintain the boundaries between legality and illegality, proper and improper behavior, and how to keep the necessary respect for institutional rules without which stable government is impossible. The problem for the government is less the issues than the means. For those oppposed, it is just the other way around.

Today, all democratic countries confront the question of how to be more responsive and how responsive to be. For although it is generally true that the instruments of politics and prevailing mechanisms of representation, participation, and of course opposition, which were designed to render extra-institutional protest redundant, themselves originated as some sort of opposition—electoral reform, the expansion of the franchise, the right to organize in trade unions, the basic protection of individual liberties—now the problem is precisely how to respond when institutional innovation appears exhausted. Extra-institutional political activity can still identify the need for greater democraticization of access to power, the widening of political participation, and indeed some necessary evolution of democracy itself. But the protests themselves do not suggest good solutions.

We may be reaching the point where not only is it difficult for governments to respond to protest, but where by altering the prevailing rules and mechanisms of participation matters may be made worse. If so, the problem is uniquely troubling. For if governments have increased their responsibilities beyond the point where they can discharge them effectively, the problem of extra-institutional protest is not a matter of right or wrong or good and bad decisions but the problem of the state itself.

This is the larger issue behind our inquiry into extra-institutional protest in Japan, an issue for which we have no ready answers. If the state is the problem, not the solution, what is needed is renewed speculation on classic themes in a context of very specific case studies that show the state's limitations in many settings and at many levels. What will need reviewing in detail are all the old matters once regarded as settled: jurisdictions, political accountability, alternatives of opposition, institutional politics. These matters, while they are beyond the scope of this study, suggest its hidden political agenda.

That indeed is one reason why we chose a case in a highly successful and democratic state, one that, since the war at any rate, has put its best foot forward. We have not been dealing with circumstances where the state has performed badly, or where the government is manifestly corrupt or its leaders incapable, or where politics is so weakly institutionalized that the government is fragile. Nor is the present case one in which an authoritarian regime is slowly and haltingly being replaced by more democratic practices so that at the point of transition, when police terror is eschewed, a backlog of old grievances erupts. Still less are we dealing with a case like that of Poland, where the creation of an opposition is itself a revolutionary act. Rather in this example government policy has been successful, the results accepted, and the public reasonably satisfied.

Although we have discussed the how, why, and what of the problem of extra-institutional protest in the context of the Sanrizuka struggle, we have only hinted at its complexity as a phenomenon. Considering it from the various standpoints of those most deeply involved, we have seen that the members of the various political action groups formed shared the belief that they could not effectively utilize the prevailing structures of political participation in order to affect government policy and that the regular institutional means of politics prevented rather than facilitated the proper flow of appropriate information. To them, institutional politics represented a network of "blockages," catering to restricted clienteles, particularly those having great economic and social power. The system seemed to be based on exchanges between an ensemble of such clienteles and government officials and politicians, insulating them from the less well organized and the less powerful, those who were incapable of mobilizing an alternative plurality.

The solution would seem to be obvious. Widen the circle, expand the system, and include inside the network of effective communications those currently left out. But if our concern is correct, and if governments are having increasing difficulty in dealing with the responsibilities already incurred, then further increases in such responsibilities are likely to be counterproductive, only adding more layers of institutional politics and contributing to the growth of bureaucracy and government by committees with less accountability and less efficiency in catering to public needs. The danger is that institutional accommodation, of a kind bound up with the evolution of democracy, may produce an unaccommodating, undemocratic effect. In Japan the government had dealt with the problem in a vacillating way, now giving in, now holding firm, hoping to mediate the issues without changing the basic structure of politics. The results are increasingly frustrating on all sides, with each pointing the finger of recrimination at the other, a condition under which ideological manipulation, confrontation, and violence can easily arise.

In such a situation, what can be done? The impossibility of widening the circle means that offended groups, if they lack power, have few options. The only real alternative to passivity and compliance is force or the threat of force—hence the spread of extra-institutional protest in democratic systems in many parts of the world. Indeed, as soon as violations of legal and institutional limits of politics are advocated by a movement, no matter how small it is or insignificant, a signal goes out to those in authority, an alert. Events take on different proportions. There is a quickening of concern all around.

Not all protest is intrinsically valid, of course. Sometimes the state must fight back. Indeed, the problem of extra-institutional protest is a bit like the doctrine of just and unjust wars, one of those perpetual political predicaments that have no satisfactory general solutions. How should the state have responded to paramilitary formations like the Putschists and Nazis in Weimar Germany—by sharing power with them? (In the end it did, with results that are well known.) Not all extra-institutional protest is on the same plane; means and ends are crucial.

The Sanrizuka case can offer some criteria for distinguishing one extra-institutional protest from another, among them the principles advocated, the degree of violence favored, and the relationship of the movement to public opinion. Those seeking to mobilize broad public support will tend to avoid violence unless the mood of the public is already revolutionary. Reform is thus the main object when extra-institutional protest takes the form of citizen and community action. Indeed, this sort of extra-institutionality will be more or less limited to mobilization, demonstrations of solidarity, marches on government facilities, and symbolic challenges to authority such as the arrest of leaders and sit-ins on public property.

An opposite approach is the phenomenon that rejects public opinion but captures the greatest publicity, terrorism. Involving small groups with limited clienteles, terrorists hope that by violent means the prevailing authority can be discredited.[2] The main strategy is to convert citizens into bystanders who will remain passive while a network of counter-clienteles can be built up out of those increasingly alienated from institutional politics. The ultimate aim is the conversion of such counter-clienteles into a revolutionary mobilization— the specter that haunts governments confronted by any serious extra-institutional activities. For behind even the more innocuous forms of extra-institutionality lurks the danger of a mobilized radicalism, left or right, the target of which is the state itself.

The Sanrizuka movement falls in between the extremes of extra-institutional protest. Much concerned with public opinion, it appeals to a large coalition of reform groups interested in peace, anti-nuclear, and environmental issues. Limits on violence were imposed throughout the struggle. Rejecting terrorism, the movement has become anti-state, challenging its legitimacy, while trying to mobilize public support for its position.[3]

If most serious extra-institutional protest no longer leads to substantial adaptations of political practices and amendments in structure, effective policy will increasingly depend on the flexibility and imagination of political leaders and their understanding of the issues involved. Political learning and democracy will go together as never before. In this case a good deal of political learning has occurred, but not of a sort that might have been expected, that is, institutional learning. Rather, people have learned greater respect for one another. Jurisdictions have been widened. Nor has such learning taken place only within the government: citizens' groups as well have learned from the Sanrizuka struggle. Not only have people become more willing to fight against what appears to them to be government arbitrariness, they have also learned to join forces with other opposition groups and to appeal to public opinion in ways perhaps lacking in the past in Japan. What the government has learned is to be more shrewd, to anticipate problems better, and to avoid conflict by taking necessary preliminary steps, such as widening the scope of consultations. Moreover, local authorities are becoming more adept at bargaining with the national government and the private sector as well.

If all sides have learned to bargain more efficiently, they have also learned how to do so ,with dignity. For as we have seen, one of the crucial factors in the entire airport struggle was the way the government offended the farmers' dignity by its failure to consult and by ignoring their initial constitutionally appropriate attempts to protest.

Offended dignity gave the farmers and their cause a unique authenticity and generated much public sympathy. Even among those who disapproved of the tactics of confrontation and violence, it was obvious why ordinary bargaining and mediation rules and the ordinary processes of party and interest group politics were, from the farmers' standpoint, the cause of the problem rather than the solution. The government's willingness to co-opt leaders of the movement and compromise with them on the matter of compensation was often regarded as evidence of the government's moral laxity and duplicity. Farmers were surprisingly successful in establishing themselves as the "party of principle" confronting the "party of expediency," the government, and thus appealed to a broad spectrum of students and more liberal and socialist sympathizers.[4]

WHEN HISTORIES of twentieth-century Japan are written this long struggle may not seem important; perhaps it will be worthy only of a footnote. But the big punctuating events may mislead. Perhaps for that reason it has been useful to take a small event in a small space, an event that nevertheless deals with big issues like agriculture and industry, protest and violence, citizen rights and political decision-making, to see how, together, they create a serious confrontation. Perhaps, too, by seeing in greater detail what lies behind the events that people do take notice of, one gets a little bit under the surface of people's ordinary lives. Activities become visible in ways rarely seen, especially by outsiders.

Moreover, in doing so, one sees how extraordinary ordinary people can become. Old Ōki Yone, with her teeth knocked out, lying on a policeman's shield as she is carried out of her house in triumph, is unforgettable. So is Tomura, who joined the movement as a kind of contemporary Christ, angry at the moneychangers who violated his temple of Sanrizuka, but became more and more like an Old Testament prophet, hurling his wrath at the robot-like figures of the police. Both represent the extraordinary energy unleashed by the movement, the power of those old women who sprayed the police with human excrement and urine and shouted obscenities at them and in some cases wear on their faces the permanent deep-gouged curves of the police shields. There was power, too, in the mobilized efforts where, hamlet by hamlet, people dug into the soil, burrowed into tunnels, seeing in them everything from World War II to Vietnam war bunkers. It was a movement that did not use terms like "corps" and "commander" casually, yet it refused all efforts at military hierarchy. The curious lack of authority in the Hantai Dōmei was itself a commentary on the state and on violence. For if one aspect of the movement, and the battles it engaged in, was to show that a state of war existed against the state and the people, another was to show that the people were warriors without armies, faithful to the traditions of uprisings, peasant rebellions, and landlord-tenant class struggle, but not to organized war.

We can see, too, how good faith for one side was perceived as bad faith by the other. The government, by taking the necessary steps to proceed with the airport, did so from its own perspective, which was vastly different from that of the farmers. Its urgency stemmed in part from the five years lost between the original decision and the actual implementation of the plan at the Sanrizuka site, an embarrassment to those who wanted to get on with the matter. The big concerns were economic growth, industrialization, design innovation, and transportation. These, and the specific projects they were linked with, were a part of an even larger (indeed worldwide) ideology of development. It was the age of freeway construction, of expanding new towns, of landfill and industrial zones, a time of intoxication with economic power. If there were costs—pollution, environmental damage, and so on—they would be handled in due course. First comes the construction, the government thought; then comes the tidying up and beautification. The chief architect of the airport, a man of considerable sensitivity and sophistication, considered the main design task in terms of moving people in and out, creating a transportation space that would be attractive and efficient. If one goes to the main terminal today one sees how well he has done it. There is a lofty rotunda within the two main terminals, a vast domed cathedral, a modern version of those great glass-caged railway terminals built in capital cities at the end of the last century. And it is very efficient indeed, behind its fences, police, and security.

How can one evaluate this experience, which has led to so much expenditure of talent and energy on all sides, heroism, deaths, involvement even of whole families? For the airport, in one way or another, came to be the consuming interest and passion of all those involved—militants, who saw in it the class struggle; farmers, who saw in it the overwhelming power of the state; bureaucrats, who saw its completion as their duty and as the symbol of a dynamic and successful Japan.

Partly, of course, one can interpret the whole matter in terms of self-interest: each side wanted something and fought to attain it. But it would also have been in the farmers' interest to sell their land, and quickly. Why did a few hold out? Self-interest is not a sufficient answer to the events that followed.

Another answer is that certain institutional factors were responsible; due process was missing. But there are plenty of examples where legal proceedings and due process have been utilized by protest groups in Japan, sometimes successfully. Indeed, there are a number of court cases over public projects going on in Japan today, including Osaka International Airport, the Shinkansen and noise pollution in Nagoya, the U.S. military base at Yakota, and the Yokohama New Cargo Railway Track Opposition case. These involve air, water, soil, noise, and other issues. Pollution control and environmental matters have been particularly important. Many of the cases are based on violations of existing standards, but others are neighborhood and local issues. It is not as if the Sanrizuka farmers were totally helpless.

Was there something about this movement that required violence? (Not unlimited violence, to be sure, because there were rules that were almost always followed.) Perhaps. When only self-interest is involved, legal action is usually the course that is taken, even in a country where lawyers are only a last resort. But when principle is involved, the whole idea of following the tortuous and expensive legal route becomes preposterous. Such a course would be a recognition of the legitimacy of the state and its institutions of mediation and an acceptance of the idea that society acts according to the rule of law and the principle of fairness. The farmers knew that the law would not be on their side, and if they could not in the end win in the courts they had to escalate principle and violence, step by step. As the government proceeded with its plan, each confrontation led to more passionate attachment to principles, statements of universal claims, definitions of rights, which could only end in a challenge to the state itself and to its right to decide questions of propriety.

Offended interest is only a part of the story; lack of due process is only part of the story. Was it also a question of truncated and inadequate local government institutions? Here again, perhaps. For despite the ramified network of village and township and city governments, there is a difference in outlook and attitude on the part of local officials and governments in relation to the state as compared with Western democracies. We have seen that from the government's point of view, local government means prefectural consultation and not much more. But here, too, we must be careful not to ignore the very real power of more localized jurisdictions, a power that grows as local authorities are asked to participate more in national projects. As the need for local cooperation goes up, mayors also must respond to public concerns over issues of safety, pollution, and environmental damage. If the national government does not take local needs into account, cooperation can be withheld.

The mayor of Chiba City discovered that he had power in the "1.1 billion yen" affair; so did the mayors of Narita City, Shibayama Town, Daiei, Tako, Ichihara, Kanzaki, Sakura, and Tomisato. Each of these towns presented the government with a bill pointing to some problem caused by the airport. Building an airport is a project with an enormous impact on a huge area, and once people understand that their daily lives will be affected they make demands on the authorities nearest at hand.

Perhaps the most frequently mentioned precipitant of violence was the government's lack of consideration, the lack of consideration shown, for instance, in the fact that the government neglected to inform those most involved of its decision to change the site from Tomisato to Sanrizuka. (Of course one could argue that it was precisely because the government did not ignore the demands of the people at Tomisato that the site was changed in the first place.) There is no doubt that the Sanrizuka farmers saw lack of consideration as a serious and important factor. For Tomura it was the original sin. Why was it so important to them? One answer is obvious. Given the particular circumstances and characteristics of the area—the problems of the pioneers, the difficulties of farming, the nostalgia surrounding that imperial "Barbizon"—putting an airport there was simply an outrageous thing to do. A visible difference suddenly emerged between a government acting without humility (humility is, after all, not a common political attribute) and a government that humiliates. The humiliation of so historically important and so symbolically sensitive a sector of the population, the small farmers of Japan—those whose households were within living memory the basis for Japan as a society, as a social body, even as a political system—raised to a level of public prominence all those latent and disturbing questions which were already being asked. For while Japanese society was being modernized and transformed and income was doubling, much was also being relegated to the museum, to quaintness, to a kind of archeology in which obligation, mutual responsiveness, and a host of qualities uniquely Japanese were being made into objects so buried, so covered over, that they would have to be dug out of the national character like old pots from a grave. Particularly in the sixties, there was a great deal of ambivalence about this transformation and about Japan's power. People were afraid of a decline in moral standards and of political corruption. There was a blurring of the national image, a confusion about how to think of Japan as a powerful and prosperous nation.

There were real enough reasons for this ambivalence. Issues of peace, of treaty revision, of the Vietnam war, of capitalism and industrialism and militarism and imperialism, were at that time being raised by a variety of groups from the sects of the New Left to the larger citizen coalitions. The government's decision to ignore the Sanrizuka farmers triggered a response among all those groups. All poised themselves at the margin between legal and illegal protest. All had in common a fear of the modern industrial state. All were composed of clienteles overlapping in membership, people partly inside and partly outside party politics. With each new issue a memory of previous protest was recovered. The architecture of the future evoked an archeology of the past. In this the clienteles were like the ripples on the water after a stone is thrown, moving outward from the confrontations in Sanrizuka where the events were taking place. But it was as if the ripples reversed themselves as well, moving inward, to nourish and support what became a unifying symbol of all struggles, with the airport itself the unifying symbol of all that they were against. Among those who helped to make this symbolic conversion were writers, journalists, even filmmakers. Ogawa Productions has made some extraordinarily moving documentary films about the Hantai Dōmei, converting the dignity and beauty of Heta village into something more than picturesque nostalgia for rural life. Providing that tension and sense of tragedy which emerges slowly from the long fade-outs, the films served as a modern Nō drama. One knew what was happening; one knew what the outcome would be. It was the performance itself that counted most.

Indeed, at some point it is performance that comes to count in real life. Violence is not simply a reflex to blocked interests. The retrievals and projections enlist wider claims to universality, principles of life and liberty. Property is at the center of the controversy, the state the obstacle to solution. There is a search for alternatives—modest ones perhaps, like One-Pack's collective farming, or more ambitious ones, like universal revolution. For some Sanrizuka was an originating terrain like Mao's caves, and for sects such as Chūkaku-ha and perhaps others it was a starting point for those millennial solutions that begin with an interpretation of historical experience and the translation of that history into the hard logic of Leninist necessity.

SPECIFIC ISSUES, mobilizable clienteles, universalized principles, a plunderable history, retrieval and nostalgia, projection and millennialism, myth and theory, metaphor and metonymy—these are the properties that can be seen inside this movement. One sees the evidence in the use of tools as weapons, and in the headbands worn by militants and by old women. One sees them as a semiotic dialectic to the electronic head globes and space uniforms so obligingly worn by the police, who look rather like they have just come down from a moon walk. One sees it in the watchtowers each side has raised against the other, the one with steel cages and telescopes on top, the other with ragged red flags flapping away on top of crazy wooden constructions. Even the architecture of the fortresses suggests how violent and determined the sect is, how bristling or warlike it wants to appear. One sees, too, the electrifying effects of mass action, of snake-dances in which writhing columns press against long sticks, and where people chant and shout their solidarity, a celebration of the violence that does not break out but threatens.

This leads us to further questions: How important is violence? How necessary are the rituals of death and destruction for transforming interest into principle, commitment into devotion, anger into passion? Probably very important, very necessary. For violence is the final proof of devotion. One proves one's willingness to die— that is the ultimate claim to seriousness, the one principle that can equal or transcend all others. Moreover, it endows all others—sovereignty, rights, power itself—with that necessary symbolic infusion which takes it well beyond more cynical forms of expression, of Sorelian manipulation. For if blood is the paste of principle, and death and dying defines life and living, circumstances will easily get out of control and ordinary possibilities be eliminated. A certain terrible sequence must work itself out until a climax, a point of exhaustion, is reached. The sexual parallels are unmistakable.

In a sense, then, the ordinary acts of ordinary people carrying out their ordinary tasks are totally transformed by the movement. Nothing is as it seems. Each act represents a hidden agenda. Amelioration, negotiation, and compromise are defined as violations and corruption; power is sexual, primitive, passionate.

Perhaps, however, that goes too far. Perhaps the most pertinent question posed by the anti-airport movement is one that even the participants ask. What kind of movement is this? Is it similar to anti-pollution and environmental movements, ecology and anti-nuclear groups, each focusing on a preferred set of dangers, each seeking to mobilize public support often through extra-institutional actions like sit-ins, break-ins, and other expressions of public outrage? In some ways yes, in other ways no. In Japan such groups have attached themselves or supported the Sanrizuka movement, but there is one obvious and important difference. The Sanrizuka movement was and is basically a farmers' movement. It is linked to a "base," a way of life, a method of production. Insofar as these other bodies attach themselves to it, they become linked with something more fundamental in Japanese society than the specific issues which concern them.

Nevertheless, although it is a movement with a firm base, that base is small and shrinking. This is a protest by people becoming marginalized, their way of life rendered functionally superfluous; that is what gives the movement its special quality. It suggests, too, that it would have failed without the support of the militants seeking an AMPO 1960 on a larger and more permanent scale. Bringing in the many citizen protest groups transformed the fight over land into a fight over the nature of the state, a rural-based class struggle that would envelop the trade unions in a total mobilization for revolution. Exactly what kind of revolution might occur no one was quite sure; in any case, perspectives varied with ideological preference and between sects and individuals. Perhaps an ideal would have been an evolution similar to that of Solidarity in Poland, a workers' trade union movement, surely, but one which became much more than that—a national movement aimed at the democratization of society, animated by an ideal of socialism, a redemption of what had been corrupted and deformed by the Stalinist state.[5]

The Sanrizuka movement had neither such a clear ideological perspective nor such a power base. It wanted to correct deformities in the parliamentary democratic state by altering the course of a general evolution, but, after all, the parliamentary system in Japan is not an authoritarian or Stalinist state. In Japan there is no equivalent polarization between state and worker or between state and society. Indeed, for most farmers, being driven off the land meant better opportunities and more income from industry. And if this produced an industrial reserve army, for the most part it was one quickly and easily absorbed in an expanding industrial complex.

Nevertheless, just as the roots of the Solidarity movement can be traced to events in Hungary in 1956, so the New Left in Japan can be traced to the same events. It, too, is searching for an authentic socialist alternative to Stalinism and to the bureaucratism of the Soviet model. Some of the questions being asked by people in Solidarity about the nature of free unionism (free enterprise) and "autogestion" (worker participation), and the future of society based on such entities, have, in miniature, their counterpart in One-Pack and other farming experiments. In both movements, questions have been raised about how farming can be redesigned and made more attractive as an alternative mode of life, how it can be at once rural and sophisticated, collective but also private and family-based.

Radicalism and the move to the left became an irresistible force in Solidarity. A similar tendency toward radicalism in the Sanrizuka struggle, increasing with each confrontation and given voice by Tomura, brought the movement to the fringe of society and away from its center. Democracy does make a difference. Nevertheless, it was a large fringe. Although the figure must be taken with reservation, close to a million people, mostly young, involved themselves in the movement from its beginning days to the present. Even if one discounts this figure by half, and then by half again in terms of serious concern, it still represents a sizable number, and behind each person there were networks of friendship and kinship. We do not know, of course, to what degree participation (or friendship with a participant) permanently changed sensitivities and political attitudes.

A few of the original members of sects who came to Sanrizuka became allied with the United Red Army or with people close to it. Indeed, the sect member who served as Tomura's private secretary was for a time close to such groups and had made many trips to Beirut. He and others wanted to "internationalize" the movement, by which they meant using violent tactics, hijacking or shooting down planes, kidnapping airport officials, bombing offices, and the like. Considering how militant some of the sects are, and the fact that some have underground organizations already heavily engaged in militant operations, it is remarkable that terrorism was not used. Certainly Tomura was moving in that direction.

There are several reasons why terrorism did not become a part of the movement. First, terrorism was to the farmers simply beyond the rules of the game. They were ex-soldiers who did not want to be in a war against their own society. They were willing to protest, and if violence was involved they were prepared to use it and die. But actual terrorism would not only have violated the law; it would also have destroyed the main emphases of the movement itself, the nurture of people as well as the soil, and the handmade quality of power.

There is another answer as well: the nature of the state in Japan. If one compares the Sanrizuka movement with terrorist movements in other countries—the Montoneros in Argentina, or ERP, the Baader Meinhof in Germany, and the Red Brigades in Italy—one finds very different situations in the four cases. The first sought to establish a base in the provinces in order to create a people's army and, with peasant support, capture Buenos Aires. The object of terrorism was to create a guerrilla army by applying principles of peasant war. Although the Sanrizuka sects and farmers may have had a similar aim, it was clear that farmers were not peasants, and that Japan was no longer either a peasant or a farming society. Even the sects, who were carried away with possible parallels to Vietnam, for the most part recognized that mobilizing support in Japan did not mean recruiting a peasant force, but rallying public opinion. There is a vast difference between the force of public opinion in a democracy, and the need for revolutionary forces in an autocracy. In a sense a democracy lays itself open to terrorism, but unless its political structure is very, very weak, terrorism is not likely to win on its own terms. It is more likely to convert a democracy into an authoritarian state.

As for the Baader Meinhof (Red Army Faction) in Germany, the remarkable thing about it was that despite the tragedies it perpetrated and the equally tragic deaths of its founders and key leaders, it was more like comic opera than tragedy. Despite, too, some support among intellectuals, lawyers, psychiatrists, professors, and parts of the New Left, it was totally isolated from mainstream German life. The leaders had a penchant for fast cars, high living, and luxurious flats, and some had a fascination with weapons which bordered on the pathological. It was a lifestyle completely different from that of the Red Army sects in Japan.

The Red Brigades in Italy are a different phenomenon entirely. In a country where government corruption is longstanding, where society manages, as in Argentina, to insulate itself as much as possible from government and is remarkably efficient at managing its own networks of private deals and social arrangements, where there are large mobilizable clienteles such as a vast group of the unemployed and an army of ex-students, and where the general public is profoundly dissatisfied with politics, terrorism has a better chance. The line between clientele and public opinion begins to break down.

In Japan, Red Army groups remained "superstructures" without a base. Political movements like Sanrizuka, on the other hand, which start with a base and a clientele that depends on mobilizing popular opinion, tend to become populist rather than revolutionary, no matter how revolutionary they may sound. We have, then, some categories for evaluation. One is the base of a movement and its size, composition, and quality. Another is the clientele that supports it, its commitment, and its financial and other contributions. Still another is the role of popular opinion and the mediating effect it has on both government and the movement itself. In a democracy this is perhaps the most crucial. For while public opinion may be fickle, to a degree it can define appropriate canons of justice and discretion according to the way it sees and hears the issues.

In the Sanrizuka case, the public heard and saw. The journalists wrote of the events. The television cameras focused on critical moments—the fall of the farmers' broadcasting tower, the taking of Komaino fort, the wounded lying in the hospitals. And while reaction was partial and incomplete, it affected Dietmen and others who remonstrated with government. It caused anxiety among parents and families. It made people wonder what could be so wrong when so many things seemed to be going so right. And it revealed the hidden costs and unfinished business of Japan as number one.

Were there clear-cut rights and wrongs? It is difficult to say. The militants may have got their notions of class struggle wrong in what is probably the most mediating society in the world and where there is the least available support for Solidarity-like expression of class struggle. The labor movement moves steadily to the right, not to the left, and everyone considers himself or herself middle class. Yet, as the movement to expand the Japanese Defense Force grows, as the economy begins to show cracks and strains, as the penetration of Southeast Asia intensifies, and as the constraints on Japanese trade are imposed from outside by countries fearful of competition, something like a class struggle may make its appearance, not socially but politically. The LDP has dominated for more than thirty-five continuous years. It favors large industry, business, technology, and design as a matter of course. It depends on its factions, and since its factions require funds, there is a natural and corrupting affinity between economic and political power. Japan is both a one-party state and a multi-party state: the opposition is ineffective. The JCP has little to offer in any case except an occasional shrewd and efficient Dietman or local representative. It is the party of efficient municipalities, good at making trains run on time. But in a country where this is handled very well by the Ministry of Transportation, so much so that one can almost set one's watch by the departure and arrival of the trains, the Communist Party is redundant. As for the JSP, it is rather muddled ideologically and something of a dumping ground for ex-JCP members and intellectuals who cannot vote for the LDP or will not be co-opted by it.

THIS BRINGS US back to the role of extra-institutional protest and the role of violence in a democracy that cannot pick up many of the threads of public feeling under quickly changing circumstances. Protest and violence are, as we have said, more or less permanent features of democratic life. Extra-institutional protest, and the sporadic violence that often accompanies it, may well be an important element in the way democracies can listen and hear what they might otherwise ignore. Deeply held feelings, minority views, principles otherwise bypassed, are in any case too diverse for their continuous conversion into mediating packages, whether by interest groups or political parties. And if some of these become shared by larger sectors of the public, either in the form of latent sympathy or in a more active expression, parties may be insufficient vehicles for their conveyance to government under the best of circumstances.

Rather, extra-institutional protest and episodic violence, difficult as these are to accept in a society of laws where the principle of majority rule and the conversion of need and demand into policies and actions is the basis of good order, may require a good deal more attention than it has received, and as part of the way politics—that is, ordinary politics—works. We tend to think of protest and violence as extraordinary because they are extra-institutional, and that is right; otherwise the institutions themselves would decay and be held in contempt. But how well institutions can be made to work, and how to define the appropriate limits of government obligation, is a continuing debate, one that does not take the form of abstract principle alone, but the acting out of ends in a context of both appropriate and inappropriate means. The line between appropriate and inappropriate means fluctuates according to the principles themselves and with the views of the wider public, which in the last analysis holds the balance of legitimizing power. If the first question is what kind of movement the Hantai Dōmei represents, the last question is what kind of space there is in democratic societies for extra-institutional politics. It is a question for which there can be no entirely theoretical answer, for it deals with an area of ambiguity, a political space in which more than rational political demands are involved, and where perhaps both the logic of democracy and the institutions are challenged in ways ill-afforded by both.

Indeed, on all these matters both farmers and militants have very little to say. Ask them about solutions and they will become silent. Part of our problem is how to interpret such silence. Is it simply a reflection of ignorance, or the stubborn refusal of revolutionaries to be clear about what they are for rather than what they were against? Or is it, rather, the silence of a judgment—the judgment that the state itself is no longer an appropriate instrument of modern life and that its institutions are less and less effective in promoting development, rationality, control, and power. When pressed, our respondents argued that in making institutions more accountable, responsive, and democratic, it is the state that is the chief obstacle. But whatever their views, it seems plausible to interpret their silence as really a lack of good general solutions. To question the state so fundamentally is to deny the possibility of effective institutional solutions and to reject conventional answers to problems of modern national economies, capitalist or socialist, within a state context. One may not agree with their views, but one must also ask whether or not there is a certain wisdom in such silence. For it is not as if they are unconcerned with alternatives. They are concerned. But they seek them in actions rather than words, and not only in violence but in experimentation with new modes of social existence. Seen in this light, what was revolutionary about these farmers and the militant sects supporting them was not so much what they were against as it was how they went about finding out what they are for. Resisting the state, they sought solutions outside it, and for this there is lacking a good and appropriate language.

One has to examine not only what they said and did not say, then, but also what they did, and in some detail. In this case we were not only concerned with the specific pattern of extra-institutional protest but also with the ad hoc way a language of fresh solutions comes into being and which, more than the solutions themselves, becomes an important part of political behavior. Not that there was any agreement on such matters among the participants. The movement showed surprising variations and differences, especially for a society like Japan where collective loyalties are ordinary aspects of life, not peculiar to mobilized sects and collective entities. But the movement enabled a kind of radical individualism to express itself, a pluralism of solutions built into this radical and anti-state coalition. Not only did the movement offer opportunities for expressing individuality quite lacking in more institutional life in Japan, it also may have contributed to a self-generating vitality that accounts for the relatively long duration of the movement. As there was no final orthodoxy, so there was no final disillusionment.

A movement that keeps changing while enduring (an additional reason for studying it), the Sanrizuka struggle has involved thousands in some way or another over the eighteen years of its existence. Today the first phase of the airport has been completed. More than forty million people have used it since it first opened in May 1978. Fighting continues over the second phase. Although the government seems determined to press on and complete the airport, there are private doubts on all sides that the second phase, at least as presently envisaged, will be built. In a sense the government has won, but the cost has been great and the victory partial.

The farmers and militants, too, have won a partial victory. The government has been forced to accede to the principle that small farmers should not be obliterated by state policy. Militants have found in Sanrizuka a terrain, an arena of action, a stage for confrontation which, some believe, "reveals" the fundamental contradictions of state capitalism in Japan. Rightly or wrongly, they have made the issues more fundamental, a matter of the state versus a sector of society whose embedded symbolic value in Japan is part of the tradition of "Japaneseness." They have attached the universality of their ideologies to the particularity of the society and in doing so have helped to put the movement as a whole far beyond some conflict of rural versus industrial interests.

We have also tried to show how people react when they have been rendered superfluous in a state run by functional elites, bureaucrats who in the name of rationality, development, growth, and order stand for the intelligence and discipline that these imply. From their standpoint, farmers and militants, by the virtue of their mode of opposition even more than its substance, represented a disordering and nonrational element in society. Because of this attitude, the farmer's existence depended solely on his ability to survive after being deprived of his functions. What happened in the fields and fortresses was not mere resistance to the government's change in policy but rather a search for new forms of functionality and a call for a reappraisal by society of the farmer's role. Hence we saw in the Sanrizuka movement a variety of experiments—youth trying out new modes of farming, militants trying out the collective life, generational linkages forming between old farmers and young militants— and also the emergence and the maintenance of a loose entity of ideological and social opposites. The area of combat became a space for new meanings, even though there was little effort made to obliterate differences between individuals and groups. When each person tried to render these differences complementary, new functions and new rules of association were created. As well, the movement generated its own myths and history, building up an ideological momentum much larger in implication than the original issues. A sub-society, becoming an anti-society, defined what was being lost while seeking redemptive solutions. Yet it never became wholly separated or alienated from the larger culture.

These and other concerns are more important than the movement itself. However, as a movement in the life of postwar Japan it is unique, for it represents the most generalized expression of all postwar extra-institutional protest movements. Around the Sanrizuka struggle and within the confines of its terrain, all others rallied and all the problems of capitalism and bureaucratic power were defined. For some, indeed, it was the defining example of citizen protest. For others it was less important among protest movements, a minor tune played in a major key. Perhaps both assessments have merit. In a sense, the movement's importance has been less in terms of the impact it has had on the larger drift of Japanese politics and society than in how it has reflected the ambiguities of the drift itself.

Today, as the movement recedes and principle converts to interests, bargaining and compromise become possible. Reason is about to prevail; soon no one will understand what the fuss was all about. The variable and fluctuating quality of semiotic meaning is a little understood phenomenon of politics, for it cannot be understood without knowledge of the contexts of events themselves, in all their multiple expressions and interpretations. In retrospect it is difficult to understand how a particular moment or circumstance could appear so frightening, so loaded with menace.

We began this book with some questions about the adequacy of current thinking, especially social science thinking, about such phenomena as the Sanrizuka movement and its meanings. Most social science thinking is strangely out of touch with these problems. Some think that the events described require psychological explanations. But what happened is not much different from what happens in other circumstances, small or large, where protest changes to violence. The rationalistic bias of choice theory and the need to convert our subject matter into vectors of interest or another negotiable principle are entirely laudatory, but used as explanations of these kinds of events the results are empty, devoid of explanatory power beyond the most obvious truths, and thus not true at all.

Indeed, as we have suggested, one of the problems of contemporary social science is the overgeneralized nature of its theories and the overkill quality of its categories. This is true for both the liberal variety and the radical. A neo-Marxism which tries to fit events into the class struggle is as much guilty of forcing complexity into a terrifyingly oversimple mold as any militant in a fortress; so is the view that the whole Sanrizuka movement is a fight by farmers to bid up the price of their land and strike a better deal with the government at the appropriate time.

There is a need, then, to go back to the drawing boards, to cases, to field studies, to observation of multiple perspectives and contexts. There may also be a need for wholly different categories and ways of thinking about what people actually do when they fight, protest, and organize, and what these do to the ordinary commonsense world in which most of us live, anticipate, and act. It is for this reason that the small events described here can offer us a few of the phenomenological raw materials for a review not only of the events but also of the way we think about them, the language of protest and the language of violence, and, in the end, the seriousness of the issues themselves. For in the last analysis, if this was a struggle over land and principle, the principles themselves were among the most significant we have: rights, obligations, peace, power, the citizen and the state, stability and change, and of course just living itself.

Postscript

THE SANRIZUKA MOVEMENT has lasted for a generation. During that period Japan has experienced many changes. So has the movement. It still goes on, but many of the tensions that we have described, tensions that were successfully held in check for a long time, have proved impossible to contain. The movement is now divided. Differences of principle and personality are only a part of the story of the split. Not only have the sects and the Hantai Dōmei had to adapt to changing circumstances since the airport opened, they have also had to confront the remarkable economic success of Japan, which far surpassed the expectations of 1960 when the new economic policy was launched. The public mood has shifted. Most Japanese today would be surprised to learn that the Sanrizuka struggle is still going on. For the sects, Sanrizuka is perhaps a last stand. Their stake in it goes up even as the number of farmers and supporters dwindles.

Whatever its future, the importance of the Sanrizuka movement is independent of its immediate successes or failures. It retrieved a tradition of protest in Japan and added to a history of movements standing against the authority of the state. By projecting a different future, it helped redefine the character of that future itself. Extra-institutional protest will continue to wax and wane, but it is rapidly becoming as much a part of contemporary politics as the conventional practices of governments. Movements in countries all over the world oppose the state on grounds of principle by questioning policies involving militarism, nuclear missiles, disarmament, the environment, and a host of other critical issues. Many such movements hover between parliamentary and extra-institutional means. Although the Sanrizuka struggle may be coming to an end, then, the phenomenon it represents is, if anything, more widespread.

Not that all in Sanrizuka is completely finished. The militants have not yet packed up their fortresses, and the farmers in the second-stage construction site have not yet sold their land. There are now two Hantai Dōmei organizations, one representing the influence of the Fourth International and its allies, the other representing the influence of Chūkaku-ha and its allies. The split was brought on by more than mere sectarianism, although both sects have in fact intervened more and more forcefully while the Hantai Dōmei has lost much of its original power. The latter never recaptured its momentum after the government changed its tactics and began to avoid direct physical confrontation. Once the Airport Authority began to pursue indirect and secret negotiations with the farmers, cracks in the Hantai Dōmei appeared, and the sheer public visibility of the movement sharply declined. As popular interest waned, efforts to bolster support took on a greater urgency. The sects, invoking a wider range of principles in support of the movement, became more ambitious. Rural claims were universalized, and the Sanrizuka movement was internationalized. The effect these changes had was opposite to what was intended. The more general the principles invoked by the movement, the more they could be defended on other terrains. The airport served less and less as a mobilization space, and the movement itself became less and less important.

All these factors played a part in what happened inside the Hantai Dōmei. As time went on the central Executive Committee became increasingly peripheral; ordinary policy was conducted by hamlet Hantai Dōmei organizations. Without the discipline and cooperation engendered by direct confrontation with the authorities, rifts appeared. The Youth Corps, deeply concerned about the future of farming, openly ventilated its grievances against Chūkaku-ha, which it saw as usurping power. Events in which the Hantai Dōmei participated—rallies, demonstrations, joint mobilizations with other protesting groups—were mainly arranged by Kitahara, who was moving closer to Chūkaku-ha. The political preferences of groups outside the Sanrizuka area were imposed on the groups within, a process that was troubling to farmers; they refused to serve as surrogates for sects and to become involved in internecine struggles that they did not approve of. This situation festered until early 1983, when the Executive Committee of the Hantai Dōmei rebelled.

Perhaps it was Kitahara himself who, by losing his sense of the limits of appropriate action, precipitated the split. Certainly many farmers who had had serious reservations about him held back from open antagonism until Chūkaku-ha initiatives against Ishibashi in early 1982. After Ishibashi and the others were forced to resign on charges that they had violated the rules against negotiation with the government (charges brought by Chūkaku-ha), there were many who expressed the view that such treatment of high and trusted Hantai Dōmei officials was unacceptable. Moreover, personal antagonism between Kitahara and Ishibashi was well known, and it appeared that Kitahara was positioning himself to act as the most powerful person in the Hantai Dōmei, using Chūkaku-ha rather than farmers as his base of support. True, Chūkaku-ha had served as the watchdog of the farmers in the second-stage site with commendable energy and vigilance. But its zeal had had negative political consequences within the Hantai Dōmei that the sect had done little to curtail. Its actions were taken by farmers as a violation of the original charter governing relations between the sects and the Hantai Dōmei. The alliance between Chūkaku-ha and Kitahara was, in many farmers' eyes and in the view of the Fourth International, a breach of the charter itself.

Growing conflict between the Fourth International and Chūkaku-ha over such issues divided the loyalties of farmers according to whether they lived inside the designated second-stage airport site, which remained pro-Chūkaku-ha, or outside. Government policies, too, seemed to be designed to exacerbate differences between the two groups of farmers. The Airport Authority advanced generous proposals for the rehabilitation of farm areas immediately outside and adjacent to the airport, to mitigate noise pollution, to halt the deterioration of irrigation, to introduce new measures of water control, and to assist farmers with many other problems. Farmers inside the second-stage site feared that the promises of government assistance and improved facilities for farmers outside would in the end be effective, leaving those inside helpless and expendable.

If both farmers and sects were increasingly divided over strategy and tactics, so too was the government. Despite pledges to proceed to the completion of the airport with all due and deliberate speed, the circumstances were proving to be increasingly problematic. Growing construction costs, reduced projections of air traffic, and delays to travelers caused by highway congestion all made Narita a less than satisfactory prospect as the sole international airport serving the Tokyo metropolitan area. Some government officials began to favor the expansion of Haneda, and although no one envisaged the actual abandonment of existing facilities at Sanrizuka, a scaling-down of the project seemed more and more likely.

These and other ambiguous aspects of the situation eroded the original objectives of all three groups, the government, the farmers, and the sects. Trying to establish a forward-looking policy in support of the Hantai Dōmei, the Fourth International decided to renew the "one-*tsubo*" land movement. Leaders of the sect reasoned that this would revitalize public support and make it more difficult for the government to acquire those lands remaining outside their control. Supporters throughout Japan were asked to pay 10,000 yen each to become part-owners of pieces of land scattered about in twenty-three places on the second-stage site. The object was to so complicate the pattern of land ownership that not only would government acquisition be deterred but any ensuing legal processes would be made infinitely more tortuous.

Chūkaku-ha strenuously objected to this policy. Selling property in any form, Chūkaku-ha said, would violate the Hantai Dōmei rule that the farmers should stick to the land at all cost. In Chūkaku-ha's view, the authenticity of the movement depended on farmers' remaining inside the second-stage site rather than becoming outsiders. This position gained Chūkaku-ha the loyality of the farmers who were inside the site. Kitahara openly supported Chūkaku-ha's position and indeed went a step further: he tried to convince the supporting organizations throughout Japan of the correctness of the position and urged them not to participate in the "one-*tsubo*" movement.

In turn, the Hantai Dōmei Executive Committee's ire was aroused. It considered Kitahara's stance to be a challenge to its authority. Charging that Kitahara had become a puppet of Chūkaku-ha, the Executive Committee decided to expel him. Kitahara replied, however, that the Executive Committee lacked the authority to take such an action, and he refused to step down. The farmers inside the second-stage area sided with Kitahara; those outside supported the decision of the Executive Committee. And so the Hantai Dōmei split

Postscript

into two separate organizations, each replicating the structure of the parent organization and each claiming Tomura as its symbolic progenitor. Each Executive Committee expelled those who accepted positions in the other.

Important people who joined the Kitahara-line Hantai Dōmei include Shimamura Ryōsuke and Ogawa Kakichi. Those who joined the Atsuta-line Hantai Dōmei (named after Atsuta Hajime, commander of the Action Corps after Uchida's resignation in 1982) come mainly from outside the second-stage site. Each group has its own publication and holds its own rallies. The Kitahara-line Hantai Dōmei's spring 1983 rally was held at Sanrizuka Park with supporters from Chūkaku-ha and Liberation. The Atsuta-line Hantai Dōmei met at Yokobori Cemetery with its supporters from the Fourth International. Hamlet Hantai Dōmei organizations supporting Atsuta have publicly forbidden Chūkaku-ha and Liberation to enter their hamlets.

Some of the farmers outside the second-stage site have joined the Kitahara-line Hantai Dōmei, most notably Hagiwara Susumu of Yokobori village, who has become its deputy secretary general. And some farmers inside the site, like Ogawa Gen of Kinone hamlet (where the Hantai Dōmei windmill is located), have joined the Atsuta-line Hantai Dōmei because members of the hamlet believe the government has now decided against constructing the side-wind runway that would have obliterated Kinone. (The hamlet is thus now technically outside the second-stage site.) No doubt some of those living inside the second-stage area who have joined the Kitahara-line Hantai Dōmei have misgivings about Kitahara and the power of Chūkaku-ha. No doubt others, like Hasegawa Take, who was commander of the Women's Corps in the original Hantai Dōmei and has assumed the same post in the Atsuta-line Hantai Dōmei, will retain links to Chūkaku-ha, with which she once was close. Each side has its contingent of well-respected old Hantai Dōmei figures. The divisions also extend outward from Sanrizuka to the networks of supporters, who are forced to take sides. The rupture, then, will have many repercussions, so many that, whatever its future, the Sanrizuka movement can no longer serve as the rallying point for extra-institutional protest in Japan.

Notes
Index

Notes

Introduction

1. See *Fight,* a pamphlet in English and German published by Mobilization for Sanrizuka and Dōrō Chiba (Tokyo: June 1982).

2. See D. E. Apter, "Notes on the Underground: Left Violence in the National State," in Stephen R. Graubard, ed., *The State* (New York: W. W. Norton, 1979), pp. 155–172.

3. A long list of pollution and environmental struggles and cases reaches back to the turn of the century and the Ashio Copper Mine case. The most notorious in recent years was the Minamata case, which involved the mercury poisoning of fishermen and their families. See Kazuko Tsurumi, "Aspects of Endogenous Development in Modern Japan," Part III: "Man, Nature and Technology: A Case of Minamata" (Tokyo: Institute of International Relations, Sophia University, 1979).

4. See Ezra Vogel, *Japan as Number One* (Cambridge, Mass.: Harvard University Press, 1979).

5. See *Le Monde,* Dossiers and Documents, No. 86, December 1981, *Japan:* "Undoubtedly one of the keys to the rapid mutation of the Japanese productive system is the intensive utilization of information. As one sociologist put it, there is a clear correlation between productivity and the ability of business to exploit information" (translation mine). For a discussion of the crucial political role of high information see D. E. Apter, *Choice and the Politics of Allocation* (New Haven, Conn.: Yale University Press, 1971).

6. See Apter, *Choice and the Politics of Allocation.* See also G. A.

Cohen, *Karl Marx's Theory of History* (Princeton, N.J.: Princeton University Press, 1978).

7. See Pierre Bourdieu, *Outline of a Theory of Practice* (Cambridge, Eng.: Cambridge University Press, 1977).

8. See Lafcadio Hearn, *Japan: An Interpretation* (New York: Macmillan, 1924), pp. 107–108.

1. Sanrizuka and Shibayama

1. For a somewhat dated but still useful account of local and rural life in Japan, see Richard K. Beardsley, John W. Hall, and Robert E. Ward, *Village Japan* (Chicago: University of Chicago Press, 1959).

2. Hamlets and Households

1. See Thomas C. Smith, *The Agrarian Origins of Modern Japan* (Stanford: Stanford University Press, 1959).

2. Inheritance is not in fact strictly limited to eldest sons. A daughter, an adopted son, or a son-in-law may also receive the patrimony.

3. Ronald P. Dore, *Shinohata: Portrait of a Japanese Village* (New York: Pantheon Books, 1978), pp. 123–124. The best account of Japanese agricultural practices and policies is Ronald P. Dore, *Land Reform in Japan* (London: Oxford University Press, 1959).

4. See Japan Institute of International Affairs, *White Papers of Japan, Annual Abstract of Official Reports and Statistics of the Japanese Government, 1971–72* (Tokyo: 1973).

5. See Ronald P. Dore, "The Socialist Party and the Farmers," in Allan B. Cole, George O. Totten, and Cecil H. Uyehara, eds., *Socialist Parties in Post-War Japan* (New Haven, Conn.: Yale University Press, 1966), pp. 370–417.

6. Tsurumi, "Aspects of Endogenous Development in Modern Japan," Part I, pp. 11–12.

7. Ibid., p. 27.

8. For a study of the practical and working relationships between party, government, cooperatives, and local farmers, see Michael W. Donnelly, "Setting the Price of Rice," in T. J. Pempel, ed., *Policy-Making in Contemporary Japan* (Ithaca, N.Y.: Cornell University Press, 1977).

9. Ogasawara Nagakazu and Kawamura Masaru, *History of Chiba Prefecture,* 2d ed. (Tokyo: Yamakawa Shuppaun, 1980).

10. See Richard J. Smethurst, *A Social Basis for Prewar Japanese Militarism* (Berkeley: University of California Press, 1974).

11. See Tadashi Fukutake, *Rural Society in Japan* (Tokyo: University of Tokyo Press, 1978).

12. See the interesting discussion of this point in Joji Watanuki, *Politics in Postwar Japanese Society* (Tokyo: University of Tokyo Press, 1977), pp. 65–100.

13. See Robert J. Smith, *Kurusu: The Price of Progress in a Japanese Village* (Stanford: Stanford University Press, 1978).

3. Past and Present

1. See Irwin Scheiner, "Benevolent Lords and Honorable Peasants: Rebellion and Peasant Consciousness in Tokugawa Japan," in Tetsuo Najita and Irwin Scheiner, eds., *Japanese Thought in the Tokugawa Period* (Chicago: University of Chicago Press, 1978), pp. 39–62.

2. See Roger Bowen, *Rebellion and Democracy in Meiji Japan* (Berkeley: University of California Press, 1980).

3. See Ann Waswo, "Origins of Tenant Unrest," in Bernard S. Silberman and H. O. Harootunian, eds., *Japan in Crisis.* (Princeton, N.J.: Princeton University Press, 1974), pp. 374–397.

4. See E. Herbert Norman, *Soldier and Peasant in Japan* (Vancouver, B.C.: University of British Columbia Press, 1965).

5. See E. Herbert Norman, *Japan's Emergence as a Modern State* (New York: Institute of Pacific Relations, 1940), pp. 70–80.

6. Thomas R. H. Havens, *Farm and Nation in Modern Japan* (Princeton, N.J.: Princeton University Press, 1974), p. 7.

7. Ibid., p. 8.

8. Ibid., pp. 55–73.

9. Ibid., pp. 186–187.

10. See Kazuko Tsurumi, "Religious Beliefs: State Shintoism vs. Folk Belief," Research Papers, Series A-37 (Tokyo: Institute of International Relations, Sophia University, 1979), p. 7.

11. Ronald Dore, *Land Reform in Japan* (London: Oxford University Press, 1959), p. 57. See also Smethurst, *A Social Basis for Prewar Japanese Militarism.*

12. See Mikiso Haive, *Peasants, Rebels, and Outcasts* (New York: Pantheon, 1982), pp. 64–68.

13. See D. B. Simmons and John H. Whitmore, *Notes on Land Tenure and Local Institutions in Old Japan* (Tokyo: Asiatic Society of Japan, 1919), p. 58. A precise and unromantic rendering of village life is Thomas C. Smith, *The Agrarian Origins of Modern Japan* (Stanford: Stanford University Press, 1959).

14. See Japan Institute of International Affairs, *White Papers on Japan,* Annual Abstract of Official Reports and Statistics of the Japanese Government (Tokyo: 1974–75).

15. See Chalmers Johnson, *MITI and the Japanese Miracle* (Stanford: Stanford University Press, 1982).

4. Fields and Fortresses

1. The Kita-Fuji movement came to represent protest against the violation of Article Nine of the Japanese constitution, which renounces war and the threat of force.

2. The Sunagawa movement came to represent protest against the United States–Japan Security Treaty of June 18, 1960. The people who fought in Sunagawa became the major force in the AMPO movement of 1960.

3. Reprinted in *AMPO: Japan-Asia Quarterly Review,* Vol. 9, No. 4 (1977), p. 3.

4. A reference to the prime minister.

5. Matsumoto Yuko, "A Report from the Front," *AMPO: Japan-Asia Quarterly Review,* No. 9–10 [1971], pp. 8–9.

6. Ibid., p. 9.

7. She "adopted" Koizumi Hidemasa, who was born in Hokkaido in 1948, the second son of a poor settler. He became a student. Interested in existentialism, he worked part-time to support himself, and became involved in the movement over the Vietnam War, Okinawa, and AMPO 1970. He met his wife in the movement. He joined Beheiren, moved to Sanrizuka, and came to live with Ōki Yone. After his marriage he built a hut in which several militants lived, including Higashiyama Kaoru, who was killed by the police. Koizumi Hidemasa is a leading member of the One-Pack Movement.

8. The best single account of the movement is Sato Bunsei, *Harukan-aru Sanrizuka* (Tokyo: Kodansha, 1978), published in Japanese. We have made extensive use of this account throughout Chapter 4.

5. New Left Sects and Their History

1. The "one-*tsubo*" movement is a strategy of small-scale purchases of land within the second-stage airport site. Even if all the farmers drop out of the Hantai Dōmei, the government will still not possess all of the land and will have to negotiate with the owners of the "one-*tsubo*" plots.

2. See Bowen, *Rebellion and Democracy in Meiji Japan.* See also H. D. Harootunian, "Introduction: A Sense of Ending and the Problems of Tai-shō," in Bernard S. Silberman and H. D. Harootunian, eds., *Japan in Crisis* (Princeton, N.J.: Princeton University Press, 1974), pp. 3–28.

3. The topic has been dealt with in both novels and social science inquiry. See, for an example of the latter, Masao Maruyama, *Thought and Behavior in Modern Japanese Politics* (London: Oxford University Press, 1963). Maruyama suggests (pp. 8–10) that absolute values were embodied in the person of the emperor, who became the personification of the good, the true, and the beautiful, an "external culmination" so that the locus of Japanese morality was not in the consciousness of the individual but in the affairs of the nation.

4. See Okada Osamu, "Sanrizuka: Universalizing the Struggle," *AMPO: Japan-Asia Quarterly Review,* Vol. 9, No. 3 (1977), p. 15.

5. Ibid.

6. See Masamichi Asukai, "Kōtoku Shūsui," in Nobuya Bamba and John F. Howes, ed., *Pacifism in Japan: The Christian and Socialist Tradition* (Vancouver: University of British Columbia Press, 1978), pp. 123–141.

7. See Henry Dewitt Smith II, *Japan's First Student Radicals* (Cambridge, Mass.: Harvard University Press, 1972), p. 27.

8. See F. G. Notehelfer, *Kōtoku Shūsui: Portrait of a Japanese Radical* (Cambridge, Eng.: Cambridge University Press, 1971), p. 74.

9. See Sir Isaiah Berlin, *Russian Thinkers* (New York: Viking, 1978). See also Sandra T. W. Davis, *Intellectual Change and Political Development in Early Modern Japan* (Cranbury, N.J.: Associated University Presses, 1980).

10. See Kazuko Tsurumi, *Social Change and the Individual* (Princeton, N.J.: Princeton University Press, 1970).

11. Smith, *Japan's First Student Radicals,* pp. 178–179.

12. Ibid., p. 179.

13. Ibid., p. 249.

14. Ibid.

15. See D. E. Apter and James Joll, *Anarchism Today* (New York: Doubleday Anchor Books, 1973).

16. See Margaret A. McKean, "Political Socialization through Citizens' Movements," in Kurt Steiner, Ellis S. Krauss, and Scott Flanagan, eds., *Political Opposition and Local Politics in Japan* (Princeton, N.J.: Princeton University Press, 1980), pp. 228–273.

17. The system is called the "Potsdam Student Body" because its organizational principles were based on the Occupation policy according to the Potsdam Declaration.

18. See Kōji Takazawa, Masayuki Takagi, and Kazunari Kurata, *A Twenty-Year History of the New Left* (Tokyo: Shinsensha, 1981).

19. See the account of AMPO events in Robert A. Scalapino and Junnosuke Masumi, *Parties and Politics in Contemporary Japan* (Berkeley: University of California Press, 1962), pp. 125–153.

20. There is inconsistency in both the names used by many of the sects and the translations given. This makes the analysis of sects both confusing and difficult to follow. Actually the above discussion is a simplified version of a much more complex process.

21. For a more detailed analysis from which this material was drawn see Akiyama Katsuyuki, *Zengakuren Wa Nani O Kangaeruka* [*What Does Zengakuren Think about It?*] (Tokyo: Jiyū Kokumin-sha, 1968).

22. See J. L. Austin, *How to Do Things with Words* (Oxford: Oxford University Press, 1975).

6. The Sects at Sanrizuka

1. See Joseph A. Massey, *Youth and Politics in Japan* (Lexington, Mass.: D. C. Heath, 1976).

2. See McKean, "Political Socialization through Citizens' Movements."

3. See Tsurumi, *Social Change and the Individual.*

4. Ibid.

5. Hans Toch, *The Social Psychology of Social Movements* (Indianapolis, Ind.: Bobbs-Merrill, 1965), p. 127.

6. See Erik H. Erikson, *Identity, Youth, and Crisis* (New York: W. W. Norton, 1968), pp. 91–141.

7. See Neil J. Smelser, *Theory of Collective Behavior* (New York: Free Press of Glencoe, 1963), p. 313.

8. Mutō Ichiyō, born in 1931, went to Tokyo University but dropped out. A translator and critic, he was one of the organizers of anti-nuclear movements and a leader of Beheiren. He runs the Asian Pacific Information Center in Tokyo.

9. Corruption in the sense that some sect members manipulate farmers for sectarian purposes and some farmers use sect members for self-enrichment.

10. Maruki Iri was born in Hiroshima, the first son of a farm family. He began studying painting in 1923 in Tokyo. Toshi was born in 1912 in Hokkaido, the eldest daughter of a Buddhist priest. Married in 1941, they went to Hiroshima in 1945, shortly after the A-bomb was dropped, and lived in what remained of Maruki Iri's home. They began working on the Hiroshima panels in 1948 and completed them in 1972. The panels have been shown to 650,000 people in fifty-one cities in Japan and were exhibited in twenty countries abroad, including the United States. Maruki Iri and Toshi joined the JCP in 1946 but were expelled in 1965.

11. She claims that during this period she was not allowed to see a lawyer and the police applied pressure on her. The courts have refused to accept testimony obtained under such circumstances. The matter is ambiguous, since police cannot legally hold a suspect for more than a few days without cause.

12. Her arrest had been reported in the newspapers, with her picture. Children would run after her in the street, shouting, "Militant, militant!"

7. The Christ of the Crossroads

1. One of Tomura's schoolmates died after being taken by the police, charged with being a Communist Party spy, and tortured. In the same year military officers came to train students for the military reserve. These events affected Tomura very deeply and stiffened his resolve to live a life dedicated to principles.

2. See Smethurst, *A Social Basis for Prewar Japanese Militarism.*

3. The incident in question was the culmination of a period of political struggle involving young officers who were acting against a "constitutional elite." On February 26, 1936, some 1,400 rebel officers and their troops invaded central Tokyo and captured key members of the imperial household and cabinet. See Tetsuo Najita, *Japan* (Englewood Cliffs, N.J.: Prentice-Hall, 1974), pp. 132–133.

4. See Kenneth Strong, *Against the Storm* (Tenterden, Kent: Paul Norbury Publications, 1977), pp. 65–127.

5. See Gail Lee Bernstein, *Japanese Marxist* (Cambridge, Eng.: Cambridge University Press, 1976), pp. 13, 31–32.

6. Even the telephone number of the church, 0139, could be read to stand for characters of Tomura's first name.

8. The Hantai Dōmei

1. In villages divided between Hantai Dōmei and non–Hantai Dōmei families, some matters, such as irrigation, might be discussed by the whole village as a single body. Among themselves Hantai Dōmei representatives would discuss matters affecting the Hantai Dōmei. Disputes were not uncommon. The Hantai Dōmei had to be concerned with the effects of discisions not only on its own membership but on supportive non-members as well.

2. The argument is best summarized in Tomura Issaku, "Ten Years of Struggle: Sanrizuka and Its Links with Asia," quoted in *AMPO: Japan-Asia Quarterly Review,* Vol. 7, No. 4 (Oct.–Dec. 1975), pp. 39–44.

3. See Joyce Lebra, Joy Paulson, and Elizabeth Powers, eds., *Women in Changing Japan* (Boulder, Colo.: Westview Press, 1976).

9. The View from the Top

1. See the discussion of the inverse relationship between coercion and information in Apter, *Choice and the Politics of Allocation.*

2. PARC has a chairman, vice-chairmen (six from the House of Representatives, one from the House of Councillors), committees, and a secretariat. PARC discusses and defines party policy in the LDP and helps to facilitate bills' smooth passage. The committees themselves parallel ministries in the Cabinet, covering such areas as local administration, defense, foreign affairs, justice, finance, construction, social welfare, labor, commerce and industry, transportation, agriculture and forestry, fishing, education, science and technology, and environment. The chairman of PARC is one of the three top LDP posts and is chosen by the prime minister with the approval of the Executive Council. Among former PARC chairmen were ex-prime ministers Miki Takeo, Fukuda Takeo, Tanaka Kakuei, and Ohira Masayoshi.

3. The Executive Council consists of thirty members: fifteen elected by LDP Dietmen in the House of Representatives, seven elected by LDP Dietmen, in the House of Councillors, and eight appointed by the prime minister, who is of course the president of the LDP. This is the most sensitive political committee and meets regularly twice a week. See Murakawa Ichiro, *Policy Affairs Decision-Making Process* [*Seisaku Kettei Katei*] (Tokyo: Kyoikusha Co., n.d.).

4. Many of the former presidents were ex-bureaucrats. Their previous positions include the Japan National Railways tourism chief, a high court judge, a Maritime Bureau chief, and a deputy minister of justice.

5. Out of 185 senior administrative positions in fifteen ministries in 1977, 147 were University of Tokyo graduates. (Data from the National Personnel Authority.)

6. See the discussion of this point in Ide Yoshinori, "Administrative Culture in Japan: Images of the *'Kan'* or Public Administration," *Annals of the Institution of Social Science* (University of Tokyo), No. 22 (1981), pp. 152-182.

7. Ibid., p. 179.

8. Another reason often alleged is that Kawashima had a friend who owned a 30-hectare golf course adjacent to the site and that Kawashima and Tomonō arranged the sale of some of its land to the Airport Authority for very substantial sums of money.

10. Reflections on Protest

1. See Pierre Bourdieu, *Outline of a Theory of Practice* (Cambridge, Eng.: Cambridge University Press, 1977).

2. See Martha Crenshaw, "The Causes of Terrorism," *Comparative Politics,* Vol. 13, No. 4 (July 1981), pp. 379-399.

3. Georges Sorel, *Reflections on Violence,* trans. T. E. Hulme and J. Roth (Glencoe, Ill.: Free Press, 1950). See also Claude Lévi-Strauss, "The Structural Study of Myth," in *Structural Anthropology* (New York: Basic Books, 1963), pp. 206-231, and Paul Ricoeur, *The Symbolism of Evil* (Boston, Beacon Press, 1967), pp. 161-174.

4. See Margaret A. McKean, *Environmental Protest and Citizens' Movements in Japan* (Berkeley: University of California Press, 1981).

5. See Alain Touraine, François Dubet, Michel Wieviorka, and Jan Strzelecki, *Solidarité* (Paris: Fayard, 1982), p. 14.

Index

Index

Confrontations, 2, 8, 79, 81–81, 98–106. *See also* Arrests, from confrontations; Casualties, from confrontations; Demonstrations; Iwayama steel tower confrontation; Rallies; Sanrizuka airport, control tower takeover
Constitution, 208
Construction Ministry, 215, 219
Consumer Supply Federation, 46
Cooperative, 50, 52, 53, 57, 60, 68, 183, 184, 190
Crenshaw, Martha, 260n2

Daily Life Improvement Schemes, 47
Daughter-in-law. *See Yomé*
Davis, T. W., 257n9
Decision-making, 226; in government, 201, 203, 204–205, 207–209, 211–212, 213–222. *See also* Airports, locational decisions; Cabinet, decisions; Negotiation
Democracy, 50, 60, 201, 226, 227, 229, 234, 238, 240, 241–242
Democratic Socialist Party, 52
Demonstrations, 124, 155–156, 162, 217, 230. *See also* Rallies
Development. *See* Economic growth
Diet, 50, 199, 202–203, 215, 218, 222
Dokō Toshio, 204
Donnelly, Michael W., 254n8(chap. 2)
Dore, Ronald, 45–46, 47, 67, 254nn3,5, 255n11
Dōrō Chiba. *See* Chiba branch of the locomotive union
Dubet, François, 260n5
Due process, 56, 69, 86, 233

Ebara Masako, 178
Ecology, 27, 43, 109, 188
Economic growth, 4, 38–39, 47, 60, 205, 232, 253. *See also* Industrial development; Rural development
Edo period, 52
Educational system, 10, 70–71, 75, 206
Elders' Corps. *See* Old People's Corps
Elections, 125, 159–160, 202
Emperor, 67, 256. *See also* Imperial estate
Erikson, Erik H., 135, 258n6
Experimental agriculture, 22, 23, 27, 90, 91, 192, 238

Expropriations. *See* Land, expropriations

Factories, 26, 34
Family, 5, 10, 42–43, 58–59, 67, 70, 192–193, 254. *See also* Household; Kinship; *Yomé*
Farmers, 22–23, 26, 42–43, 54–59, 188–190, 243–244; position of, 4–5; political experience of, 8, 50, 52, 59–60, 133, 185; as fighters, 23–24, 39; relations of, with ex-farmers, 28, 183
Farmers' broadcasting tower, 87, 101, 240
Farmers' movement, 63–64, 143, 168, 237. *See also* Sanrizuka movement
Farmers' Union, 183–184
Farmer-Workers Solidarity Hut (Rōnō Gasshuku-jo), 143–144, 146–147
Farm Implement Modernization Fund, 46
Farm income, 45, 47, 184, 189
Farming. *See* Agriculture
Farms, 21, 54–55, 57, 58. *See also* Agriculture; Collective farming
Farm Successor's Fund, 47
"Father movement." *See* Sunagawa movement
Feudalism, 52–53, 63, 65–66, 67
Finance Ministry, 215, 219
Firefighters, 49, 50
Fishermen: protests by, 35. *See also* Minamata movement
Flanagan, Scott, 257n16
Fortifications: by Hantai Dōmei, 23–24, 80–81, 95–97, 100, 159, 183; by police, 24, 33, 130. *See also* specific fortifications, e.g. Watchtowers
Fortresses, 25, 85, 94, 100, 104, 105, 129–130, 235; life in, 71, 82, 116–117, 132–133, 135–136
Forts, 23, 33, 86. *See also* Kinone fort; Komaino fort; Tennami fort
Fourth International, 8, 100, 104, 118, 121–122, 127, 141, 143, 144–145; and Sanrizuka airport, control tower takeover, 106–107, 122; leadership of, 131, 138. *See also* Chūkaku-ha, and Fourth International
France, 143, 206, 208
Freud, Sigmund, 133

Index